THE *Miracle* OF *Faith*

THE *Miracle* OF *Faith*

J. L. THOMPSON

CFI
An imprint of Cedar Fort, Inc.
Springville, Utah

ISBN 13 Paperback: 978-1-4621-4562-1
ISBN 13 Ebook: 978-1-4621-45-63-8

Published by CFI, an imprint of Cedar Fort, Inc.
2373 W. 700 S., Suite 100, Springville, UT 84663
Distributed by Cedar Fort, Inc., www.cedarfort.com

Library of Congress Control Number: 2023935314

Cover design by Shawnda T. Craig

Printed in the United States of America

10 9 8 7 6 5 4 3 2 1

Printed on acid-free paper

Dedication

For my children.

Other books by this author

Worlds without Number, Cedar Fort, Inc. (2022)

Enoch in the City of Adam, Leicester Bay Books (2015)

Contents

1

What Is Faith?

After reading, thinking, studying, and thoughtfully praying about the formidable principle of faith for much of my life, I have distilled my understanding of it into an easily comprehended concept.

Faith is trust developed through experience.

We could similarly define faith as *confidence based on one's experience.*

We might say, "I've never heard that definition of faith. Is that really what faith is?" This is a definition that one can glean from a thorough reading of the scriptures and the words of all the prophets ancient and modern. Although none of them actually put it in those words, the principles are well detailed in this definition.

We hear of "faith" in varied contexts and must first ask what type of "faith" we are discussing. If we ask diverse people about their faith, they might share their feelings about beliefs that they hold, especially about the existence of God, Christ, angels, miracles, saints, or earth spirits; talismans, spirit guides, crystal energy, and so forth. Is this faith? It is often referred to as faith, but it is not. It is belief—or in these particular cases, a belief system, just as those beliefs outlined in what we call our own Articles of Faith. As we see in our discussion on the following pages, faith is a principle of action, and additionally, it must be founded on truth—we cannot exercise faith in something that is untrue. Therefore, faith is not the object of our worship or veneration. Faith is something we do—and it must be done in the proper manner in order to receive the desired results.

The Prophet Joseph Smith Taught the High Value of Faith

How important is faith in this life and in the world to come? In the School of the Prophets,[1] Joseph Smith taught the then current and future leaders of The Church of Jesus Christ of Latter-day Saints (the "Church") that faith is the first principle in revealed religion and the foundation of all righteousness (*Lectures on Faith*, 1:11).[2] Faith is the very bedrock on which all other principles of salvation and exaltation are developed in time and in the eternities (ibid., 7:5).[3] No other principles or ordinances can be established or sustained without it. Faith in the Lord Jesus Christ is the purest form of faith and is essential to any progress beyond our present condition, as explained in the fourth article of faith: "We believe that the first principles and ordinances of the Gospel are: first, Faith in the Lord Jesus Christ."

Extolling the foundational importance of faith, the ancient Apostle Paul provides us a working definition of the principle thus: "Faith is the substance of things hoped for, the evidence of things not seen" (Hebrews 11:1).

To comprehend the complete meaning of this definition, we must view its components separately. Before we do so, let us consider its companion scriptures found in the Book of Mormon:

---

1. In the early days of the restoration of the gospel, the School of the Prophets was a select group of early leaders of The Church of Jesus Christ of Latter-day Saints who began meeting on January 23, 1833, in Kirtland, Ohio under the direction of the Prophet Joseph Smith for both theological and secular learning. The *Lectures on Faith* publication was presided over by Joseph Smith, and some of the lectures therein were personally written and delivered by him; but all will be attributed to him herein by reference, because they all received his personal approval.
2. "Faith being the first principle in revealed religion, and the foundation of all righteousness, necessarily claims the first place in a course of lectures which are designed to unfold to the understanding the doctrine of Jesus Christ."
3. ". . . then faith is truly the first principle in the science of Theology . . ."

> And now as I said concerning faith—faith is not to have a perfect knowledge of things; therefore if ye have faith ye hope for things which are not seen, which are true (Alma 32:21).

> And now, I, Moroni, would speak somewhat concerning these things; I would show unto the world that faith is things which are hoped for and not seen; wherefore, dispute not because ye see not, for ye receive no witness until after the trial of your faith (Ether 12:6).

These and other scriptural definitions of the principle of faith provide us with a hierarchy of principles—or concepts—which we can list in ascending order of certainty.

1. Belief —> 2. Hope —> 3. Faith —> 4. Knowledge

So, on our scale, the oracles of God tell us that faith is something less certain than knowledge but something more certain than hope. They instruct us that faith is our hope for things that are true (factual or real) that are not visually or otherwise evidenced by outward proof in the moment.

In order to understand the meaning of the ascending grades of certainty, these principles, and the true nature of faith, let us review them in order from lowest to highest, starting with definitions of the concepts of belief and hope.

Belief

Belief is any understanding, tenet, principle, theory, opinion, view, ideology, hypothesis, conjecture, speculation, assumption, premise, presumption, supposition, guess, concept, or precept that a person accepts as being real. There is no requirement of quality of actuality associated with belief. People can believe anything, regardless of its basis in fact or reality. All concepts held by someone to be possible, no matter how improbable or actually impossible, can be believed and constitute belief. To believe in something that is untrue does not in itself necessarily lessen the quality of a person's belief. To believe in something that is true does not in itself necessarily improve the quality of a person's belief. Belief can be entirely independent of truth or fallacy. It is merely human acceptance of the status of a thing or concept unrestricted by legitimacy.

Throughout human history people have believed nearly every possible idea. They have believed truth, and they have believed error; foolishness, and lies. Belief can be obtained or developed through any possible thought process or any course of discovery, regardless of its authenticity or suitability. Belief can be based on sloppy and shoddy discovery or thought processes, invariably leading to false beliefs, or it can be based on revealed truth or verified scientific method, often resulting in belief in correct principles or facts. All myths, legends, rumors, and false doctrines are based on someone's mistaken belief in those tenets. Most of human history has been driven by humanity's beliefs—mistaken or correct. To the extent the beliefs were invested in truth, humanity prospered. To the extent those beliefs were devoted to erroneous principles, humanity suffered.

Hope

Hope, in the context of our discussion, can be defined as a *desire* for something to be factual. It is of a higher quality and certainty than mere belief because it actively seeks legitimacy. It is of a lower quality and certainty than faith, because it may seek after something that ultimately turns out to be untrue, or not based in reality. Like belief, hope can vary in its value based on the quality of one's inquiry or the promise upon which it is based. For instance, to hope that one will win a lottery is feeble hope, because its basis is so tenuous—so uncertain. Surely, one may have a *desire* to win the lottery, but the probability of success is so low that it renders the quality of hope very poor in such a case. One cannot develop true confidence in this low quality of certainty. However, the more probable and predictable the outcome of the thing desired, the greater the hope.

How can hope develop into faith? As an example of increasing mere hope, which is little more than desire, a child can "hope" their daddy catches them when he tosses them in the air. Although it's possible that their father may not catch them due to accident or miscalculation, that hope will be of higher quality, because fathers generally have the ability and desire to catch a tossed child, and the child will have already developed a relationship of trust with their father. The child's hope increases in quality and becomes justified in the child's mind as they gain experience in the principle. In this case, the first time a child is tossed in the air, there may be skepticism of their father's ability to catch their fall, resulting in a low level of hope, despite the child having a strong desire. With experience, hope increases, eventually growing into faith. In our example, after the father has tossed the child up and caught them twenty times every day for a year, the child's hope level has risen to a high quality. Therefore, we comprehend that the value of hope is directly affected by the quality of our experience. Experience teaches us reasonable expectation. The quality of hope is based on the value of the underlying promise, which is generally dependent on the quality of the person extending the promise and their demonstrated desire and ability to fulfil their promise. A father can be a reliable person to extend a promise, especially regarding a child's safety in his arms. How much more then is the quality of a Heavenly Father's promise of salvation and eternal life or of divine intervention in troubled times?

In a gospel sense, hope is a precursor of faith. When the tossed child develops strong trust in their father and their confidence is strengthened, their hope will eventually become faith because it is invested in a factual circumstance. The prophets inform us that precursors of hope are humility and charity, charity being the pure, unconditional love of Christ. In Moroni chapter seven, the prophet shares the words of his father, Mormon, regarding the hierarchic relationship of faith, hope, and charity. As we read together, let us keep in mind our ascending order of certainty—belief, hope, faith, and then knowledge.

> And again, my beloved brethren, I would speak unto you concerning hope. How is it that ye can attain unto faith, save ye shall have hope? And what is it that ye shall hope for? Behold I say unto you that ye shall have hope through the atonement of Christ and the power of his resurrection, to be raised unto life eternal, and this because of your faith in him according to the promise. Wherefore, if a man have faith he must needs have hope; for without faith there cannot be any hope. And again, behold I say unto you that he cannot have faith and hope, save he shall be meek, and lowly of heart. If so, his faith and hope is vain, for none is acceptable before God,

> save the meek and lowly in heart; and if a man be meek and lowly in heart, and confesses by the power of the Holy Ghost that Jesus is the Christ, he must needs have charity; for if he have not charity he is nothing; wherefore he must needs have charity. And charity suffereth long, and is kind, and envieth not, and is not puffed up, seeketh not her own, is not easily provoked, thinketh no evil, and rejoiceth not in iniquity but rejoiceth in the truth, beareth all things, believeth all things, hopeth all things, endureth all things (Moroni 7:40–45).

As we see from these verses, love for God, Christ, and our fellow beings leads to a true perspective of our place in the universe and gives us humility before Christ because of our dependence on Him and His atoning sacrifice rendered in our behalf. When we have humility and charity, we can develop hope that Christ's Atonement will have a redeeming effect on us and rescue us from the fall. As the quality of our hope increases, it will develop into faith. Therefore, if the appropriate precursors of hope are in place—humility and charity—we are in a position to develop our characters to the level of hope, which is the true desire for something better. When our hope is developed and invested in something that is based in reality, it can become faith.

Faith

Faith is of higher quality and certainty than hope. It is defined as hope combined with or endowed with truth. Again, let us review the scriptural definition of faith: "Faith is the substance of things hoped for, the evidence of things not seen" (Hebrews 11:1). And also, "And now as I said concerning faith—faith is not to have a perfect knowledge of things; therefore if ye have faith ye hope for things which are not seen, which are true" (Alma 32:21).

Based on these definitions, faith is hope in things that are true, although we can't readily see the tangible proof (or substance) of their truthfulness. If we could see the proof of the truthfulness of things hoped for, it wouldn't be faith, because it would become knowledge. Knowledge comes from witnessing proof. That which we experience directly, we know. We see, hear, touch, taste, and smell that which exists, and we "know" it exists. This is knowledge. If we know a thing is true, we do not have faith in it, because faith exists only when the proof or knowledge is yet absent. Knowledge is wonderful, but the Lord has declared that faith is more powerful than knowledge in our present relationship with Deity.

Christ explained the principle to His apostles of old in this manner:

> Then saith he to Thomas, Reach hither thy finger, and behold my hands; and reach hither thy hand, and thrust it into my side: and be not faithless, but believing. And Thomas answered and said unto him, My Lord and my God. Jesus saith unto him, Thomas, because thou hast seen me, thou hast believed: blessed are they that have not seen, and yet have believed (John 20:27–29).

The Lord teaches His Apostles, through the doubting Apostle Thomas, that seeing is knowing, but having faith (because they have not yet seen) is more blessed.

The Apostle James further clarified this point when he taught the ancient Saints the necessity of acting on one's faith. In his discussion, he used the example of knowledge, explaining that it is of no particular value to those who reject the truth and benefits associated with that sure knowledge. "Thou believest that there is one God; thou doest well: the devils also believe, and tremble" (James 2:19). This is such an impactful scripture. It perfectly illustrates the reason that faith is more powerful than knowledge. Like most of the children of the earth before the great flood, these devils know perfectly well that God exists but fail to accept Him as the true God of the universe. They reject Him and His divine authority at their own certain peril. Although they have a desire (less than hope) to overthrow Him and His kingdom through their demonic efforts, they still tremble at the near certainty that He will eventually cast them into outer darkness. Yes, they *know* there is a God but tremble because of their knowledge. It is the action-oriented nature of faith that makes it more powerful than knowledge, but that action must be performed as the Lord has required to have efficacy.

We know that faith requires action, but what other elements are necessary for us to have and exercise faith? To help us better understand the full nature of faith, we can express it as a simple equation:

Faith = Hope + Truth

As we discussed, hope is a thing desired. We can desire many things, but we cannot have faith in things that are untrue. To hope that the bus will go to Havana from Seattle will never rise to the level of faith because it is not based in truth. Our lottery example illustrates that to desire a thing of a tenuous nature will not result in real faith. But to hope that Daddy catches the child when he tosses them *can* result in faith. The more experience the child cultivates with their father's actions, the more their hope grows into faith, until faith blossoms and becomes undeniable. But what do the prophets mean when they say faith is the *substance* of things hoped for and the *evidence* of things *not seen*? Let's list those elements. Faith is something higher than hope (desire) in that it is hope imbued with "substance." What is the substance that transforms hope into faith? It is truth. If it is truth, then why isn't it knowledge? It isn't knowledge, because at this point in the exercise of faith, we haven't yet witnessed the result, or outcome. This is why the prophet Alma says, "Faith is not to have a perfect knowledge of things," but faith is to "hope for things which are not yet seen, which are true." Faith can only be exercised before the outcome is "known," although we can have tremendous confidence in the eventual outcome.

This "yet unseen" nature of faith is present in our example of the child being tossed in the air by his father, because although the child has developed tremendous trust in his father's willingness and ability to catch him, he never sees the actual outcome of the next toss in advance. Therefore, regardless of how much trust and confidence the child has in his father's willingness and ability, based on the year of experience being tossed and caught, the "truth" of the matter will become evident at the time of the present toss and fulfilled safe landing. In this example, we have our experience with the integrity of the promise, or in this case, the father's ability and will to catch the child, as our "evidence of things not [quite yet] seen."

Our Heavenly Father and His Son, our Savior, have made certain promises to us. It is our goal to exercise faith in their promises, and obtain the desired results. Our ability to obtain those blessings depends on the quality of our faith. Our faith must develop from mere belief and then hope, growing into something of substance that has the ability to produce results. This is the most important task we have as mortals, which is why the prophets have repeatedly taught us that faith is the foundation on which all else is built.

The prophet Alma taught the principle of developing from a mere "desire to believe" into faith and then knowledge in his example of nurturing a good seed.

> Now, as I said concerning faith—that it was not a perfect knowledge—even so it is with my words. Ye cannot know of their surety at first, unto perfection, any more than faith is a perfect knowledge. But behold, if ye will awake and arouse your faculties, even to an **experiment** upon my words, and exercise a particle of faith, yea, even if ye can no more than desire to believe, let this desire work in you, even until ye believe in a manner that ye can give place for a portion of my words (Alma 32:26–27).

Alma says that if we begin with just desire, or hope, and allow it to grow within us, it will blossom—as long as it is rooted in truth.

Is it becoming clear how listing the levels of certainty and the elements of faith help us understand what the prophets have taught us about faith? Alma continues his explanation of how faith in the word of God grows:

> Now, we will compare the word unto a seed. Now, if ye give place, that a seed may be planted in your heart, behold, if it be a true seed, or a good seed, if ye do not cast it out by your unbelief, that ye will resist the Spirit of the Lord, behold, it will begin to swell within your breasts; and when you feel these swelling motions, ye will begin to say within yourselves—It must needs be that this is a good seed, or that the word is good, for it beginneth to enlarge my soul; yea, it beginneth to enlighten my understanding, yea, it beginneth to be delicious to me (Alma 32:28).

Like the seed that is planted in our heart, the principle upon which we exercise faith must be rooted in truth. The bus does not go to Havana, but it does go to Springville. One destination is an untruth, and one is a truth. A "good seed" is one that is based on truth. If it is true, it will begin to grow and provide your life with greater light and understanding. It will inculcate a desire for more light and understanding in your life.

The prophet next asks us the question, "Now behold, would not this increase your faith?" (Alma 32:29). He declares that this is the very process that expands our faith, but reminds us that faith is not "perfect knowledge." The process of growing our faith toward knowledge is essential, however, and he describes how we can learn for ourselves that the information or principle is true.

> But behold, as the seed swelleth, and sprouteth, and beginneth to grow, then you must needs say that the seed is good . . . And now, behold, will not this strengthen your faith? Yea, it will strengthen your faith: for ye will say I know that this is a good seed; for behold it sprouteth and beginneth to grow (Alma 32:30).

Recognizing the validity of the process of developing faith and its tangible results is essential to building confidence in the principle or trust in the person or concept. Because it grows within us, it changes our very nature and becomes part of our internal constitution. As faith grows, we literally become a person of faith.

The prophet Alma also explains how we can test the truthfulness of principles or information in which we wish to develop abiding faith.

> And now, behold, are ye sure that this is a good seed? I say unto you, Yea; for every seed bringeth forth unto its own likeness. Therefore, if a seed groweth it is good, but if it groweth not, behold it is not good, therefore it is cast away (Alma 32:31–32).

Of course, Jehovah declared in the beginning, "Let the earth bring forth grass, the herb yielding seed, and the fruit tree yielding fruit after his kind, whose seed is in itself, upon the earth: and it was so."[4] He expanded on this principle during His earthly ministry, saying,

> Even so every good tree bringeth forth good fruit; but a corrupt tree bringeth forth evil fruit. A good tree cannot bring forth evil fruit,

4. Genesis 1:11.

> neither can a corrupt tree bring forth good fruit. Every tree that bringeth not forth good fruit is hewn down, and cast into the fire.[5]

The prophet Alma uses this eternal principle to provide us with a test, wherewith we can check the validity of the information or principle we are considering. "And now, behold, because ye have tried the experiment," he explains, "and planted the seed, and it swelleth and sprouteth, and beginneth to grow, ye must needs know that the seed is good" (Alma 32:33).

It is interesting that the ancient prophet chooses the term "experiment" to describe the process of checking the validity of the principle under examination. In modern times we might think of it as an experiment where we carefully control the elements and environment to see what naturally occurs when we apply certain organic materials and control the conditions. In this case, will the seed we plant turn out to be a good seed? Will it bring forth a good plant after its own kind? Will it increase our enlightenment and understanding? If the answers all turn out to be yes, then we can be confident that this is a good choice for us, and we can exercise trust in it and invest ourselves and our lives in the principle.

Knowledge

The level of certainty above faith is knowledge. How do we acquire knowledge? How do we come to know something? How do we gain certainty of anything? We use our five senses in our daily lives to comprehend the reality around us. We see, hear, taste, smell, and touch, and that is how we inform ourselves about the actual nature of the things in our environment. I see my child drop a book on the floor, and I know she dropped the book. I don't believe it. I don't hope it. I don't have faith that she dropped the book. I know she dropped it, because I witnessed the event with my own eyes. I have knowledge. Likewise, I hear the smoke alarm go off as I'm cooking dinner and stepped out to take a call. I don't have a belief that the alarm has activated. I don't have hope or faith. I hear it. I have knowledge—personal knowledge of something I witness with my ears. I rush to the

5. Matthew 7:15–20.

kitchen and stub my toe on the cabinet corner. I know I stubbed my toe, because I feel the crippling pain in my foot. This is how we come to know things in our lives—by witnessing them with one or more of our five senses. There is another sense that we can develop, of course, which also provides us with knowledge and understanding. This is connected to our spirit, which receives communications from God through the Light of Christ and from the Holy Ghost.

The prophet Alma speaks of arriving at the level of knowledge certainty by following the instructions he provides. After we have performed the experiment suggested by Alma and cultivated a "good seed" within our hearts, have tested its validity and encouraged its growth, and have finally witnessed the eventual truth of the matter being tested, the prophet speaks about attaining this ultimate level of certainty—knowledge—which supersedes the faith we had attained.

> And now, behold, is your knowledge perfect? Yea, your knowledge is perfect in that thing, and your faith is dormant; and this because you know, for ye know that the word hath swelled your souls, and ye also know that it hath sprouted up, that your understanding doth begin to be enlightened, and your mind doth begin to expand (Alma 32:34).

The prophet then addresses the "reality" of the result of this testing process and begins teaching about the correlation of light with truth and knowledge.

> O then, is not this real? I say unto you, Yea, because it is light; and whatsoever is light, is good, because it is discernible, therefore ye must know that it is good (Alma 32:35).

We note in this verse that Alma is instructing us in the use of the sixth sense we introduced a moment ago—our spiritual sense.

It is at this point in the prophet Alma's discourse that he speaks to the limits of knowledge. As we've discussed briefly, the certainty level of faith appears to have greater power than actual knowledge. This seems counterintuitive as we think about it, so he teaches us a little more about the concept. He continues,

> And now behold, after ye have tasted this light is your knowledge perfect? Behold I say unto you, Nay; neither must ye lay aside your faith, for ye have only exercised your faith to plant the seed that ye might try the experiment to know if the seed was good. And behold, as the tree beginneth to grow, ye will say: Let us nourish it with great care, that it may get root, that it may grow up, and bring forth fruit unto us. And now behold, if ye nourish it with much care it will get root, and grow up, and bring forth fruit (Alma 32:35–37).

Knowledge has its limitations when it comes to invoking the power of God, and those who seek knowledge as a substitute for faith quickly find themselves in opposition to God. "Yea, there are many who do say: If thou wilt show unto us a sign from heaven, then we shall know of a surety; then we shall believe" (Alma 32:17). However, Alma instructs,

> Now I ask, is this faith? Behold, I say unto you, Nay; for if a man knoweth a thing he hath no cause to believe, for he knoweth it. And now, how much more cursed is he that knoweth the will of God and doeth it not, than he that only believeth, or only hath cause to believe, and falleth into transgression? Now of this thing ye must judge. Behold, I say unto you, that it is on the one hand even as it is on the other; and it shall be unto every man according to his work. And now as I said concerning faith—faith is not to have a perfect knowledge of things; therefore if ye have faith ye hope for things which are not seen, which are true. And now, behold, I say unto you, and I would that ye should remember, that God is merciful unto all who believe on his name; therefore he desireth, in the first place, that ye should believe, yea, even on his word (Alma 18–22).

Again, the key is, "If ye have faith ye hope for things which are not seen, which are true." In this there is power.

By letting belief or the desire to have faith grow into something more through experimentation and nurture, our hope develops into faith and eventually into knowledge. It is through this process that we develop power to affect our temporal and eternal lives through our own efforts, coupled with the opportunities and the Atonement provided by God and the Savior.

God Supplies the Truth

Therefore, faith is hope (desire) combined with truth (the desired thing must be based in fact or reality).

We are responsible to provide the belief and desire, but God is responsible to supply the truth. In other words, we mortals have no control over what is true or what is false. The best we can do is exercise our faculties to discover what is real, tangible, factual, and true. We can pray for the Lord to bless us in a particular matter, and we can hope that He will intervene. That is not exercising faith, however, but merely having hope. This appears to be the level at which most of us operate in our relationship with our Heavenly Father—we exercise hope.

Faith is something more than hope in quality and effect. In order for us to exercise faith, the object of our faith must be true or based in reality. If anyone asks God to perform a miracle that is contrary to the will of God, they cannot ask in faith, because the truthfulness of the object of their hope is nonexistent. Truth is the exclusive domain of God, and mortals are powerless to create truth from their own will or desire. We may create favorable circumstances through our efforts and manipulations, and that in itself may create opportunity for fulfillment of desired results, but ultimately, truth, especially eternal truth, is the exclusive domain of Deity, and the best we can do is seek out that truth and then align ourselves with it in exercising our faith.

A Principle of Action and Power

In his updated translation of the New Testament, Joseph Smith rendered Hebrews 11:1 as "NOW faith is the assurance of things hoped for, the evidence of things not seen," substituting "assurance" for the word "substance." He then explained, "From this we learn that faith is the assurance which men have of the existence of things which they have not seen, and the principle of action in all intelligent beings" (*Lectures on Faith,* 1:9).

The prophet used this concept to demonstrate the multi-faceted nature of the principle of faith, showing that it is 1) a principle of action, and 2) a principle of power. As a principle of action, the School of the Prophets was taught:

> If men were duly to consider themselves, and turn their thoughts and reflections to the operations of their own minds, they would readily discover that it is faith, and faith only, which is the moving cause of all action in them; that without it, both mind and body would be in a state of inactivity, and all their exertions would cease, both physical and mental (*Lectures on Faith*, 1:10).

Faith then is the moving cause of all action, the sole impetus of anything that is done. The hundreds of brethren in attendance for this series of lessons on the nature of faith were taught:

> Were this class to go back and reflect upon the history of their lives, from the period of their first recollection, and ask themselves what principle excited them to action, or what gave them energy and activity in all their lawful avocations, callings, and pursuits, what would be the answer? Would it not be that it was the assurance which we had of the existence of things which we had not seen as yet? Was it not the hope which you had, in consequence of your belief in the existence of unseen things, which stimulated you to action and exertion, in order to obtain them? Are you not dependent on your faith, or belief, for the acquisition of all knowledge, wisdom, and intelligence? Would you exert yourselves to obtain wisdom and intelligence, unless you did believe that you could obtain them? Would you have ever sown if you had not believed that you would reap? Would you have ever planted if you had not believed that you would gather? Would you have ever asked unless you had believed that you would receive? Would you have ever sought unless you had believed that you would have found? Or would you have ever knocked unless you had believed that it would have been opened unto you? In a word, is there anything that you would have done, either physical or mental, if you had not previously believed? Are not all your exertions of every kind dependent on your faith (*Lectures on Faith*, 1:11)?

Any exertion of energy in any manner is based in temporal faith—our desire to obtain something by an effort. Without the belief and desire that we will obtain, we are not spurred to act. We see men planting fields only when they have a predictable hope (which is yet unseen evidence, or assurance, based on their experience or another reliable promise) that the crop will grow and provide food. Conversely, we do not see men planting crops in the middle of Death Valley. This is because the "truth" or "assurance" factor is absent in that scenario. Experience tells us that there is no promise of a crop planted in such harsh conditions. Therefore, we do not see men pursuing this action, because they have no faith, or even hope, under those circumstances.

Faith is the motivating factor in more mundane matters as well. Would a parent dress their child and send them to school if there was no expectation (confidence, based on prior experience) that someone would be at the school to open it and teach? The answer is found in the number of children that are dressed and sent to school on Saturday. Would anyone take their car to the gas station if they didn't believe there would be gasoline to purchase? Would a child throw a ball against a wall and await its return if there wasn't faith that the laws of physics would return the ball to their expectant glove? Would a carpenter lay a foundation and frame up walls without an expectation that a roof would be put on the house? Would a farmer arise early and go to the hen house if there was no faith that eggs would be present to gather? Millions of examples surround us daily of the principle of faith in action. We live by faith, whether we realize it or not. We live by expectation, or confidence, based on our own experience with the matter.

The Prophet Joseph Smith taught,

> As faith then is the moving cause of all temporal actions, so it is the moving cause of all spiritual actions. Or may we not ask, what have you, or what do you possess, which you have not obtained by reason of your faith? Your food, your raiment, your lodgings, are they not all by reason of your faith? Reflect, and ask yourselves if these things are not so. Turn your thoughts on your own minds, and see if faith is not the moving cause of all action in yourselves; and if the moving cause in you, is it not in all other intelligent beings?
>
> And as faith is the moving cause of all action in temporal concerns, so it is in spiritual; for the Savior has said, and that truly, that "He that believeth and is baptized shall be saved" (Mark 16:16).

> As we receive by faith all temporal blessings that we do receive, so we in like manner, receive by faith all spiritual blessings that we do receive (*Lectures on Faith*, 1:11–13).

The principle is clear—we must *act* to set things into motion. As long as we act in the appropriate or prescribed manner based on true principles and on proven methods, we exercise a reasonable expectation that the predictable result will occur based on prior experience with similar matters. This is the very process of exercising faith and receiving the "promised" or predictable results. As the Prophet taught, this applies in both temporal and spiritual pursuits.

Ask, and You Shall Receive

The scriptures are replete with the admonition that we do certain things to obtain certain promised blessings. "And when we obtain any blessing from God, it is by obedience to that law upon which it is predicated" (Doctrine and Covenants[6] 130:21). We must note that the scripture is clear that specific laws are associated with specific blessings, and we must obey the law associated with a particular blessing in order to receive the blessing we seek. This was quite a surprising concept to the world of Joseph Smith's day, but as we contemplate the model, it becomes clear in our minds that it is a universal law that is applicable at all times. *For every action, there is an equal and opposite reaction.* Humans often painfully discovered this law through experience and observation. We have tested it, and tested it, until we have concluded that it is always applicable. There are many universal laws governing how things react and interact. We can't break the laws with any degree of success, so we find ways to obey the laws while getting the things we desire. There are laws associated with all of the commandments. Receiving blessings in countless forms requires us to 1) discover the underlying law, and 2) fulfil it. One of the main reasons that our Heavenly Father commanded the ancient prophets to write their experiences is to provide subsequent generations with a record of how they obtained blessings in this way. In general conference we

---

6. Hereafter, D&C.

likewise hear talks from seasoned veterans of life, sharing wisdom of how to obtain the blessings of a loving Father in Heaven.

One of the key commandments we have received associated with obtaining blessings from God is the need to ask Him for the blessing we seek. We are instructed, even commanded, to ask for the assistance of God in our pursuit of such desired results in both spiritual and temporal realms. With the commandment comes a promise that He is faithful in giving us what we ask. God shares the formula thus: "But ye are commanded in all things to ask of God, who giveth liberally" (D&C 46:7). Asking God for a blessing is a key element in receiving something from Him. And, in truth, all things, temporal and spiritual, come from Him, because they are under His control. In the same way that we might exercise our faith by planting seeds in the spring, asking God for His blessing is the exercise of our faith in spiritual matters, spiritual meaning things beyond the physical or worldly restrictions of our temporal existence. Surely, as we lift our eyes above the carnal and decaying landscape that makes up our daily lives and look to heavenly realms for higher learning and purpose, we find that we are far from our heavenly home and that the distance must be bridged with means not readily at our mortal disposal. God has informed us of the great gulf that separates us. "For as the heavens are higher than the earth, so are my ways higher than your ways, and my thoughts than your thoughts" (Isaiah 55:9).

Because of this great disparity between mankind and God, between our ways and His ways, our thinking and His thinking, He has put systems, methods, mechanisms, and devices into place to enable us to bridge that gulf. He builds the bridge halfway to us and has provided us with means to overcome the remainder of the distance and differences, and those means are spelled out in the scriptures and elucidated by His earthly representatives, the prophets. The mechanics of how we can bridge that gulf and how we can employ the means provided by Him are based on systems and methods that He has devised. He has instructed us that strict adherence to these systems and methods is required if we are to obtain what we seek from Him. His declaration that "when we obtain any blessing from God, it is by obedience to that law upon which it is predicated"[7] is His gift of love and compassion to His children to ensure that we are not left alone as we walk through this sometimes lone and dreary world.

By following the system that our Heavenly Father has put into place, and by obeying the governing principles as He has established and outlined them for our understanding, we are able to obtain blessings from His hand through our own efforts. The principle of obedience as illustrated in the above scripture is defined by the Lord as adherence to a system or set of instructions as outlined in the following scripture.

> Therefore, prepare thy heart to receive and obey the instructions which I am about to give unto you; for all those who have this law revealed unto them must obey the same (D&C 132:3).

By following the prescribed instructions or the formula that the Lord has given us, we may fulfil the law that He has established and thereby obtain any sought-after blessing.

Faith Is Power

Not only is faith a principle of action, temporal and spiritual, but it is also a principle of power. Joseph Smith taught quite clearly that all things of a miraculous or spiritual nature performed by man or God are accomplished through faith.

> But faith is not only the principle of action, but of power also, in all intelligent beings, whether in heaven or on earth. Thus says the author of the epistle to the Hebrews 11:3, "Through faith we understand that the worlds were framed by the word of God, so that things which are seen were not made of things which do appear." By this we understand that the principle of power, which existed in the bosom of God, by which the worlds were framed, was faith; and that it is by reason of this principle of power existing in the Deity, that all created things exist—so that all things in heaven, on earth, or under the earth, exist by reason of faith, as it existed in Him.

7. D&C 130:20–21.

> Had it not been for the principle of faith, the worlds would never have been framed, neither would man have been formed of the dust. It is the principle by which Jehovah works, and through which he exercises power over all temporal, as well as eternal things. Take this principle or attribute (for it is an attribute) from the Deity, and he would cease to exist. Who cannot see that if God framed the worlds by faith, that it is by faith that he exercises power over them, and that faith is the principle of power? And that if the principle of power, it must be so in man as well as in the Deity? This is the testimony of all the sacred writers, and the lesson which they have been endeavoring to teach to man (*Lectures on Faith*, 1:13–17).

Here is the value of faith. Without it, nothing happens, and all things cease to exist, including God Himself—at least in the role of God. Even we mortals live by faith, and it is the foundation of all that we seek and accomplish, just as it is with Deity. Here is the problem, however: although we accomplish all that we do by faith, we often lack faith necessary to accomplish more than the mundane. We are, by and large, a faithless people when it comes to conscious faith. We are sometimes unable to call upon God to receive His specific blessings and favors through our faith. Most of us look at others, those of greater spiritual prominence or of ancient reputation as being more capable of obtaining the promised blessings of the Lord. We generally do not account ourselves as capable to do the same. We believe that we have faith but are reluctant to call upon God to intervene or to perform His miracles for our benefit or that of others. This is nothing new, either. It has always been the state of men to reflect upon better times when miracles seemed plentiful and the Spirit of the Lord was had among people in greater abundance.

Even great prophets of antiquity have lamented that things in their times were not so spiritually grand as in former times. Nephi, the son of Helaman, returned to the land of Zarahemla from the land northward where the people had rejected his testimony and gospel message. He, like many of us, lamented that he had not been born in the good old days.

> Oh, that I could have had my days in the days when my father Nephi first came out of the land of Jerusalem, that I could have

> joyed with him in the promised land; then were his people easy to be entreated, firm to keep the commandments of God, and slow to be led to do iniquity; and they were quick to hearken unto the words of the Lord—Yea, if my days could have been in those days, then would my soul have had joy in the righteousness of my brethren. But behold, I am consigned that these are my days, and that my soul shall be filled with sorrow because of this the wickedness of my brethren (Helaman 7:7–9).

Also, like many of us, this prophet Nephi nurtured a view of the past that would probably have surprised his ancient father Nephi. The former Nephi, with those who chose to follow him, suffered great afflictions and lived a life of isolation and deprivation. They were hunted and despised by those of their brethren who hated and persecuted them. He spent a great deal of his time and energy comforting his people in these sore afflictions with recitations of the Lord's dealings with ancient Israel, reminding them of God's former kindness and mercy to His children and of His willingness to do the same for them if they would be obedient and seek His righteousness. The first Nephi had nothing of an easy, cheerful life filled with the constant outpourings of blessings from on high. He struggled, just as the later Nephi, who wished he had lived in those fonder, earlier times. The lesson is clear—these are the times the Lord has allotted to us, and we must make of them whatever we will and make of our lives whatever we will with the Lord's assistance and blessings.

Our present prophet, President Russell M. Nelson, recently delivered an inspiring general conference address in which he shared that these are the times of great blessings and manifestations of the power of the Lord.

> I assure you that our Heavenly Father and His Beloved Son, Jesus Christ, love you. They are intimately aware of your circumstances, your goodness, your needs, and your prayers for help . . . In coming days, we will see the greatest manifestations of the Savior's power that the world has ever seen. Between now and the time He returns "with power and great glory," He will bestow countless privileges, blessings, and miracles upon the faithful. Nonetheless, we are presently living in what surely is a most complicated time in the history

> of the world. The complexities and challenges leave many people feeling overwhelmed and exhausted.[8]

The prophet Joseph Smith told the brethren of his time that all things are accomplished through our faith, and that if we fail to accomplish anything, it is because of our lack of faith.

> The Savior says Matthew 17:19–20, in explaining the reason why the disciples could not cast out the devil, that it was because of their unbelief: "For verily I say unto you," said he, "If ye have faith as a grain of mustard seed, ye shall say unto this mountain, Remove hence to yonder place; and it shall remove; and nothing shall be impossible unto you."
>
> Moroni, while abridging and compiling the record of his fathers, has given us the following account of faith as the principle of power: He says, [Book of Mormon] page 746 [Ether 5:14], that it was the faith of Alma and Amulek which caused the walls of the prison to be rent, as recorded on the 356th page [Alma 10:77–85]; that it was the faith of Nephi and Lehi which caused a change to be wrought upon the hearts of the Lamanites when they were immersed with the Holy Spirit, and with fire, as seen on the 747th page [Ether 5:15; also Helaman 2:79–118]; and that it was by faith that the mountain Zerin was removed, when the Brother of Jared spake in the name of the Lord. See also 748th page [Ether 5:30–31].
>
> In addition to this we are told in Hebrews 11:32–35, that Gideon, Barak, Samson, Jephthah, David, Samuel, and the prophets through faith subdued kingdoms, wrought righteousness, obtained promises, stopped the mouths of lions, quenched the violence of fire, escaped the edge of the sword, out of weakness were made strong, waxed valiant in fight, turned to flight the armies of the aliens, and that women received their dead raised to life again, etc.
>
> Also, Joshua, in the sight of all Israel, bade the sun and moon to stand still, and it was done Joshua 10:12–13.
>
> We here understand that the sacred writers say that all these things were done by faith. It was by faith that the worlds were

8. "Overcome the World and Find Rest," October 2022 general conference, Sunday morning session.

framed—God spake, chaos heard, and worlds came into order, by reason of the faith there was in Him.

So with man also—he spake by faith in the name of God, and the sun stood still, the moon obeyed, mountains removed, prisons fell, lions' mouths were closed, the human heart lost its enmity, fire its violence, armies their power, the sword its terror, and death its dominion; and all this by reason of the faith which was in them.

Had it not been for the faith which was in man, they might have spoken to the sun, the moon, the mountains, prisons, lions, the human heart, fire, armies, the sword, or to death in vain (*Lectures on Faith*, 1:18–22)!

"Faith then," the Prophet Joseph concludes,

> . . . is the first great governing principle which has power, dominion, and authority over all things; by it they exist, by it they are upheld, by it they are changed, or by it they remain, agreeable to the will of God. Without it, there is no power, and without power there could be no creation, nor existence (*Lectures on Faith*, 1:23–24)!

We have seen that faith is twofold in its nature, or that it has two aspects—a principle of action, and a principle of power. In daily living it is a motivating principle reflected in the law of the harvest. We reap what, where, and how we sow. It spurs us to act that we may obtain the natural fruits of our efforts. In higher living, faith empowers us on a much higher level. It enables us to obtain what we desire for ourselves, our loved ones, and the good of humanity by employing the systems and mechanisms put into place by our Heavenly Father for those very purposes. Even Christ learned "obedience"[9] and thereby achieved power to acquire desired "higher than mundane" results through employing "the finger of God," as he explained it, to perform miracles during His earthly ministry.[10] Most of us assume that Christ was born to His innate abilities and powers. We tend to believe that His extraordinary manifestations and accomplishments were unique

9. "Though he were a Son, yet learned he obedience by the things which he suffered;" Hebrews 5:8.

10. "But if I with the finger of God cast out devils, no doubt the kingdom of God is come upon you." Luke 11:20.

to Him and came to Him naturally as if He were imbued with superhuman influence and abilities from His birth. Although Christ was the Only Begotten Son of God in the flesh literally and was born with higher innate abilities, He told His Apostles, "Verily, verily, I say unto you, He that believeth on me, the works that I do shall he do also; and greater works than these shall he do; because I go unto my Father" (John 14:12).

Although the Lord told us that His followers would do even greater things than He did, we somehow tend to discount the statement. However, history has recorded quite clearly that many mortals, from the first man to the present time, have performed all of the same miracles that Christ performed, save His Atonement. So, can we, mere humans of these latter days, perform those same miracles in the same manner as the Christ? We may parrot a perfunctory *yes* thinking upon the question academically, but do we truly believe it? If we do, then why are our lives not filled with miraculous interventions from on high? Why do we not employ the "finger of God" frequently as the prophet Enoch did and as Melchizedek did as well as many others? Is there some power or ability that we lack? Is there some understanding that we still require?

This is the very mission of this work—to examine the question of faith as a principle of action and power and how it *should* and *can* work in our lives. The Lord's instructions are extremely clear to us in this regard. Yet, most of us appear to lack faith sufficient to accomplish those things that the Lord has commanded us to do. We seem to shrink from the tasks that he has required at our hands, resulting in a famine of the blessings that He has prepared for us. Those blessings and gifts await our "obedience" to His commands. He is powerless to do anything until we exercise our faith. Even the Lord Jesus found it difficult to call upon the powers of heaven when those around Him lacked appropriate faith. "And he could there do no mighty work, save that he laid his hands upon a few sick folk, and healed them. And he marvelled because of their unbelief" (Mark 6:5–6).

God stands ready to bless us, yet we have failed to bridge the gulf that separates us from Him and His blessings. God has not changed. The fault is ours, as demonstrated so eloquently by the prophet Moroni, who had thought that he would no longer be spared to write anything additional to us but was allowed to add the following testimony before his demise.

> Wherefore, my beloved brethren, have miracles ceased because Christ hath ascended into heaven, and hath sat down on the right hand of God, to claim of the Father his rights of mercy which he hath upon the children of men? For he hath answered the ends of the law, and he claimeth all those who have faith in him; and they who have faith in him will cleave unto every good thing; wherefore he advocateth the cause of the children of men; and he dwelleth eternally in the heavens. And because he hath done this, my beloved brethren, have miracles ceased? Behold I say unto you, Nay; neither have angels ceased to minister unto the children of men. For behold, they are subject unto him, to minister according to the word of his command, showing themselves unto them of strong faith and a firm mind in every form of godliness. And the office of their ministry is to call men unto repentance, and to fulfil and to do the work of the covenants of the Father, which he hath made unto the children of men, to prepare the way among the children of men, by declaring the word of Christ unto the chosen vessels of the Lord, that they may bear testimony of him. And by so doing, the Lord God prepareth the way that the residue of men may have faith in Christ, that the Holy Ghost may have place in their hearts, according to the power thereof; and after this manner bringeth to pass the Father, the covenants which he hath made unto the children of men. And Christ hath said: If ye will have faith in me ye shall have power to do whatsoever thing is expedient in me (Moroni 7:27–33).

We learn some important principles related to the exercise of faith to obtain the blessings of God in these passages. First, we learn that Christ claims and advocates those who have faith in Him, and such people cleave to every good thing. It also clarifies that even though Christ left the earth to dwell in the presence of the Father, the miracles that He performed have not ceased, and angels continue to minister to people on Earth. It additionally informs us that God prepares a way for us to have "faith" in Christ, which is facilitated by the gift and the power of the Holy Ghost. In this, the Lord gives us a tripartite formula for receiving miraculous blessings:

1. If we will have faith in Christ
2. We shall have power to do whatsoever thing
3. But the thing must be expedient in Christ

Of course, having faith in Christ is the very object of our course of study. As we come to better understand it, we will also come to discover that we are fully capable of developing such faith in Him through the confidence that we cultivate based on our experience. With that faith in Christ, we will be capable and have the "power" to do what Moroni terms as "whatsoever thing." We divide "whatsoever thing" from "is expedient in me" for a moment to facilitate a better understanding of the two steps involved. "Whatsoever thing" denotes a range of things from the mundane to the divine. Through faith in Christ, I can prepare the sacrament for blessing and distribution to my ward. Through faith in Christ, I can open my mouth and my heart and ask my neighbor if they would like to know about the Restoration of the gospel. Through faith in Christ, I can counsel a daughter whose heart has been disappointed, or lay my hands on her head to give her a father's blessing of comfort and guidance. Is that where the range of possibilities ends? Sadly, for most of us, this is the highest level of "whatsoever thing" we accomplish. What about higher things? What about healing the sick? What about defying the armies at our borders, as did Enoch and others? What about diverting rivers from their courses with a word? The answer is number 3—so long as the thing is expedient in Christ. Discerning the will of the Lord is of utmost importance in our quest to exercise tremendous faith in this life and in the world to come. We discuss it in depth below. For now, let us remember the simple formula the Lord provides for achieving great things with the Lord's help and blessings: Have faith in Christ to accomplish anything that is expedient in Him.

Continuing his discussion on faith, Moroni quotes his father, Mormon, who asks the test question: *If miracles have ceased, and God is unchangeable, what happened to cause their cessation?* He lays out his argument carefully.

> And who shall say that Jesus Christ did not do many mighty miracles? And there were many mighty miracles wrought by the hands

> of the apostles. And if there were miracles wrought then, why has God ceased to be a God of miracles and yet be an unchangeable Being? And behold, I say unto you he changeth not; if so he would cease to be God; and he ceaseth not to be God, and is a God of miracles. And the reason why he ceaseth to do miracles among the children of men is because that they dwindle in unbelief, and depart from the right way, and know not the God in whom they should trust (Mormon 9:18–20).

There are many promised blessings and unfulfilled covenants awaiting our obedience. Angels are waiting to come to men and women to fulfill all that the Father has decreed and promised. When will miracles fill our lives and the windows of heaven be opened and pour out great blessings upon us as a church, families, and individuals? It is entirely up to us.

2

Ask and Receive

THE LORD HAS BEEN QUITE DIRECT IN HIS INSTRUCTION TO US ABOUT how we can receive blessings at His hand. As we mentioned previously, one of the clearest promises found in the scriptures is that if we will ask anything of Him, He will give it to us. He says it often, and He says it in many contexts. Let us explore the principle of asking and receiving that we may fully understand its intent, ramifications, and boundaries.

This dispensation of the gospel on the earth began when young Joseph Smith read the promise of the Apostle James in the New Testament; "if any of you lack wisdom, let him ask of God, that giveth to all men liberally, and upbraideth not; and it shall be given him" (James 1:5). The principle is clear—ask, and you shall receive that which you requested. However, as with most of the occasions when this promise is extended, we are taught to ask in faith:

> But let him ask in faith, nothing wavering. For he that wavereth is like a wave of the sea driven with the wind and tossed. For let not that man think that he shall receive any thing of the Lord. A double minded man is unstable in all his ways (James 1:6–8).

Like most of us, Joseph recounts that this scripture had always seemed like nothing more than a truism to him. He had read it before with no particular interest or compelling feelings. Something changed within him while he read the promise upon that special occasion in his fifteenth year, and the full import of the promise was seared into his soul.

> Never did any passage of scripture come with more power to the heart of man than this did at this time to mine. It seemed to enter with great force into every feeling of my heart. I reflected on it again and again, knowing that if any person needed wisdom from God, I did (Pearl of Great Price, Joseph Smith—History, verse 12).

Young Joseph was suddenly filled with faith—faith that the promise was true and was from the Lord. Faith that, if he did what he was instructed to do, the promised blessing would be fulfilled exactly as the Lord had pledged. Joseph recounts,

> At length I came to the conclusion that I must either remain in darkness and confusion, or else I must do as James directs, that is, ask of God. I at length came to the determination to "ask of God," concluding that if he gave wisdom to them that lacked wisdom, and would give liberally, and not upbraid,[11] I might venture (Ibid., verse 13).

I find this last comment to be endearing of the young prophet. "I might venture" seems like he didn't have a lot of faith to propel him to call upon the Lord. Yet, Jesus specifically taught that faith is faith, and even a small amount, as in the case of a mustard seed, is sufficient to perform miracles. In Matthew 17:20, Jesus declared, "If you have faith as small as a mustard seed, you can say to this mountain, move from here to there and it will move. Nothing will be impossible for you."

As a direct result of Joseph's acceptance of the truthfulness of this promise of the Lord, the dispensation of the fullness of times was opened, and "all things" are being restored preparatory to the Lord's

---

11. Biblical meaning of UPBRAID: transitive verb. 1) to criticize severely : find fault with. 2) to reproach severely : scold vehemently. The promise included the assurance that God will not criticize, find fault with, reproach or scold anyone who asks Him something in this manner.

return to the earth (Matthew 17:11;[12] Acts 3:21[13]). Joseph's experience in exercising his faith in the Lord's promise eventually and even naturally led to the next level of certainty—knowledge. Joseph reports that he "had found the testimony of James to be true—that a man who lacked wisdom might ask of God, and obtain, and not be upbraided" (Joseph Smith—History 1:26). The prophet *asked* mighty and marvelous things of the Lord many times during his life and was blessed with monumental miracles and visited by heavenly messengers on dozens of occasions. Every visitation, every miracle, every wisp of inspiration, and every act of divine intervention was the direct result of that initial, foundational step—to ask, and thereby, receive—which the Prophet repeated continually throughout his life.

In this example of the Prophet Joseph Smith, we establish that the Lord has promised that if we ask Him for wisdom, He will give it to us, just as He promised through the Apostle James. In fact, the promise covers all topics, all things, and all people, and all times in the earth's history—including today. The promise is to all God's children; men and women. The promise is not an idle invitation, however. It is, in fact, a commandment of the Lord.

> But ye are commanded in all things to ask of God, who giveth liberally; and that which the Spirit testifies unto you even so I would that ye should do in all holiness of heart, walking uprightly before me, considering the end of your salvation, doing all things with prayer and thanksgiving (D&C 46:7).

As we see in this statement by the Lord, we are to remain close to the Spirit of the Lord, and act in accord with that Spirit, with the correct attitude guiding our resolve to accomplish His divine will.

The ancient prophet Enoch was one of the most successful practitioners of "asking and receiving" of which we have a record. His accomplishments are remarkable and extensive. He makes clear to us

---

12. "And Jesus answered and said unto them, Elias truly shall first come, and restore all things."

13. ". . . whom the heaven must receive until the times of restitution of all things, which God hath spoken by the mouth of all his holy prophets since the world began."

in one of his revelations that he learned to ask for divine help and intervention by way of commandment.

> And Enoch beheld the Son of Man ascend up unto the Father; and he called unto the Lord, saying: Wilt thou not come again upon the earth? Forasmuch as thou art God, and I know thee, and thou hast sworn unto me, and commanded me that I should ask in the name of thine Only Begotten; thou hast made me, and given unto me a right to thy throne, and not of myself, but through thine own grace; wherefore, I ask thee if thou wilt not come again on the earth (Moses 7:59).

Enoch knew the Lord, and knew that all things are made by Him, and come through His grace—as a gift of love and kinship. His remarkable statement, "and given unto me a right to thy throne," sets the unlimited nature of the promised blessings of the Lord, and reminds us of Christ's declaration, "for in my Father's house are many mansions, and I have prepared a place for you; and where my Father and I am, there ye shall be also" (D&C 98:18; see also John 14:2).

Enoch explained to the people of his time that upon his expulsion from the Garden of Eden, Father Adam was told to repent and be washed in the waters of baptism in the name of Jesus Christ, that he might receive the gift of the Holy Ghost, by which he would ask "all things" in Christ's name, and they would be given to him.

> If thou wilt turn unto me, and hearken unto my voice, and believe, and repent of all thy transgressions, and be baptized, even in water, in the name of mine Only Begotten Son, who is full of grace and truth, which is Jesus Christ, the only name which shall be given under heaven, whereby salvation shall come unto the children of men, ye shall receive the gift of the Holy Ghost, asking all things in his name, and whatsoever ye shall ask, it shall be given you (Moses 6:52).

In this, we see that the promise and commandment of "asking and receiving" is foundational in the relationship between God and his children. We see that it was in the same breath that repentance, baptism, and the gift of the Holy Ghost, through the grace of the Savior, were first revealed. The commandment and promise of "asking and receiving" was extended to all humanity. Not only is the entire gospel plan of salvation and exaltation outlined in this single scripture, but the interactive relationship of asking and faith is revealed to us as well.

Faith Is Action

Faith, we see, is more than just a feeling or an attitude; it is something that we do. Faith is an act; it is effort. The Apostles of Jesus explained the "action" aspect of faith abundantly to the Saints of their time. The Apostle James teaches us that true faith is a combination of faith and action.

> What doth it profit, my brethren, though a man say he hath faith, and have not works? can faith save him? . . . Even so faith, if it hath not works, is dead, being alone. Yea, a man may say, Thou hast faith, and I have works: shew me thy faith without thy works, and I will shew thee my faith by my works. . . . But wilt thou know, O vain man, that faith without works is dead? . . . Seest thou how faith wrought with his works, and by works was faith made perfect? . . . For as the body without the spirit is dead, so faith without works is dead also (James 2:14, 17–18, 20, 22, 26).

This functional aspect of acted upon faith was considered paramount by the Apostles. As we see, mere belief, even if it rises to the level of faith, is useless unless we employ or engage it in some manner. For example, if we had faith that planting seeds in the proper season and the proper soil would result in abundant crops, but we failed to plant them, our faith would be of no value to us. It is in exercising our faith in acts that we receive the blessings—or that we qualify ourselves to receive the blessings. It is in doing what we are instructed to do that we obtain. The fastest automobile in the world is of little value if its owner never fills it with fuel and ignites the engine. The Apostle James chided those of his time, teaching them that belief and faith are dead and useless to us without something more. "Thou believest that there is one God; thou doest well: the devils also believe, and tremble" (James 2:19). The scorn in his statement borders on sarcasm, causing modern students of holy writ to grin, if only slightly, to know that we are not alone in our battle against skepticism and inaction when it comes to exercising faith in the Lord's promises. It is also a perfect illustration of the value of testimony over knowledge. I can know that Jesus existed, but unless I have faith in Him as the Savior of humanity, and our Mediator and Advocate with the Father, that knowledge has no power to improve my life, or standing with God.

Let us further examine the Lord's promise that if we will ask, He will give, to the end that we might more fully appreciate its significance in the Lord's purposes, and His plan for us. The promise is fully laid out for us by the Lord Jesus Christ Himself, and is found in many places in the scriptures, because it was made to all people in all places in all dispensations of time. It was at the conclusion of the Sermon on the Mount that the Lord specifically directed:

> Ask, and it shall be given you; seek, and ye shall find; knock, and it shall be opened unto you: For every one that asketh receiveth; and he that seeketh findeth; and to him that knocketh it shall be opened (Matthew 7:7–8; see also Luke 11:10[14]; 3Nephi 14:8[15]).

The principle is simple and extraordinary. The Lord elucidates it on this sacred occasion: if we ask something of the Father, He will give it to us; if we seek something, He will make sure we find it; if we knock at the door, He will open it. This last promise is glorious in its implication and significant in ways that are not readily apparent to everyone. As shared by the ancient prophet Jacob,

> O then, my beloved brethren, come unto the Lord, the Holy One. Remember that his paths are righteous. Behold, the way for man is narrow, but it lieth in a straight course before him, and the keeper of the gate is the Holy One of Israel; and he employeth no servant there; and there is none other way save it be by the gate; for he cannot be deceived, for the Lord God is his name (2 Nephi 9:41).

14. "Every one that asketh receiveth; and he that seeketh findeth; and to him that knocketh it shall be opened."
15. "For every one that asketh, receiveth; and he that seeketh, findeth; and to him that knocketh, it shall be opened."

The Lord Jesus Christ is the Holy One, and will Himself be the gatekeeper on that holy day when we shall knock and He shall extend His scarred hand to help us pass through the veil into the celestial kingdom (2 Nephi 9:41).

Did the listeners on the mount understand what the Lord Jesus was telling them? To ensure that they did, Jesus gave them a familiar comparison to their own lives. They, as parents, sought to give good gifts to their own children, and thereby recognized the sincerity of the Father's promise and relationship to them. He explained:

> Or what man is there of you, whom if his son ask bread, will he give him a stone? Or if he ask a fish, will he give him a serpent? If ye then, being evil, know how to give good gifts unto your children, how much more shall your Father which is in heaven give good things to them that ask him (Matthew 7:9–11; Luke 11:11–13; 3 Nephi 14:11–14)?[16]

Luke records the Lord making a specific promise to the children of Israel: "Ye then, being evil, know how to give good gifts unto your children: how much more shall your heavenly Father give the Holy Spirit to them that ask him?" (Luke 11:13). We should not think that the specific promise of the Holy Spirit is a promise to be taken lightly. The light and knowledge that the Lord gives His children on Earth through the medium of the Holy Spirit is powerful and transformational. It is a direct link to the mind of God. Receiving the pure intelligence of the Holy Spirit is so unyielding in its confirmation of truth that denying carried heavy consequences. Having once received such a communication and then denying it is one of the few ways that a person disqualifies themself from a kingdom of glory in the eternities. They are abandoned to the hopelessness of outer darkness with Satan and his league of rebellious spirit followers (Hebrews 6:4–6). The ministration of the Holy Spirit is one of the very best gifts that God gives His children. We do well to seek it and to ask for it in unshakeable faith to the end that we might receive knowledge and testimony of all truth.

---

16. Luke records an additional question: "Or if he shall ask an egg, will he offer him a scorpion" (Luke 11:12)?

Could the Lord be any clearer in explaining the sacred principle that loving parents give good things to their children? Like the parents in ancient Israel, we receive our children as sacred gifts from the Father, and we hold them in high esteem as our inheritance from the Lord. We love our children with all of our hearts, and we would do anything for their welfare—including laying down our lives for them if necessary. Against this backdrop, the Savior said that we give to our children those things which they ask of us, and that we would never think to give them something less than what they ask. Understanding that God's ways and thoughts are higher than ours as the heavens are higher than the earth (Isaiah 55:9), Jesus explained that our love and devotion toward our children is mere indifference in comparison to our Father's love and devotion toward us. To the same amplified degree, God is that much more anxious to give us those good things that we ask of Him than we are anxious to give good things to our own little children when they ask good things of us. If we are able to come to a proper understanding of this concept—to fully appreciate the love that the Father has for us, it becomes clear just how much He is willing to give us those things that we ask of Him. Can there be any doubt of this great and powerful principle?

The Lord Frequently Commands Us to Ask

Is the Lord's promise that if we ask something of Him, He will give it to us, a passing or insignificant phrase that we find tucked away in a cobwebbed corner of the Old Testament? No, it is prominent, and frequent throughout all of the scriptures. He said it to Adam, and to Enoch. He said it repeatedly to all of Israel throughout recorded history, and He said it to the Saints of the early part of the Restoration. He says it to us, now. He says it to you—and He says it in this very moment.

Let us explore the command to ask that we might receive from the Lord in holy writ, to see if there are limits to His promises. Below are several scriptural passages in which the Lord and His prophets extend the promise—ask and receive. There are many here so that we may see them in the strength of their numbers, and that we may consider them in proper context.

And whatsoever ye shall ask the Father in my name, which is right, believing that ye shall receive, behold it shall be given unto you (3 Nephi 18:20).

And now I go unto the Father. And verily I say unto you, whatsoever things ye shall ask the Father in my name shall be given unto you. Therefore, ask, and ye shall receive; knock, and it shall be opened unto you; for he that asketh, receiveth; and unto him that knocketh, it shall be opened (3 Nephi 27:28–29).

And now, if God, who has created you, on whom you are dependent for your lives and for all that ye have and are, doth grant unto you whatsoever ye ask that is right, in faith, believing that ye shall receive, O then, how ye ought to impart of the substance that ye have one to another (Mosiah 4:21).

And after that he came men also were saved by faith in his name; and by faith, they become the sons of God. And as surely as Christ liveth he spake these words unto our fathers, saying: Whatsoever thing ye shall ask the Father in my name, which is good, in faith believing that ye shall receive, behold, it shall be done unto you (Moroni 7:26).

Ask, and ye shall receive; knock, and it shall be opened unto you. Amen (D&C 4:7).

Therefore, if you will ask of me you shall receive; if you will knock it shall be opened unto you (D&C 6:5).

AND the Lord said unto me: John, my beloved, what desirest thou? For if you shall ask what you will, it shall be granted unto you (D&C 7:1).

And, therefore, whatsoever you shall ask me to tell you by that means, that will I grant unto you, and you shall have knowledge concerning it (D&C 8:9).

Ask that you may know the mysteries of God, and that you may translate and receive knowledge from all those ancient records which have been hid up, that are sacred; and according to your faith shall it be done unto you (D&C 8:11).

Therefore, if you will ask of me you shall receive; if you will knock it shall be opened unto you (D&C 11:5).

Therefore, if you will ask of me you shall receive; if you will knock it shall be opened unto you (D&C 12:5).

Therefore, if you will ask of me you shall receive; if you will knock it shall be opened unto you (D&C 14:5).

And, as it is written—Whatsoever ye shall ask in faith, being united in prayer according to my command, ye shall receive (D&C 29:6).

Behold, I say unto you, go forth as I have commanded you; repent of all your sins; ask and ye shall receive; knock and it shall be opened unto you (D&C 49:26).

He that asketh in the Spirit asketh according to the will of God; wherefore it is done even as he asketh (D&C 49:30).

And if ye are purified and cleansed from all sin, ye shall ask whatsoever you will in the name of Jesus and it shall be done (D&C 50:29).

Draw near unto me and I will draw near unto you; seek me diligently and ye shall find me; ask, and ye shall receive; knock, and it shall be opened unto you. Whatsoever ye ask the Father in my name it shall be given unto you, that is expedient for you; And if ye ask anything that is not expedient for you, it shall turn unto your condemnation (D&C 88:63–65).

And in that day whatsoever any man shall ask, it shall be given unto him (D&C 101:27).

Behold this is my will; ask and ye shall receive; but men do not always do my will (D&C 103:31).

Therefore, as I said unto you, ask and ye shall receive; (D&C 103:35) . . .

Let my servant William Law also receive the keys by which he may ask and receive blessings; let him be humble before me, and be without guile, and he shall receive of my Spirit, even the Comforter, which shall manifest unto him the truth of all things, and shall give him, in the very hour, what he shall say (D&C 124:97).

I am the Lord thy God, and I gave unto thee, my servant Joseph, an appointment, and restore all things. Ask what ye will, and it shall be given unto you according to my word (D&C 132:40).

And all things, whatsoever ye shall ask in prayer, believing, ye shall receive (Matthew 21:22).

And I say unto you, Ask, and it shall be given you; seek, and ye shall find; knock, and it shall be opened unto you. For every one that asketh receiveth; and he that seeketh findeth; and to him that knocketh it shall be opened (Luke 11:9–10).

And whatsoever we ask, we receive of him, because we keep his commandments, and do those things that are pleasing in his sight (1 John 3:22).

> And this is the confidence that we have in him, that, if we ask any thing according to his will, he heareth us: And if we know that he hear us, whatsoever we ask, we know that we have the petitions that we desired of him (John 5:14–15).
>
> But I know, that even now, whatsoever thou wilt ask of God, God will give [it] thee (John 11:22).
>
> And whatsoever ye shall ask in my name, that will I do, that the Father may be glorified in the Son (John 14:13).
>
> If ye shall ask any thing in my name, I will do [it] (John 14:14).
>
> If ye abide in me, and my words abide in you, ye shall ask what ye will, and it shall be done unto you (John 15:7).
>
> Ye have not chosen me, but I have chosen you, and ordained you, that ye should go and bring forth fruit, and [that] your fruit should remain: that whatsoever ye shall ask of the Father in my name, he may give it you (John 15:16).
>
> And in that day ye shall ask me nothing. Verily, verily, I say unto you, Whatsoever ye shall ask the Father in my name, he will give [it] you (John 16:23).
>
> Hitherto have ye asked nothing in my name: ask, and ye shall receive, that your joy may be full (John 16:24).

In addition to these several general instructions to ask and receive, the Lord has given the commandment with respect to obtaining specific blessings by asking.

> Do ye not remember the things which the Lord hath said?—If ye will not harden your hearts, and ask me in faith, believing that ye shall receive, with diligence in keeping my commandments, surely these things shall be made known unto you (1 Nephi 15:11). [Receive knowledge].
>
> Wherefore, I knowing that the Lord God was able to preserve our records, I cried unto him continually, for he had said unto me: Whatsoever thing ye shall ask in faith, believing that ye shall receive in the name of Christ, ye shall receive it (Enos 1:15).
>
> [God would preserve their records]
>
> And again, believe that ye must repent of your sins and forsake them, and humble yourselves before God; and ask in sincerity of heart that he would forgive you; and now, if you believe all these things see that ye do them (Mosiah 4:10).
>
> [Seek forgiveness]

Therefore, go ye unto your homes, and ponder upon the things which I have said, and ask of the Father, in my name, that ye may understand, and prepare your minds for the morrow, and I come unto you again (3 Nephi 17:3).

[Gain understanding]

And when ye shall receive these things, I would exhort you that ye would ask God, the Eternal Father, in the name of Christ, if these things are not true; and if ye shall ask with a sincere heart, with real intent, having faith in Christ, he will manifest the truth of it unto you, by the power of the Holy Ghost (Moroni 10:4).

[Learn truth]

OLIVER Cowdery, verily, verily, I say unto you, that assuredly as the Lord liveth, who is your God and your Redeemer, even so surely shall you receive a knowledge of whatsoever things you shall ask in faith, with an honest heart, believing that you shall receive a knowledge concerning the engravings of old records, which are ancient, which contain those parts of my scripture of which has been spoken by the manifestation of my Spirit (D&C 8:1).

[Receive a knowledge of ancient scriptures]

And it shall come to pass, that if you shall ask the Father in my name, in faith believing, you shall receive the Holy Ghost, which giveth utterance, that you may stand as a witness of the things of which you shall both hear and see, and also that you may declare repentance unto this generation (D&C 14:8).

[Receive the Holy Ghost]

Ask the Father in my name, in faith believing that you shall receive, and you shall have the Holy Ghost, which manifesteth all things which are expedient unto the children of men (D&C 18:18).

[Receive the Holy Ghost]

And whoso shall ask it in my name in faith, they shall cast out devils; they shall heal the sick; they shall cause the blind to receive their sight, and the deaf to hear, and the dumb to speak, and the lame to walk (D&C 35:9).

[Perform miracles]

Thou shalt ask, and my scriptures shall be given as I have appointed, and they shall be preserved in safety (D&C 42:56);

[Preserve scriptures]

If thou shalt ask, thou shalt receive revelation upon revelation, knowledge upon knowledge, that thou mayest know the mysteries and peaceable things—that which bringeth joy, that which bringeth life eternal (D&C 42:61).

[Receive revelations, knowledge and mysteries]

Therefore, he that lacketh wisdom, let him ask of me, and I will give him liberally and upbraid him not (D&C 42:68).

[Receive wisdom]

Lay your hands upon the sick, and they shall recover. Return not till I, the Lord, shall send you. Be patient in affliction. Ask, and ye shall receive; knock, and it shall be opened unto you (D&C 66:9).

[Perform healing miracles]

Let them ask and they shall receive, knock and it shall be opened unto them, and be made known from on high, even by the Comforter, whither they shall go (Id., 75:27).

[Holy Ghost will instruct and direct]

In 2 Nephi, the Lord specifically scolds the people for their lack of faith and their apathy in doing the basic things that they knew would enlighten their minds and spirits. "Wherefore, now after I have spoken these words, if ye cannot understand them it will be because ye ask not, neither do ye knock; wherefore, ye are not brought into the light, but must perish in the dark" (32:4). The answer is always "ask and receive.'

How We Imbue Our Faith with Power

To dispel any notion that all of these promises were given to specific people at specific times, thereby excluding us—we who read of them and claim them for ourselves in these latter days—the prophet Moroni clarifies that the commandment and promise to ask and receive is for everyone, everywhere. "Behold, I say unto you that whoso believeth in Christ, doubting nothing, whatsoever he shall ask the Father in the name of Christ it shall be granted him; and this promise is unto all, even unto the ends of the earth" (Mormon 9:21). This specifically broadens our understanding of the promise to include all people, in all places, at all times in the earth's history. Moroni additionally instructs us in this scripture that the promise to ask and receive has a requirement that we "ask in faith." The promise is often couched in such qualifying terms. Specifically, the prophet says that we must 1) believe in Christ, and 2) doubt nothing.

To illustrate the principle of exercising powerful faith, without doubt, we cite an example of Christ teaching His Apostles in the New Testament. As Jesus returned to His Apostles and disciples from the Mount of Transfiguration, he was met by a man whose son was possessed by an evil spirit, which tortured him day and night. The Apostles had been attempting to cast out the spirit, without success. Jesus asked the youth's father about the lad.

> How long is it ago since this came unto him? And he said, Of a child. And ofttimes it hath cast him into the fire, and into the waters, to destroy him: but if thou canst do any thing, have compassion on us, and help us. Jesus said unto him, If thou canst believe, all things are possible to him that believeth. And straightway the father of the child cried out, and said with tears, Lord, I believe; help thou mine unbelief (Mark 9:21–24).

How often have we found ourselves to be like this concerned father? He immediately declared his belief, but upon a moment's reflection perceived that he required something more. "Increase my faith," was his prayer. Like us, this man walked by faith, and additionally he even followed Jesus, perhaps having witnessed miracles imparted by the Savior for the benefit of others. Now, it was his turn to receive a blessing at the Lord's hand. He stepped up and asked. Jesus reminded him of the requirement of faith, to which the man replied that he had faith, but immediately recognized that the kind of faith Jesus spoke of was beyond his daily level of conviction. He thereupon asked the Lord to make up the difference between the amount of faith he possessed, and the amount of faith necessary to obtain the promised blessing of the Lord—to heal this beloved son of his grave affliction.

Was there ever a clearer or more profound demonstration of the effects of Christ's Atonement? This son of Israel understood the Savior's role in our lives better than most of us. He knew that Christ's Atonement makes possible all things—especially those things that seem out of reach due to sin. Perhaps we tell ourselves that we are imperfect, and therefore unworthy to receive the Lord's promised blessings. Is this true? Are His promises ineffectual to us if we have fallen short of His own level of perfection? Do we harbor this belief somewhere in the dark recesses of our hearts—that because of our imperfections the Lord's promises will not be true with regard to us? Is that why we place limitations on His ability to heal us or our loved ones, or to intercede in our lives in some remarkable manner? Is that why we fail to ask Him for those things that we lack to make our lives magnificent reflections of our heavenly stature? Do we fail to ask Him, that we might receive, because we fall short of "the measure of the stature of the fulness of Christ" (Ephesians 4:13[17])? If this is the case, it is time to repent—repent of listening to the negative and limiting voice of evil. It is time to cleanse ourselves of the stains of the world. These are the doctrines of the evil one, whose intent is to nullify the Atonement of the Redeemer by convincing us that it is ineffectual for us personally. To the extent we have believed these lies and have limited the Lord's ability to help us through our failure to ask Him, and to exercise our faith that we will receive of Him, we have nullified His atoning sacrifice in our own hearts, and crucified Him afresh, putting Him to an open shame (Hebrews 6:6; D&C 76:35).

The father of the possessed youth understood that it is the Messiah's mission to elevate us from our fallen state, to stand tall before God, and to make up the difference between where we are and where we could be—who we are, and who we could be. It is Christ who has purchased us with his atoning blood, and who has reached down his pierced hand to a fallen race. He pleads with us to reach up and grasp His rescuing grip that He might elevate us to stand next to Him, on His level, before the Father. He wants us to receive His name, and His inheritance from the Father. He wants us to dwell with Him eternally on an equal footing, doing the things He does, enjoying all that has been prepared for Him and those who accept His invitation. He makes up the difference between what we are and what He is. We struggle in attempts at righteousness to close the gap, it is true, but the difference is too great, and without His efforts to elevate us we will never bridge the boundless gulf. To recognize our dependence on

---

17. "Till we all come in the unity of the faith, and of the knowledge of the Son of God, unto a perfect man, unto the measure of the stature of the fulness of Christ."

Him in this regard is not to be discouraged, or to hang our heads in defeat. It is to accept our temporal humanity, our imperfections, and our need to avail ourselves of His divine help.

Surely, we are the offspring of Deity, sons and daughters of God, as clarified in this passage.

> Behold, what manner of love the Father hath bestowed upon us, that we should be called the sons of God: therefore the world knoweth us not, because it knew him not. Beloved, now are we the sons of God, and it doth not yet appear what we shall be: but we know that, when he shall appear, we shall be like him; for we shall see him as he is (1 John 3:1–2).

Thus, we could have come into this world bearing the perfection and glory that we enjoyed in the eternal worlds before this world was created. That was contrary to the plan of salvation and exaltation, however, and it was decreed by the Father that we should come to this earth in an imperfect and fallen state. We are "natural men and women." As such, we must struggle to return to a loftier status, developing, and eventually becoming like God Himself. That is the possibility that God has given us, and the goal which we should all have constantly in mind. King Benjamin explained this struggle to his people in his sermon from the tower.

> For the natural man is an enemy to God, and has been from the fall of Adam, and will be, forever and ever, unless he yields to the enticings of the Holy Spirit, and putteth off the natural man and becometh a saint through the atonement of Christ the Lord, and becometh as a child, submissive, meek, humble, patient, full of love, willing to submit to all things which the Lord seeth fit to inflict upon him, even as a child doth submit to his father (Mosiah 3:19).

If we follow this process, we will become more like Christ. We will reach up to Him and allow Him to grasp our hand and pull us up to His level. We will allow Him to make up the difference between where we are, and where we could be; between what we are, and what we could be. We will believe His promises—that if we believe in Him and accept Him as the Savior, the Son of God, He will save us from death and from the fall. If we believe Him, we will keep His promise that anything we ask for, we will receive. Just as the father of the possessed child, we must look to the Lord, who bridges the gap between our human weakness, and His divine strength, and allow His Atonement to make up the difference for our weakness, and lack of faith. As we seek to imbue our faith with power, 1) believing in Christ, and 2) doubting nothing, we must look to the Savior, our Mediator and Advocate with the Father, who has *already* paid the price for our success, and say, "help thou mine unbelief." We must rely on the Lord of Hosts, who recognizes our personal weakness and shortcomings, but nevertheless invites us, "Take my yoke upon you, and learn of me; for I am meek and lowly in heart: and ye shall find rest unto your souls. For my yoke is easy, and my burden is light" (Matthew 11:29–30). Taking upon us His name, and His burden, is His price to avail ourselves of the blessings and opportunities that flow from His atoning sacrifice. He strengthens our weakness, to the very degree we ask Him to strengthen us, and makes up the difference between what we can do on our own and what is required. He strengthens our faith, so that it is sufficient to call upon the heavens to accomplish the things we must do. Through Him, we exercise faith in Him, doubting nothing.

To illustrate this point, let us consider for just a moment the case of the Roman Centurion's dying servant, reported in Luke, chapter 7. The Centurion, a Roman soldier who commanded 100 soldiers at Capernaum, had a servant whom he cared deeply for, and was profoundly concerned that the man lay near death. "And when he heard of Jesus, he sent unto him the elders of the Jews, beseeching him that he would come and heal his servant" (verse 3). In everything we read about the relationship between Jesus and the elders of the Jews, they were anything but supportive of His ministry among the people. Yet, backed by the might of the Roman Empire, this Centurion imposed on them that they might "ask" Jesus if he would come to the dying man, and heal him. The politics of this request is astonishing, but the implication of the Centurion's "faith" that Jesus could simply heal his beloved servant is astounding. The Romans did not accept Jesus as a man who represented the true God; moreover, a man with innate power to heal the sick and dying. Yet, this Roman had heard of the miraculous works of the Redeemer, and had developed a testimony that He would be able to heal his servant. The elders of the Jews did come to Jesus, and implored Him, making a report of the Centurion, "That he was worthy for whom he should do this: For he loveth our nation, and he hath built us a synagogue" (verses 4–5).

Jesus agreed to follow the Jewish elders to the house of the Centurion, and as they grew close to the house, the Centurion's servants met them, and said to Jesus, speaking for their master, "Lord, trouble not thyself: for I am not worthy that thou shouldest enter under my roof" (verse 6): Jesus paused and listened to their unusual message. They related that the Centurion considered himself to be unworthy of Jesus's visit to his home, but asked Him, "but say in a word, and my servant shall be healed" (verse 7). Jesus and the elders looked at the men, who had just passed on the Centurion's message, that it would be sufficient for Jesus to merely speak the word, and the Centurion knew his servant would be healed thereby. The servants quickly added the Centurion's reasoning to their explanation, rehearsing their master's explanation, "For I also am a man set under authority, having under me soldiers, and I say unto one, Go, and he goeth; and to another, Come, and he cometh; and to my servant, Do this, and he doeth it" (verse 8). This Roman Centurion was a man who understood power and authority, and how it is shared and transferred through lines of authority. He suggested that pursuant to this wielding of God's power, Jesus could speak the word, and it would be done according to His authority. "When Jesus heard these things, he marvelled at him, and turned him about, and said unto the people that followed him, I say unto you, I have not found so great faith, no, not in Israel" (verse 9).

The promise is unto all people, at all times, and in all places. Ask, believing that you shall receive, having faith in the ability and authority of Him who implores us to seek Him, and ask that which we desire. As long as it is within His righteous will, He will sustain the person and their request. As promised, the Centurion's beloved servant was immediately healed of his affliction and lived. The Centurion did not doubt the Lord's ability, or His will, to heal the servant.

Doubting Nothing

The "ask and receive" promise is elucidated by the Lord, and found in a somewhat unusual place in the scriptures. As the Prophet Joseph rendered a more accurate translation of the New Testament, he was working on the book of Mark, the ninth chapter, where the Lord taught His disciples about offenses. In it the Lord presents a child to them and declares that those who offend the innocent shall reap an evil reward, and further teaches that if there are things in our lives that are offensive, we must pare them to ensure that we enter into the celestial kingdom. In the middle of these examples of ridding ourselves of evil and offensive obstacles to eternal happiness, the Lord says: "Seek unto my Father, and it shall be done in that very moment what ye shall ask, if ye ask in faith, believing that ye shall receive" (JST Mark 9:45). The scripture is unique, not only because of its unusual insertion in the middle of a famous discourse by the Savior, but because it gives us insight into the parameters of the promise that we will receive what we ask for. As with many scriptural references to the promise, it tells us that we must ask in faith, and further states that we must believe that we will receive the thing we request—both of which are quite important in the process of asking and receiving. Here, however, in the inspired translation, the Prophet includes a timing instruction for the Saints to understand.

As an obstacle to implementing the Lord's promise, ask and receive, many of us make excuses why the Lord won't answer our requests. These excuses are as numerous as they are tedious and erroneous. One such self-imposed obstacle is that even if the Lord does send His blessing, it will be done "in His own time." This tends to "let the Lord off the hook" in the requester's mind, which actually only serves to let the requester off the hook, evidencing the requester's lack of faith in the Lord. Even if we believe the Lord will bless us, for instance, it is left up to a future fulfillment in our mind . . . possibly even after the resurrection. In other words, by making the excuse that the Lord won't bless us now (but may bless us at some unknown point in the future), we are demonstrating that we have no faith that the Lord will bless us at all. This is not the commandment or the promise. The commandment and promise is, ask and ye shall receive. It is unequivocal, except for the parameters discussed herein. There is no evidence in the scriptures or revealed word that the Lord provides opportunities to escape His promise, if anyone was of the thought that He might seek to escape it.

The timing issue raised in the JST Mark scripture is essential to our understanding of how the Lord intends for us to receive those things which we ask of Him. It declares clearly that "it shall be done in that very moment what ye shall ask." There is no mention of the Lord's own due time, or perhaps someday, or maybe even in a future phase of our eternal life—perhaps during "the Millennium." These common excuses for our lack of faith in the Lord are entirely absent from His words, His commandments or His promises, anywhere in the scriptures. Because this particular declaration was specifically restored through the prophet's revelation, we cannot use the excuse that perhaps mistranslation rendered it thus. The promise is clear and unequivocal—"it shall be done in that very moment what ye shall ask." Due to generations of faithlessness, we have become dull in our understanding of the principle of timing. We have become slow to recognize the importance of timing to the Lord. We make excuses about it based on our own lack of faith, but the Lord has never excused it as an important aspect of our lives or His relationship with us.

To demonstrate this principle, let us consider the importance of timing in other aspects of the gospel. Does timing matter when we are baptized? In fact, we must be of the age of accountability, and we must first repent of our sins, then we can be baptized for a remission of our sins. This is why baptizing those who have not arrived at the age of accountability is entirely repugnant to the Lord (Moroni 8:4–16). Does timing matter in the eating of fruit? If we eat it before it is ripe, it does, or if we eat it before we weigh it and pay for it at the store, it matters a great deal. If we eat it after paying for it, it is justified—even if we eat it before leaving the store—but eating it before we pay for it constitutes a sin. Does timing matter in the instance of intimacy between a man and a woman? Timing is everything, because if it happens before they are married, it is grievous sin, but if it happens after they are married, it is blessed by the Lord. The principle holds true across the board that timing is an important concept to the Lord. So, with this understanding, why do we excuse our lack of faith by telling ourselves that the Lord will bless us eventually, at some ambiguous point in the future . . . maybe . . . ? It is true that all things will be done in the Lord's own time, because all things will be done according to His righteous will, and the timing is part of His will. Here is the answer to our timing question, however—the Lord's own time is generally now. In fact, unless the Lord specifically tells us that now is not the time and provides us with the proper time, the time is usually now.

This point is illustrated in all of the scriptures that recount Christ's miracles. In reading the New Testament and the Book of Mormon we find where Jesus and His Apostles, as well as many others endowed with the high priesthood, exercised that priesthood to bless others. We can find hundreds of examples where the priesthood and faith of those involved were employed to bless and restore, and with only a few exceptions we see that the results were immediate—in that very moment. In fact, with only a single exception, all of Christ's miracles were performed instantly, as the need became apparent. It was the case of the blind man who after the first application of spit to his eyes saw only "men as trees, walking." After that Christ "put his hands again upon his eyes, and made him look up: and he was restored, and saw every man clearly" (Mark 8:22–25). The reason for this two-stage healing, a mere thirty second delay, is not explained, and although it was not delayed to a future time for its fulfillment, we can contrast it with hundreds of other healings and blessings wherein the effects were instant. "Immediate" is the normal course of the Lord, both in giving us assignments, and in fulfilling our requests of Him—again, unless He specifies another time.

The main requirement in receiving what we ask of the Lord is that we have faith that He will give it to us, as included in the JST Mark 9:45 scripture already discussed, as well as many others. An equally important element of our formula for asking in faith, is that we ask not amiss—but ask for that which is right in the eyes of the Lord.

Ask for That Which Is Right

As we seek to understand the method of receiving the Lord's blessings, as established by Him, we look to the scriptures for clarification.

Most of the prophets have understood the formula for receiving blessings at the Lord's hand, including King Benjamin, who says,

> And now, if God, who has created you, on whom you are dependent for your lives and for all that ye have and are, doth grant unto you whatsoever ye ask that is right, in faith, believing that ye shall receive, O then, how ye ought to impart of the substance that ye have one to another (Mosiah 4:21).

The formula outlined by King Benjamin is:

1. Ask that which is right
2. Ask it in faith
3. Believing that ye shall receive

In this scripture we see the additional requirement, that the thing being asked is "right." This is similar to the requirement that the requested thing not be superfluous or unrighteous. "Yea, I know that God will give liberally to him that asketh. Yea, my God will give me, if I ask not amiss" (2 Nephi 4:35; see also James 4:2–3;[18] D&C 8:10;[19] D&C 46:9[20]). Similarly, the prophet Moroni counsels us,

> Be wise in the days of your probation; strip yourselves of all uncleanness; ask not, that ye may consume it on your lusts, but ask with a firmness unshaken, that ye will yield to no temptation, but that ye will serve the true and living God (Mormon 9:28).

Note that Moroni describes our third element in the formula as "firmness unshaken." Also, we must ask ourselves, what things are amiss, wrong, incorrect, lustful, sign seeking, otherwise selfish,

18. "Ye lust, and have not: ye kill, and desire to have, and cannot obtain: ye fight and war, yet ye have not, because ye ask not. Ye ask, and receive not, because ye ask amiss, that ye may consume it upon your lusts."
19. "Remember that without faith you can do nothing; therefore ask in faith. Trifle not with these things; do not ask for that which you ought not."
20. "For verily I say unto you, they are given for the benefit of those who love me and keep all my commandments, and him that seeketh so to do; that all may be benefited that seek or that ask of me, that ask and not for a sign that they may consume it upon their lusts."

or ungodly? We are specifically commanded not to tempt the Lord (Matthew 4:7; Alma 30:44). All of this means that we must ask that which is right, according to everything we learn from studying the precepts of the gospel, plus, we must receive the confirmation of the Holy Ghost that the thing we are asking is correct, and in accord with the will of the Lord. With regard to the requirement that we ask only for that which is right, a similar requirement is that we do not ask for that which is contrary to God's explicit will.

> And now, because thou hast done this with such unwearyingness, behold, I will bless thee forever; and I will make thee mighty in word and in deed, in faith and in works; yea, even that all things shall be done unto thee according to thy word, for thou shalt not ask that which is contrary to my will (Helaman 10:5).

In truth, we must specifically seek to ask for those things that are the will of God. Discerning what is God's will, and separating it from our own internal will can be a difficult task. The Lord corrected Oliver Cowdery in a revelation given through Joseph Smith the Prophet, at Harmony, Pennsylvania, in April 1829. Oliver had desired to emulate the work of the prophet, and asked if he could translate some of the passages from the gold plates that contained the writings of the ancient Nephite people. The Lord granted his request, and Oliver made the attempt, but was unable to translate. He was disappointed, and asked the prophet why he had failed in the matter. The Lord responded to his question through revelation. "Behold, you have not understood; you have supposed that I would give it unto you, when you took no thought save it was to ask me" (D&C 9:7).

In our three-step formula, Oliver had fulfilled number one, to ask—and it was a thing that was "right." But in steps two and three, he was lacking. Here is the remainder of the Lord's instruction to Oliver.

> But, behold, I say unto you, that you must study it out in your mind; then you must ask me if it be right, and if it is right I will cause that your bosom shall burn within you; therefore, you shall feel that it is right. But if it be not right you shall have no such feelings, but you shall have a stupor of thought that shall cause

> you to forget the thing which is wrong; therefore, you cannot write that which is sacred save it be given you from me. Now, if you had known this you could have translated (D&C 9:8-10).

The Lord confirms in this His earlier instructions on asking and receiving; that we must ask in faith, nothing wavering, and that we must receive the confirmation of the Holy Ghost. The Lord generously provides us with a token of the process involved in discerning the Lord's will. He tells us 1) study it out in our own mind, 2) ask if our conclusion is correct, and 3) await a feeling of confirmation, which manifests as a burning in our bosom. Although we often hear this passage discussed, we have little guidance on what constitutes a burning feeling in our bosom. Of course, the process and result will be unique to each of us. In my own experience, the burning in my bosom comes as an overwhelming feeling that something clicked into place, and that sensation of alignment produces a tremendous sense of calm.

To know what is God's will, we must seek the counsel of the Holy Spirit, approaching with clean hearts and hands, as explained by the prophet Joseph.

> And if ye are purified and cleansed from all sin, ye shall ask whatsoever you will in the name of Jesus and it shall be done. But know this, it shall be given you what you shall ask; and as ye are appointed to the head, the spirits shall be subject unto you. Wherefore, it shall come to pass, that if you behold a spirit manifested that you cannot understand, and you receive not that spirit, ye shall ask of the Father in the name of Jesus; and if he give not unto you that spirit, then you may know that it is not of God (D&C, 50:29–30).

This particular revelation about receiving the confirmation of the Holy Ghost to discern truth from falsehood, was received by Joseph in Kirtland, Ohio, on May 9, 1831, in response to "manifestations of different spirits abroad in the earth" that caused many of the members to err. It was intended to provide a sort of litmus test of true manifestations of the Spirit, and separate them from satanic counterfeits. Discerning the will of God through the confirmation of the Holy Ghost is paramount in our quest to "ask and receive" that which we seek. We must practice and draw close to the Spirit to refine our ability to recognize the will of God as it is manifest through the Holy Ghost.

Enoch Is Our Exemplar

Enoch was a mighty prophet, and he exercised the power of asking and receiving as much as any man that we know of. When he was first called of the Lord to be His prophet, however, Enoch responded, "Why is it that I have found favor in thy sight, and am but a lad, and all the people hate me; for I am slow of speech" (Moses 6:31); The Lord replied, "Go forth and do as I have commanded thee, and no man shall pierce thee. Open thy mouth, and it shall be filled, and I will give thee utterance, for all flesh is in my hands, and I will do as seemeth me good." Because Enoch was humble, and willing to do whatever God commanded him, the Lord particularly told Enoch, "Behold my Spirit is upon you, wherefore all thy words will I justify; and the mountains shall flee before you, and the rivers shall turn from their course; and thou shalt abide in me, and I in you; therefore walk with me" (Moses 6:34). The key to understanding Enoch's great power over the earth and its elements is to know that he listened to the Spirit of the Lord and acted upon its promptings. The Spirit instructed him to preach to the people, and what to teach them, and that is what he did. The Spirit told Enoch to go to a certain place, or perform service for people in need, or heal the sick, or to command the mountains and the rivers to be moved to protect his people, and he commanded them in the name of the Only Begotten, and they were moved.

This is the key to exercising faith sufficient to call down miracles from heaven. We must invite the Holy Spirit to dwell with us, and live carefully to ensure we always have that Spirit with us. We must additionally seek the will of Deity through the Spirit, and yield our own will to that of God. By aligning our life and our own will with the Lord, we become of one mind and purpose. As we do so, we build greater confidence that God will support us in the things we undertake, and the Lord trusts us to always do the right thing.

> And so great was the faith of Enoch that he led the people of God, and their enemies came to battle against them; and he spake the

> word of the Lord, and the earth trembled, and the mountains fled, even according to his command; and the rivers of water were turned out of their course; and the roar of the lions was heard out of the wilderness; and all nations feared greatly, *so powerful was the word of Enoch*, and so great was the *power of the language* which God had given him (Moses 7:13).

We note that in the beginning, Enoch was considered to be nothing but a backward stammering "lad,"[21] and the people of the land disrespected him (Moses 6:31). When he put aside his personal inadequacies and obeyed the instructions of the Lord, exercising great faith in Him, we see that "the word of Enoch" became "powerful," to the point of commanding the elements, the earth, and even entire nations feared his word.

2,000 Stripling Warriors

One need not be called upon to serve in Church leadership positions, or to be the oracle of God on Earth, to receive miraculous blessings and divine intervention by exercising faith. In Alma, we read the account of young men who were ordinary foot soldiers in a great war between nations, whose faith saved them from death. In chapter 56, Helaman sends an epistle to Moroni, sharing details of their war against the Lamanites. Helaman recounts that these 2,000 young men were the children of tribes who were formerly quite bloodthirsty, but who had made an oath to God that they would not take up arms and shed the blood of man again. These sons had not made such an oath, however, and felt that they should defend their families from the approaching enemy. They followed Helaman, and their very presence stayed the enemy for a long time. There came a point when combat was inevitable, however, and Helaman tells us,

> And now I say unto you, my beloved brother Moroni, that never had I seen so great courage, nay, not amongst all the Nephites. For as I had ever called them my sons (for they were all of them very young) even so they said unto me: Father, behold our God is with

---

21. "Enoch was twenty-five years old when he was ordained under the hand of Adam; and he was sixty-five and Adam blessed him" D&C 107:48.

> us, and he will not suffer that we should fall; then let us go forth; we would not slay our brethren if they would let us alone; therefore let us go, lest they should overpower the army of Antipus. Now they never had fought, yet they did not fear death; and they did think more upon the liberty of their fathers than they did upon their lives; yea, they had been taught by their mothers, that if they did not doubt, God would deliver them. And they rehearsed unto me the words of their mothers, saying: We do not doubt our mothers knew it (Alma 56:45–48).

The key concepts that come to mind in this account are, 1) that if they did not doubt, God would deliver them; and 2) they did not doubt, because they were convinced through the strong faith of their mothers.

This principle of building faith on the foundation of someone else's faith might seem a little counterintuitive in our discussion of faith. The Prophet Joseph Smith shares the Lord's teaching on the various gifts of the Spirit, by enumerating two distinct, yet intertwined particular spiritual gifts:

> To some it is given by the Holy Ghost to know that Jesus Christ is the Son of God, and that he was crucified for the sins of the world. To others it is given to believe on their words, that they also might have eternal life if they continue faithful (D&C 46:13–14).

These two, distinct spiritual gifts are, 1) to know through the Holy Spirit that Jesus Christ is the Son of God, and 2) to believe the testimonies of those. We often hear that we cannot prosper very well on what some term "borrowed light," yet, aren't most of us in that situation? For instance, we believe in the intervention of angels, yet, few of us have actually seen an angel. We have faith in the existence and intervention of angels, based on the testimonies of others who have witnessed angels—like Joseph Smith, and the other witnesses of the resurrected angel Moroni presenting the gold plates. I have not seen something, so I do not have knowledge of it. Yet, I have received the testimony of one who is a witness, and the Spirit testifies of its truthfulness. I have faith, based on the testimony of the witness, and the testimony of the Holy Ghost.

Such was the case of the 2,000 young warriors, who did not fear, because they did not doubt that God would protect them. They borrowed a little light from their mothers. In fact, we might better think of it as borrowing a little flame from others, that we may use to light our own flame. Of course, we must provide the fuel for the flame, which consists of all of the elements we are discussing together. For the 2,000 stripling warriors, the flame was their mothers' firm conviction that God would protect them. The fuel they provided came from their own hearts—their willingness to develop faith based on the testimony of others, and willingness to act on that faith. I would challenge all of us to pay closer attention at the next fast and testimony meeting we attend. We all have two choices: go through the experience ourselves, to obtain the knowledge firsthand; or, accept the testimonial of someone else who has gone through it, and learn from their experience. It's the perfect example of building on the efforts of those who went before, and avoiding the same pitfalls and difficulties. Pay close attention.

What do we learn of the fate of those 2,000 young men who doubted not the promised blessings of the Lord, based on the sure testimonies of their own mothers? Helaman concludes his account, that after a terrible and bloody battle, the enemy had surrendered,

> I numbered those young men who had fought with me, fearing lest there were many of them slain. But behold, to my great joy, there had not one soul of them fallen to the earth; yea, and they had fought as if with the strength of God; yea, never were men known to have fought with such miraculous strength; and with such mighty power (Alma 56:55–56).

Can our faith protect us—even when we are in the midst of tremendous danger? The answer is yes—one hundred percent of these young men were so protected.

Priesthood Power

Of course, the power to engage "the finger of God" is greatly amplified by the Priesthood of God. Those who are endowed with the holy priesthood, as was Enoch, and all of the Patriarchs, which is termed the Priesthood After the Order of the Son of God, are afforded tremendous power by God, to act in His holy name, in all matters related to His children throughout the earth. Joseph Smith shared the following revelation concerning the priesthood of God.

> There are, in the church, two priesthoods, namely, the Melchizedek and Aaronic, including the Levitical Priesthood. Why the first is called the Melchizedek Priesthood is because Melchizedek was such a great high priest. Before his day it was called the Holy Priesthood, after the Order of the Son of God. But out of respect or reverence to the name of the Supreme Being, to avoid the too frequent repetition of his name, they, the church, in ancient days, called that priesthood after Melchizedek, or the Melchizedek Priesthood (D&C 107:1–4).

This higher priesthood, called the Melchizedek Priesthood, is the highest priesthood power that any man can hold, regardless of the office or Church authority he holds within the priesthood. It contains the power to perform any act in the name of God, invoking the "finger of God," including every ordinance and miracle ever performed throughout history.

Although the revelation was given to outline the bearers' "authority" or position of leadership in the body of the priesthood and The Church of Jesus Christ, the power to act in the name of God is also touched upon in the passage.

> The power and authority of the higher, or Melchizedek Priesthood, is to hold the keys of all the spiritual blessings of the church— To have the privilege of receiving the mysteries of the kingdom of heaven, to have the heavens opened unto them, to commune with the general assembly and church of the Firstborn, and to enjoy the communion and presence of God the Father, and Jesus the mediator of the new covenant (D&C 107:18–19).

This fusion of priesthood power and asking God for any good thing is the ultimate combination of power in the universe. For those who were inspired to become members of Christ's Church, and to obtain the priesthood—at the point they realize that they have been endowed with the power of God through their appointment, it behooves them to immerse themselves in priesthood power, and explore its operation and abilities.

It is interesting that as I began to write these words a moment ago, my daughter telephoned me to tell me that she and my grandson were having a nice discussion about the difference between magic that he had seen on a television show, and the power of the true priesthood of God—a theme I was contemplating for this very text. Through apostasy, satanic worship, mistake, and general falling away from the truth, history and legend are replete with accounts of those who practice counterfeits of priesthood power (*See, e.g.,* Acts 8:9, Simon the Sorcerer; 1 Kings 18, Priests of Baal). Jesus foretold of our days, predicting, "For there shall arise false Christs, and false prophets, and shall shew great signs and wonders; insomuch that, if it were possible, they shall deceive the very elect" (Matthew 24:24). President Brigham Young spoke about his contemporaries who practiced their folk form of magic and sorcery.

> Why do we lay hands on the sick? Is there virtue in doing so? There is, and the wicked world as well as the Saints prove this. Since Joseph Smith received revelations from God, Spiritualism has taken its rise, and has spread with unprecedented rapidity; and they will lay hands on each other—one system proving another—spiritualism demonstrating the reality of animal magnetism. Is there virtue in one person more than another? Power in one more than another? Spirit in one more than another? Yes, there is. I will tell you how much I have. You may assemble together every spiritualist on the face of the earth, and I will defy them to make a table move or get a communication from hell or any other place while I am present (*Journal of Discourses*, 14:72).

As we learn from President young's assessment of spiritualists, shamans, channelers, mediums and practitioners of magic in the world at his time, there is power associated with human consciousness, and there is also power derived from falling in league (knowingly or unwittingly) with the evil one.

Whatever power that may be innate to the human being, or available through nature, is something heretofore unexplored by the Church to a large extent, because it pales in comparison to the power of God, unwavering faith in Him, and His holy priesthood, which He bestows upon members of His Church. However, there appears to be a tendency among those so endowed with priesthood power, to allow it to lie fallow, dormant, and generally untapped. Tales of wizards and Jedi Knights are loosely based on ancient bearers of the true priesthood, which is after the Order of the Son of God. In those legends, myths and romantic fables we learn that the practitioners are very devoted to their avocation, and practice their art, for good or evil, on a regular basis, to constantly expand their abilities and influence. I would that the priesthood bearers of these latter days were so devoted to their avocation and would daily exercise priesthood power in every aspect of their lives, calling upon the powers of heaven to bless and influence those around us, walking daily among the ill and needy, and bringing support to those who call upon God in their hearts for healing and relief, like the apostles of old.

> Now Peter and John went up together into the temple at the hour of prayer, being the ninth hour. And a certain man lame from his mother's womb was carried, whom they laid daily at the gate of the temple which is called Beautiful, to ask alms of them that entered into the temple; Who seeing Peter and John about to go into the temple asked an alms. And Peter, fastening his eyes upon him with John, said, Look on us. And he gave heed unto them, expecting to receive something of them. Then Peter said, Silver and gold have I none; but such as I have give I thee: In the name of Jesus Christ of Nazareth rise up and walk. And he took him by the right hand, and lifted him up: and immediately his feet and ankle bones received strength. And he leaping up stood, and walked, and entered with them into the temple, walking, and leaping, and praising God. And all the people saw him walking and praising God (Acts 3:1–9).

This is what the men who are endowed with the Priesthood of God should be doing on a daily basis, as a testimony to the world of the power of God and love of His children, and the triumph of the atoning Savior.

> And righteousness will I send down out of heaven; and truth will I send forth out of the earth, to bear testimony of mine Only Begotten; his resurrection from the dead; yea, and also the resurrection of all

> men; and righteousness and truth will I cause to sweep the earth as with a flood, to gather out mine elect from the four quarters of the earth, unto a place which I shall prepare, an Holy City, that my people may gird up their loins, and be looking forth for the time of my coming; for there shall be my tabernacle, and it shall be called Zion, a New Jerusalem (Moses 7:62).

Reviewing the elements of what is necessary to ask and receive of the Lord, we see that we must:

1. Repent of our sins and become clean,
2. Have faith that God can, and desires, to give us what we ask,
3. Believe that we shall receive, and
4. Ask according to the will of God.

The Lord, and his prophets and apostles, ancient and modern, have told us quite clearly that we are capable of doing these four things, and have instructed us how to accomplish them. As we examine these steps in greater depth, we will see that they are fundamental to our religion, and not extraordinary in their application, and that it is the Lord's desire that we be able to approach Him on a daily basis and ask Him for those things that we desire and need, and receive them at His hand.

3

In Whom Do We Exercise Faith?

The prophet Joseph Smith taught that in order to exercise faith in God we must first have a correct understanding of who and what He is. We gain this understanding, to the extent we are able to comprehend Him in our present mortal state (Isaiah 55:9[22]), through a correct understanding of His attributes. In our initial definition of faith, we learned that trust in God, developed through our experiences with Him, is essential to exercising strong faith in Him. The prophet instructed:

> We here observe that God is the only supreme governor and independent being in whom all fullness and perfection dwells; who is omnipotent, omnipresent, and omniscient; without beginning of days or end of life; and that in him every good gift, and every good principle dwells; and that he is the Father of lights. In him the principle of faith dwells independently; and he is the object in whom the faith of all other rational and accountable beings centers for life and salvation (*Lectures on Faith*, 2:2).

God, our Heavenly Father, is the ultimate Being, and all other beings look up to Him as the source of all things, material and spiritual.

22. "For as the heavens are higher than the earth, so are my ways higher than your ways, and my thoughts than your thoughts."

Our Father has all power, and His influence and comprehension extend into every particle and corner of the vast universe. He knows all things, immense and infinitesimal—past, present, and future. "Through faith we understand that the worlds were framed by the word of God, so that things which are seen were not made of things which do appear" (Hebrews 11:3). We have come to learn of God and His attributes through His revelations to us, and by those who came before us who interacted with Him. Thereby, learning for themselves who and what He is, they passed on their knowledge of Him to us, by their testimonies, written or spoken. The prophet Joseph Smith taught that an understanding of God begins by one receiving these testimonies and by developing an understanding of God's historical interaction with humanity. This leads to three very necessary steps in developing our faith. The Prophet Joseph taught:

> Let us here observe. Three things are necessary in order that any rational and intelligent being may exercise faith in God, unto life and salvation: First, the idea that he actually exists. Second, a correct idea of his character, perfections, and attributes. Third, an actual knowledge that the course of life which he is pursuing, is according to his [God's] will. For without an acquaintance with these three important facts, the faith of every rational being must be imperfect and unproductive, but with this understanding, it can become perfect and fruitful, abounding in righteousness unto the praise and glory of God the Father, and the Lord Jesus Christ (*Lectures on Faith*, 3:2–5).

Perfect faith becomes a reality in our life as we grasp and apply these three simple concepts.

1. God exists
2. God's character
3. Live God's will

Trust in God, which comes through understanding these three principles, will infuse our faith with great power. Our confidence in Him will grow and strengthen as we focus and keep them present in our mind. One of the best ways to keep these concepts ever-present in our minds is to keep our Heavenly Father constantly engaged in our lives, in everything we do, at all times of the day and night. The prophet Amulek teaches us,

> Therefore may God grant unto you, my brethren, that ye may begin to exercise your faith unto repentance, that ye begin to call upon his holy name, that he would have mercy upon you; Yea, cry unto him for mercy; for he is mighty to save. Yea, humble yourselves, and continue in prayer unto him. Cry unto him when ye are in your fields, yea, over all your flocks. Cry unto him in your houses, yea, over all your household, both morning, mid-day, and evening. Yea, cry unto him against the power of your enemies. Yea, cry unto him against the devil, who is an enemy to all righteousness. Cry unto him over the crops of your fields, that ye may prosper in them. Cry over the flocks of your fields, that they may increase. But this is not all; ye must pour out your souls in your closets, and your secret places, and in your wilderness. Yea, and when you do not cry unto the Lord, let your hearts be full, drawn out in prayer unto him continually for your welfare, and also for the welfare of those who are around you (Alma 34:17–27).

If we follow this wise counsel, we will develop faith, and our power to exercise faith in God will be strengthened every day. Let us consider together each of the three elements of exercising faith in God, to ensure we are fully able to develop the necessary confidence to foster power in our lives.

God Actually Exists

The idea that God actually exists is a matter of historical fact, to those who accept the testimonies of the prophets and millions among us who have received the testimony of His presence in their lives. For each of us, it is a matter of individual, personal testimony, revealed through the Holy Spirit, and comes in particular abundance to those who enjoy the gift of the Holy Ghost. The Apostle Paul confirmed,

> But as it is written, Eye hath not seen, nor ear heard, neither have entered into the heart of man, the things which God hath prepared for them that love him. But God hath revealed them unto us by his Spirit: for the Spirit searcheth all things, yea, the deep things

> of God. For what man knoweth the things of a man, save the spirit of man which is in him? even so the things of God knoweth no man, but the Spirit of God. Now we have received, not the spirit of the world, but the spirit which is of God; that we might know the things that are freely given to us of God. Which things also we speak, not in the words which man's wisdom teacheth, but which the Holy Ghost teacheth; comparing spiritual things with spiritual (1 Corinthians 2:9–13).

The accumulation of knowledge that God actually exists comes to us in this very manner—a natural process, like any other learning gained through experiment, observation, or personal experience. Paul instructs that the difference is His Holy Spirit, which conveys knowledge of God to us at a spiritual level. We know that the Light of Christ, a spiritual gift with which we are all endowed from the womb, also bears witness of the Father and the Son. The lord instructs the Prophet Joseph Smith that this light, which is "the Spirit of Jesus Christ . . . giveth light to every man that cometh into the world; and the Spirit enlighteneth every man through the world, that hearkeneth to the voice of the Spirit" (D&C 84:45–46). To the extent we open ourselves to the light that radiates throughout the universe and passes through us, or in the case of the Holy Ghost, lingers with us, we receive constant testimonials that speak of the existence of God to our spirit.

The prophet Alma addressed the issue of the existence of God with a skeptic, Korihor. Korihor denied the existence of God, but conceded that if Alma would prove His existence through the showing of a sign, he might believe.

But Alma said to him,

> Thou hast had signs enough; will ye tempt your God? Will ye say, Show unto me a sign, when ye have the testimony of all these thy brethren, and also all the holy prophets? The scriptures are laid before thee, yea, and all things denote there is a God; yea, even the earth, and all things that are upon the face of it, yea, and its motion, yea, and also all the planets which move in their regular form do witness that there is a Supreme Creator (Alma 30:44).

In fact, the more we learn about the structure, function and intricate workings of the universe the more we understand the vision and infinite genius of the intelligence that created and governs its operation. That intelligence is God, our Heavenly Father. All things in existence evidence the existence of God. With our limited understanding of the true nature of things, we may have difficulty comprehending the relationships of the things God has created with Him, but the more we learn about the actual physical universe in which we live, the more we learn about its creator.

> And behold, all things have their likeness, and all things are created and made to bear record of me, both things which are temporal, and things which are spiritual; things which are in the heavens above, and things which are on the earth, and things which are in the earth, and things which are under the earth, both above and beneath: all things bear record of me (Moses 6:63).

One of the surest testimonials of the actual existence of God the Father, and His glorious Son, Jesus Christ, is provided by the Prophet of the Restoration. Joseph bears his solemn witness:

> When the light rested upon me I saw two Personages, whose brightness and glory defy all description, standing above me in the air. One of them spake unto me, calling me by name and said, pointing to the other—This is My Beloved Son. Hear Him (Joseph Smith—History 1:17)!

The reality of the First Vision and the coming forth of the Book of Mormon through the Prophet of the latter-day Restoration helps us believe and have faith that God exists. God's existence is fundamental to every aspect of our life. Through the prophet, Joseph Smith, God has said, "By these things we know that there is a God in heaven, who is infinite and eternal, from everlasting to everlasting the same unchangeable God, the framer of heaven and earth, and all things which are in them" (D&C 20:17).

We discussed earlier that the ancient prophet Alma shared a test we can perform to confirm to us the truth of anything. Perhaps as we approach the subject of God's existence, we only have hope that there is a God—a mere desire to believe He exists. Yet, if we nurture that desire and allow it to grow within us, it will blossom into faith, and that faith will grow until it fills us and imbues us with power (Alma 32:26–27). The key to this process is to nurture the good seed, which requires activity and effort on our part. Knowledge, of all things, including the existence of God, can be learned by "asking," as the prophet Moroni taught in his famous promise that we can know the truth of all things if we will but ask God with a sincere heart.

> And when ye shall receive these things [whatever information we wish to examine to know the truth], I would exhort you that ye would ask God, the Eternal Father, in the name of Christ, if these things are not true; and if ye shall ask with a sincere heart, with real intent, having faith in Christ, he will manifest the truth of it unto you, by the power of the Holy Ghost. And by the power of the Holy Ghost ye may know the truth of all things (Moroni 10:4–5).

Of course, it is a little "chicken and egg" if we think about it. We pray to God, to obtain knowledge that there is a God. However, the promise includes a method that allows us to build—to bootstrap, if you will—beginning at a low level of hope. Then, by exercising even a miniscule amount of faith in Christ, "if" God and Christ exist, that They will assist the requester in his or her faith. Then applying that small amount of faith to nurture and grow it into a larger, surer faith and eventually, knowledge. The Light of Christ testifies to all of God's children that He exists. We need only open our hearts and minds to its universal influence to hear its confirmation of this wonderful truth.

> Therefore it is given to abide in you; the record of heaven; the Comforter; the peaceable things of immortal glory; the truth of all things; that which quickeneth all things, which maketh alive all things; that which knoweth all things, and hath all power according to wisdom, mercy, truth, justice, and judgment (Moses 6:61).

Therefore, we must obtain an understanding of God's existence through a study of His works and creations (1) and the testimonies of others (2), coupled with the witness of the Holy Ghost (3). If we will pursue a study of the existence of God, ponder the information that we discover, and ask God to confirm the truth of those things through a manifestation of the Holy Ghost, He has promised to reveal the truth of it through the Holy Spirit. He holds Himself responsible to reveal truth to us and has promised us to do so. Therefore, He will follow through and confirm the truth of His existence to us. Our faith in His existence will increase as we progress from belief to hope, then to faith. Ultimately, our faith will become knowledge as we experience communion with Him and His divine Son.

God's Character, Perfections, and Attributes

In order to exercise faith in God, Joseph Smith taught the Saints, we must not only understand that He actually exists, but we must additionally comprehend who He is, through understanding his character, perfections and attributes. Joseph cited the testimony of the scriptures to illuminate these aspects of our Heavenly Father. First, the prophet Moses taught us important concepts about God's character. "And the Lord passed by before him, and proclaimed, The Lord, the Lord God, merciful and gracious, longsuffering, and abundant in goodness and truth" (Exodus 34:6).

Understanding that our Heavenly Father is merciful assures us that He will forgive us our weaknesses and mistakes. If we truly comprehend and accept this principle, we will know that we can approach Him with confidence as we exercise our faith in Him and ask Him for that which we desire, so long as we repent of our sins and errors, and accept His Son, Jesus Christ, as the Savior and Redeemer.

Knowing that God is gracious teaches us that He is pleasantly kind, benevolent, and courteous. He is characterized by comfort and ease in our regard, or, in other words, He is indulgent and beneficent toward us.

Knowing that God is longsuffering helps us understand that He endures our injuries and insults to His love and kindness over long periods of time, in the same way we might endure wounds inflicted by our own young or teenaged children—on a limited or temporary basis. He is happy when the rebellious and errant child comes to Him in humility, confesses his wrongs, and asks His forgiveness.

This parent and child relationship further helps us appreciate how abundant He is in goodness and truth. His feelings and desires for us are as ours for our own little children, only amplified to an incomprehensible degree. Take a moment to ponder your love for a special child. Think of how much you desire good things for that beloved one. Think of how willing you are to bless the child, to work and sacrifice for his or her happiness and future. Now, realize that your profound and abiding love for that child is indifference, neglect, or even hatred, compared with our Heavenly Father's love and concern for you. To our Father, you are that child—that beloved, sweet, beautiful little one. He lives to make you happy. His only desire and joy is to bless you. He has said it often. "For behold, this is my work and my glory—to bring to pass the immortality and eternal life of man" (Moses 1:39). He has also taught us that "men are, that they might have joy" (2 Nephi 2:25). This is His driving purpose for our creation and our sojourn on this earth and into the eternities—that our Heavenly Father can bless us with all that He possesses and help us to become exactly like Him. We are His children and heirs.

> Behold, what manner of love the Father hath bestowed upon us, that we should be called the sons of God: therefore the world knoweth us not, because it knew him not (1 John 3:1).
>
> And if children, then heirs; heirs of God, and joint-heirs with Christ; if so be that we suffer with him, that we may be also glorified together (Romans 8:17).
>
> All things that the Father hath are mine: therefore said I, that he shall take of mine, and shall shew it unto you (John 16:15).
>
> And hath made us kings and priests unto God and his Father; to him be glory and dominion for ever and ever. Amen (Revelation 1:6).

We further learn of the attributes of our Heavenly Father from the Psalmist:

> The LORD executeth righteousness and judgment for all that are oppressed. He made known his ways unto Moses, his acts unto the children of Israel. The Lord is merciful and gracious, slow to anger, and plenteous in mercy. He will not always chide: neither will he

> keep his anger for ever. He hath not dealt with us after our sins; nor rewarded us according to our iniquities. For as the heaven is high above the earth, so great is his mercy toward them that fear him. As far as the east is from the west, so far hath he removed our transgressions from us. Like as a father pitieth his children, so the LORD pitieth them that fear him (Psalm 103:6–13).

Our Father in heaven is a beautiful, kind and loving personage. He is filled with mercy toward us, His children, and, importantly, He is slow to anger. We may think that He is instantly filled with hate and spite toward us when we do something contrary to His commandments or His righteous will, but the prophets assure us that such is not the case. The scriptures are filled with accounts of His patience toward His children, always willing to forgive them if they will just turn to Him.

The Lord declares of His children that He always stands ready to openly love and bless them, as long as they are willing to receive His love and blessings,

> Jerusalem, Jerusalem, thou that killest the prophets, and stonest them which are sent unto thee, how often would I have gathered thy children together, even as a hen gathereth her chickens under her wings, and ye would not (Matthew 23:37; see also 3 Nephi 10:4–6[23])!

We also learn that the Lord God is eternal, steadfast, unchangeable, and has no end.

> And Thou, Lord, in the beginning hast laid the foundation of the earth; and the heavens are the works of thine hands: they shall

23. "O ye people of these great cities which have fallen, who are descendants of Jacob, yea, who are of the house of Israel, how oft have I gathered you as a hen gathereth her chickens under her wings, and have nourished you. And again, how oft would I have gathered you as a hen gathereth her chickens under her wings, yea, O ye people of the house of Israel, who have fallen; yea, O ye people of the house of Israel, ye that dwell at Jerusalem, as ye that have fallen; yea, how oft would I have gathered you as a hen gathereth her chickens, and ye would not. O ye house of Israel whom I have spared, how oft will I gather you as a hen gathereth her chickens under her wings, if ye will repent and return unto me with full purpose of heart."

> perish; but thou remainest; and they all shall wax old as doth a garment; and as a vesture shalt thou fold them up, and they shall be changed: but thou art the same, and thy years shall not fail (Hebrews 1:10–12).

This teaches us that He will always be there for us, that He will never cease in His works or His love toward us. Furthermore, the scriptures assure us that as He lives eternally, that He will never change; we will always know what to expect from Him. Let us read a few of the scriptures that confirm His eternal and undeviating devotion to us, His children. The Apostle James assures us that our Heavenly Father blesses us with gifts, and is steady in His feelings, opinions and operations. "Every good gift and every perfect gift is from above, and cometh down from the Father of lights, with whom is no variableness, neither shadow of turning" (James 1:17). To Malachi Jehovah declared, "For I am the Lord, I change not; therefore ye sons of Jacob are not consumed" (Malachi 3:6). Joseph Smith assured the Saints that our Father is consistently and predictably good, and we can rely on Him and His promises to us. "For God doth not walk in crooked paths; neither doth he turn to the right hand nor the left; neither doth he vary from that which he hath said; therefore his paths are strait and his course is one eternal round" (D&C 3:2). "Listen to the voice of the Lord your God, even Alpha and Omega, the beginning and the end, whose course is one eternal round, the same today as yesterday and forever" (ibid., 35:1).

All of God's words are true because He is incapable of lying. "God is not a man, that he should lie; neither the son of man, that he should repent" (Numbers 23:19). This gives us the assurance that when God speaks, whether by His own voice or through His prophets, every word that He says is true. He will uphold His promises to us no matter how lofty we may feel they appear. In the case of "ask and receive," the promise is clear. He is bound by His promise to give us that which we ask, so long as we ask in the manner He has decreed.

We also learn from the scriptures that God is the very embodiment of love. "He that loveth not knoweth not God; for God is love" (1 John 4:8). With our limited understanding of the concept of love we are able to glimpse how our Father feels about each of us. Again, we must comprehend that our own feelings toward our children are a mere faint shadow of His immense love for us, His children. How much does he love us? Does He love others more than he loves you or me, and therefore, we, due to some defect or circumstance, rate lower on His list of children than others? The answer is found in the scriptures. He is no respecter of persons (Acts 10:34;[24] Romans 2:11[25]), meaning He does not prefer some of His children to others. There are many in the world who do not believe this principle. There are those among us who feel that they are loved less by Heavenly Father, evidenced by the circumstances or location of their birth or opportunities, or by their personal weaknesses. There are still others who believe that they are preferred above others, evidenced by the family into which they were born or by some other outward manifestation of inheritance, preference, or beauty. All of these assumptions are incorrect. The Lord declares very clearly that He is no respecter of persons.

> And for your salvation I give unto you a commandment, for I have heard your prayers, and the poor have complained before me, and the rich have I made, and all flesh is mine, and I am no respecter of persons (D&C 38:16).

We are all made partakers of the heavenly gift (4 Nephi 1:3;[26] Ether 12:8[27]). The gift of God's Only Begotten in the Flesh whom He offered up a sacrifice for all of us (1 John 4:9–10[28]), that we all might

24. "Then Peter opened his mouth, and said, Of a truth I perceive that God is no respecter of persons:"
25. "For there is no respect of persons with God."
26. "And they had all things common among them; therefore there were not rich and poor, bond and free, but they were all made free, and partakers of the heavenly gift."
27. "But because of the faith of men he has shown himself unto the world, and glorified the name of the Father, and prepared a way that thereby others might be partakers of the heavenly gift, that they might hope for those things which they have not seen."
28. "In this was manifested the love of God toward us, because that God sent his only begotten Son into the world, that we might live through him. Herein is love, not that we loved God, but that he loved us, and sent his Son to be the propitiation for our sins."

be saved from the ravages of death and return to His eternal presence. "For God so loved the world, that he gave his only begotten Son, that whosoever believeth in him should not perish, but have everlasting life" (John 3:16).

This is the level of love that God has for each of His children—without exception. He loves each of us as much as any other. He may be pleased with the progress and gratitude of some of His children more than others, as we may be more pleased with those attributes in some of our own children, but that does not diminish His love for any of His other children. This may be a difficult lesson for many of us to learn because we tend to feel that those who don't do the things that we believe will please God, are outside of His love or, at least, lower down on His list of preferred children. In fact, we know that before we came to the earth, there were many among us who had performed much better than others, and who were destined to become the "rulers" thereafter.

> Now the Lord had shown unto me, Abraham, the intelligences that were organized before the world was; and among all these there were many of the noble and great ones; And God saw these souls that they were good, and he stood in the midst of them, and he said: These I will make my rulers; for he stood among those that were spirits, and he saw that they were good; and he said unto me: Abraham, thou art one of them; thou wast chosen before thou wast born (Abraham 3:22–23).

Notwithstanding this elevated premortal status among the sons and daughters of God, when we come to the earth and take upon us this mortal tabernacle of flesh and the veil of forgetfulness is drawn over our minds, we are all placed into something of a "reboot" mode—each beginning afresh, to prove ourselves, whether we will choose good, or choose evil (Abraham 3:25; Moses 3:17; 2 Nephi 2:27). God does not interfere in those choices,[29] nudging His preferred children

---

29. "Of every tree thou mayest freely eat;" Genesis 2:16. "Choose you this day whom ye will serve" Joshua 24:15; Alma 30:8; Moses 6:33. "Man could not act for himself save it should be that he was enticed" 2 Nephi 2:15–16. "Men are free to choose liberty and eternal life or captivity and death" 2 Nephi 2:27. "Ye are free; ye are permitted to act for yourselves" Helaman 14:30. "A third

in the right direction, and others in the opposite direction. Judas, an Apostle of the Lord Jesus Christ, was chosen before the foundations of the world to fulfil that high and noble calling. He was provided every opportunity as one of the "rulers" to rise to the level of the celestial. Yet, he fell, and his second estate is left barren, in shambles. The same can be said of Cain, the son of Adam, as well as millions of others who had every opportunity to be great, and to shine forever in the mansions that Christ has prepared. Conversely, many lukewarm sons of heaven have come to Earth, and when called upon to stand on the side of the Lord, have chosen the good, and kept their feet on the path that leads to celestial exaltation in the kingdoms of eternity. They may eventually be strengthened and become joint heirs with Christ.

Joseph Smith tells us that from the foregoing, we learn the following principles regarding the character, perfections and attributes of God:

1. He was God before the world was created, and the same God that He was after it was created, and will be God forever;

2. He is merciful and gracious, slow to anger, abundant in goodness, and that he was so from everlasting, and will be to everlasting;

3. He changes not, neither is there variableness with Him; He is the same from everlasting to everlasting, being the same yesterday today and forever; His course is one eternal round, without variation;

4. He is a God of truth and cannot lie;

5. He is no respecter of persons;

---

part of the hosts of heaven turned he away because of their agency" D&C 29:36. "It must needs be that the devil should tempt men, or they could not be agents" D&C 29:39. "Let every man choose for himself" D&C 37:4. "Every man may act according to the moral agency which I have given unto him" D&C 101:78. "Satan sought to destroy the agency of man" Moses 4:3. "The Lord gave unto man his agency" Moses 7:32.

6. He is love, or that all love is embodied in Him.

The prophet Joseph taught the Church leaders in the School of the Prophets, "An acquaintance with these attributes in the divine character, is essentially necessary, in order that the faith of any rational being can center in him for life and salvation" (*Lectures on Faith*, 3:19). It is salvation from the effects of death and the obtaining of eternal life, that we seek as children of God on this sojourn of mortality. Linking these attributes of God together, we are instructed how they function to help us attain sufficient confidence in our Heavenly Father to *exercise* great faith in Him.

> For if he did not in the first instance believe him to be God, that is, the creator and upholder of all things, he could not center his faith in him for life and salvation; for fear there should be a greater than he, who would thwart all his plans; and he, like the gods of the heathen, would be unable to fulfill his promises; but seeing he is God over all, from everlasting to everlasting, the creator and upholder of all things, no such fear can exist in the minds of those who put their trust in him, so that in this respect their faith can be without wavering (Ibid.).

"But second," the lecture continues,

> Unless he was merciful and gracious, slow to anger, long-suffering, and full of goodness, such is the weakness of human nature, and so great the frailties and imperfections of men, that unless they believed that these excellencies existed in the divine character, the faith necessary to salvation could not exist; for doubt would take the place of faith, and those who know their weakness and liability to sin, would be in constant doubt of salvation, if it were not for the idea which they have of the excellency of the character of God, that he is slow to anger, and long-suffering, and of a forgiving disposition, and does forgive iniquity, transgression and sin (Ibid.).

To the extent we imprint our own mortal weaknesses and frailties on God, we might tend to discount His infallible nature, and lose trust and confidence in Him. This is why it is so important for us to realize that He is perfect, and not subject to our imperfections.

He is faultless, flawless, and unchanging. He will never do anything contrary to what He has said He will do. We can trust Him with everything—our lives, and our children's lives. Our fortunes, and our eternal progression. He is trustworthy—and we know it because He has always been trustworthy, and has never done a single thing to make us fear that He might be untrustworthy.

Keeping these attributes of perfection and trustworthiness in mind does away with doubt, and allows our faith in our Heavenly Father to become exceedingly strong. We need not ever wonder if God will fulfil His word, in the slightest. We can trust Him. We can exercise supreme confidence in Him. He is eternally steadfast in everything He does, and He is predictable in every aspect of His character. If we haven't yet come to that understanding, at a personal, visceral level, it's because we haven't yet interacted with Him enough to experience His unwavering character. We haven't placed our trust in Him enough times and in sufficient quantity to put His loyalty to the test, and come to our own personal understanding of His faithfulness. Many of us trust only in "the arm of flesh," having confidence only in what we can do, or what we can cause to be done with human resources and devices. In much of our lives, human resources and devices are the daily, reasonable methods available to us. It is unavoidable. If we need a fish, we cast a line in the water and bring in a fish. If we need a paycheck, we get a job and exchange our time and effort for money. That is life, and it's okay to live it in a normal manner. However, think a moment how much better, and more productive life would be if we allowed the creator of the universe to be our partner in life. If we need a fish, we pray for inspiration to know where the fish are.

> [Jesus] said unto Simon, Launch out into the deep, and let down your nets for a draught. And Simon answering said unto him, Master, we have toiled all the night, and have taken nothing: nevertheless at thy word I will let down the net. And when they had this done, they inclosed a great multitude of fishes . . . And they came, and filled both the ships, so that they began to sink (Luke 5:4–7).

It is when we do all we can do, but imbue that effort with the inspiration that God is happy to share with us, that we begin to see our exertions blessed with success, and even multiplied. God knows where the fish are, and if we ask Him, in faith, doubting nothing, He will reveal many wonderful, useful things to us, enriching our lives and multiplying our blessings from Him.

The Prophet sums up the characteristics of God, and how an understanding of them leads to faith in Him, and His promises.

> But it is equally as necessary that men should have the idea that he is a God who changes not, in order to have faith in him, as it is to have the idea that he is gracious and long-suffering. For without the idea of unchangeableness in the character of the Deity, doubt would take the place of faith. But with the idea that he changes not, faith lays hold upon the excellencies in his character with unshaken confidence, believing he is the same yesterday, today, and forever, and that his course is one eternal round. And again, the idea that he is a God of truth and cannot lie, is equally as necessary to the exercise of faith in him, as the idea of his unchangeableness. For without the idea that he was a God of truth and could not lie, the confidence necessary to be placed in his word in order to the exercise of faith in him could not exist. But having the idea that he is not man that he can lie, it gives power to the minds of men to exercise faith in him. But it is also necessary that men should have an idea that he is no respecter of persons; for with the idea of all the other excellencies in his character, and this one wanting, men could not exercise faith in him, because if he were a respecter of persons, they could not tell what their privileges were, nor how far they were authorized to exercise faith in him, or whether they were authorized to do it at all, but all must be confusion; but no sooner are the minds of men made acquainted with the truth on this point (that he is no respecter of persons), than they see that they have authority by faith to lay hold on eternal life, the richest boon of heaven, because God is no respecter of persons, and that every man in every nation has an equal privilege. And lastly, but not less important to the exercise of faith in God, is the idea that he is love; for with all the other excellencies in his character, without this one to influence them, they could not have such powerful dominion over the minds of men; but when the idea is planted in the mind that he is love, who cannot see the just ground that men of every nation, kindred, and tongue, have to exercise faith in God so as to obtain eternal life (*Lectures on Faith*, 3:19–24)?

Understanding the true character of God assists us in building our faith in Him because we come to comprehend who He is and what He does, and that as our literal Father, His purposes are centered in our own fulfillment and joy. Armed with this understanding we are in a position to trust Him and His promises in relation to us. This empowers us to exercise faith sufficient to call upon the powers of heaven to fulfill our righteous desires, in this life and in the world to come. To better know God, we can learn more about Him through His characteristics. Joseph Smith taught the brethren that there are six attributes that our Heavenly Father possesses that, if we understand them, enable us to place sufficient faith and confidence in Him to obtain salvation and eternal life. (*Lectures on Faith*, 4:1–11) These six attributes are knowledge, faith or power, justice, judgment, mercy, and truth. Let us consider these attributes in greater detail to more fully comprehend the true nature of our Heavenly Father. We may acquire such trust and confidence in Him, and in His promises to us, that we will be capable of accomplishing great and marvelous things as we rely on His promises to give to us the things that we ask, according to our faith.

God Possesses All Knowledge

God knows all things. The Apostle Paul says, "Known unto God are all his works from the beginning of the world" (Acts 15:18). Not only does He know everything that has ever happened, but He knows everything that is happening now, and everything that will ever happen—all things pertaining to His sphere and stewardship. God declares,

> And I have a work for thee, Moses, my son; and thou art in the similitude of mine Only Begotten; and mine Only Begotten is and shall be the Savior, for he is full of grace and truth; but there is no God beside me, and all things are present with me, for I know them all . . . But only an account of this earth, and the inhabitants thereof, give I unto you. For behold, there are many worlds that have passed away by the word of my power. And there are many that now stand, and innumerable are they unto man; but

> all things are numbered unto me, for they are mine and I know them (Moses 1:6, 35).

Likewise, the pre-mortal Savior declared, "My name is Jehovah, and I know the end from the beginning; therefore my hand shall be over thee" (Abraham 2:8). Because God knows everything—past, present, and future—we can trust that when God tells us to do something. He knows the outcome, and we can exercise ultimate confidence in His instructions, knowing that only good will come from it.

Certain angels know all things as well—at least those things pertaining to our Father's kingdom. We learn from revelation that these angels "reside in the presence of God, on a globe like a sea of glass and fire, where all things for their glory are manifest, past, present, and future, and are continually before the Lord" (D&C 130:7). One day, we too will know all things.

> This earth, in its sanctified and immortal state, will be made like unto crystal and will be a Urim and Thummim to the inhabitants who dwell thereon, whereby all things pertaining to an inferior kingdom, or all kingdoms of a lower order, will be manifest to those who dwell on it; and this earth will be Christ's (Ibid., verse 9).

And,

> Then the white stone mentioned in Revelation 2:17, will become a Urim and Thummim to each individual who receives one, whereby things pertaining to a higher order of kingdoms will be made known (Ibid., verse 10).

This is complete knowledge, and the very definition of "truth." "And truth is knowledge of things as they are, and as they were, and as they are to come" (D&C 93:24);

For now, our personal knowledge of the past, present and future is quite limited. We may believe that we have a broad understanding of the universe and our place in it due to the revelations received through modern prophets and recent leaps in scientific discovery. We do not. As the Apostle Paul said, "For now we see through a glass, darkly; but then face to face: now I know in part; but then shall I know even as also I am known" (1 Corinthians 13:12). The prophet Joseph Smith taught that we can learn more about the things of God by looking into heaven for five minutes than by reading all the books ever written upon the subject of religion. Our limited understanding of the physical universe and God's relationship to it is even bleaker. Through the scientific process and the deployment of new space-based telescopes, we have learned a few things about the universe, but we are as infants possessing little more than a magnifying glass as we peer deeply into the infinite, and pronounce broad declarations about what we believe we see and how it relates to all other things in existence. We possess very little knowledge about anything (Isaiah 55:9).

The most important knowledge that we can possess in this mortality is that the course of life we are pursuing is according to God's will. Because faith must be based in truth, it is necessary that our lives are lived in harmony with truth. For this reason, it is impossible for an idol worshipper to exercise faith in his idol—faith sufficient to save them from the fall or to exalt them to the presence of God, which are the ultimate goals of faith. It is just as difficult for a heathen to exercise sufficient faith in obtaining blessings because they ask a non-existent entity for those blessings and ignore the Creator of the universe in His requests and devotions. Similarly, all forms of error separate us from the true source of power and blessing. Even Cain was ordained after the Order of the Son of God, and sought to please (or impress) God by offering a sacrifice. However, because what he offered was not in similitude of the sacrifice of the Only Begotten of the Father, which was the ordained manner of offering sacrifice, his sacrifice could not be offered in faith, and therefore, was not acceptable to God. An angel was sent to Cain with a message from the Lord, informing him of his mistake and inviting him to offer such an offering in righteousness.

> If thou doest well, thou shalt be accepted. And if thou doest not well, sin lieth at the door, and Satan desireth to have thee; and except thou shalt hearken unto my commandments, I will deliver thee up, and it shall be unto thee according to his desire. And thou shalt rule over him (Moses 5:23).

Ultimately, Cain rebelled against God and chose a different path, and lost his privileges before the Lord. Pursuing the wrong path, even if we have good or seemingly justifiable intentions, never gets us to our desired destination, and this is true of trying to exercise faith in things that are not real.

To one extent or another, all of humanity lives out of harmony with revealed truth. For those who have been informed what God requires of us, we are responsible to conform our lives to those requirements. They are not burdensome, but the Lord does expect our compliance, so that we may receive the blessings that are predicated upon our adherence to them (D&C 130:20–21[30]). He invites us, "Take my yoke upon you, and learn of me; for I am meek and lowly in heart: and ye shall find rest unto your souls" (Matthew 11:29). If we fail to conform our lives to principles and standards that He has established, we will lack the confidence necessary to stand boldly before our Father and request those things that are important to us.

What are the things we should do to live in conformity with His decrees? Christ was asked this very question. In His dispensation He plucked His reply from the Ten Commandments, which were well known to all in His hearing. "Thou shalt do no murder, Thou shalt not commit adultery, Thou shalt not steal, Thou shalt not bear false witness, Honour thy father and thy mother: and, Thou shalt love thy neighbour as thyself" (Matthew 19:18–19). Certainly, there were many other things that the people were commanded to do or prohibited from doing, especially under the Law of Moses, but the Savior enumerated these particular requirements for the purposes of His answer to the inquiring young rich man. In our day we can add programs that the Lord has established to help us resist the modern world's encroachment on our children and families—attend church meetings, pay an honest tithe, hold weekly family home evening, be vigilant about the television, internet, and cinematic programming we allow in our lives, etc. In fact, the questions that are asked of us when we renew our temple recommends might well serve to establish whether we are living lives according to God's will. If we are, then our confidence should wax strong in the presence of God (D&C 121:45[31]). We

30. "There is a law, irrevocably decreed in heaven before the foundations of this world, upon which all blessings are predicated—And when we obtain any blessing from God, it is by obedience to that law upon which it is predicated."

31. "Let thy bowels also be full of charity towards all men, and to the household of faith, and let virtue garnish thy thoughts unceasingly; then shall thy

will know that we are acceptable to the Lord and may approach Him in that spirit. If we cannot answer that we are living our lives in accordance with His divine will, there is just one thing to do—repent.

Repentance includes the process of abandoning mistaken behavior and adopting acceptable behavior. If we have failed to pay our tithes, then today we begin to pay our tithes. If we have failed to perform our duties in the priesthood, church, or family, today we begin to faithfully perform those duties. If we have done something that we are commanded to abstain from, we abstain, beginning today. If we do it with full purpose of heart, committed to continue the righteous behavior, we will find ourselves on the right side of God. We will be able to approach Him with confidence and exercise full faith in Him—knowing that He exercises confidence in us.

Satan, however, teaches us that once we make a mistake, there is no repentance, and no redemption. This is a lie perpetrated by the father of all lies. Repentance is simple, and it is easy—relatively easy—because of the Savior's Atonement. In the same way that we are eager and pleased regarding our children when they demonstrate humility and regret for their mistakes, so is our Heavenly Father toward us. He delights in repentance, as Christ explained in the story of the prodigal son (Luke 15:11–32). In the companion stories, Jesus tells of a sheep that is lost then found, and of a woman with ten pieces of silver, who, upon losing one, swept the house until she found it, then called her friends together and asked them to celebrate with her. Therein He tells us, "I say unto you, that likewise joy shall be in heaven over one sinner that repenteth, more than over ninety and nine just persons, which need no repentance" (ibid., 15:7) and, "Likewise, I say unto you, there is joy in the presence of the angels of God over one sinner that repenteth" (ibid., 15:10).

The message to us is clear and simple; if our lives are not in conformity with the will of God, put them in conformity. When we know that our lives are in accord with the will of God we can approach Him with confidence and tell Him our needs and ask in true faith what

---

confidence wax strong in the presence of God; and the doctrine of the priesthood shall distil upon thy soul as the dews from heaven."

we righteously desire, whether it is salvation, exaltation, or an act of divine intervention. President Nelson shared,

> Because the Savior, through His infinite Atonement, redeemed each of us from weakness, mistakes, and sin, and because He experienced every pain, worry, and burden you have ever had, then as you truly repent and seek His help, you can rise above this present precarious world. You can overcome the spiritually and emotionally exhausting plagues of the world, including arrogance, pride, anger, immorality, hatred, greed, jealousy, and fear. Despite the distractions and distortions that swirl around us, you can find true rest—meaning relief and peace—even amid your most vexing problems.[32]

Faith, or Power

It is instructive that the Prophet Joseph Smith equates the concepts of faith and power in the context of God's attributes. As we discussed above, in connection with this concept Joseph Smith cited Paul's declaration, "Through faith we understand that the worlds were framed by the word of God" (Hebrews 11:3). In the *Lectures on Faith* the Prophet further quotes Isaiah 14:24 and 27, which state,

> The Lord of hosts hath sworn, saying, Surely as I have thought, so shall it come to pass; and as I have purposed, so shall it stand . . . For the Lord of hosts hath purposed, and who shall disannul it? and his hand is stretched out, and who shall turn it back (*Lectures on Faith*, 4:6)?

What we learn from these passages is that the Father creates in His mind, and that His "spiritual creation" is then brought forth into the physical universe (See also Moses 3:5[33]). Although we know very

---

32. "Overcome the World and Find Rest," October 2022 general conference, Sunday morning session.

33. "And every plant of the field before it was in the earth, and every herb of the field before it grew. For I, the Lord God, created all things, of which I have spoken, spiritually, before they were naturally upon the face of the earth. For I, the Lord God, had not caused it to rain upon the face of the earth. And I, the Lord God, had created all the children of men; and not yet a man to till

little about God's process of creation, we do understand this much about it—He creates things spiritually, then physically.

A major part of the lesson taught in the scriptures as well as in the lectures and sermons of the Prophet Joseph, particularly with regard to the development and exercise of faith, is that faith is power. It is a process of developing a concept within ourselves (in our mind, or spiritually), then organizing elements to bring it forth into the physical universe. The more we can learn in this life about how God creates, first spiritually, then physically, the more we learn to be like Him, and do what he does. Of course, whenever our discussion turns to 'what God does,' our beginning place is found in Moses 1:39, where He declares, "For behold, this is my work and my glory—to bring to pass the immortality and eternal life of man." This is His purpose—it's what He does. To accomplish this, He creates worlds, innumerable to man (ibid., verse 33[34]), like our own planet Earth (ibid., verse 29[35]), and populates them with His human offspring (ibid.). He then provides his children with opportunities for learning and for testing, "to see if they will do all things whatsoever the Lord their God shall command them" (Abraham 3:25). This is who God is, and what He does. It is who we should become, and what we will do if we are to fulfill our eternal destiny.

The immortality of mankind that God brings to pass deals with the length of time we will live in the eternities, and we learn through revelation that thanks to the death and resurrection of the Only Begotten of the Father we who have been born into a mortal body will be resurrected and will live for all eternity—without end (D&C 76:39[36]). This longevity does not specify the type or quality of life that will entail, however; merely the duration. It is in the concept of eternal

---

the ground; for in heaven created I them; and there was not yet flesh upon the earth, neither in the water, neither in the air."

34. "And worlds without number have I created; and also created I them for mine own purpose; and by the Son I created them, which is mine Only Begotten."

35. "And he beheld many lands; and each land was called earth, and there were inhabitants on the face thereof."

36. "For all the rest shall be brought forth by the resurrection of the dead, through the triumph and the glory of the Lamb, who was slain, who was in the bosom of the Father before the worlds were made."

life that we gain an understanding of the quality of immortal life that awaits us in the eternities. The scriptures reveal that all who live will die, and that all who die will be raised again in the resurrection (ibid.)—those who have done good to the resurrection of the just, and those who have done evil to the resurrection of the unjust (ibid., verse 17[37]). Our understanding of our future abode is further refined by the Lord in His revelations to the Prophet Joseph. He explains the kingdoms of glory that await us, including the kingdom that lacks glory that awaits those sons of perdition (ibid., verses 31–38[38]). Those who are resurrected to a kingdom of glory, which includes everyone except the relative few who are designated sons of perdition, will be inducted into one of three main kingdoms: the highest which is designated the Celestial (ibid., verse 70[39]), the mid-level which is designated as Terrestrial (ibid., verses 71–79); and the lowest which is designated as Telestial (ibid., verses 81–90). Although we further discuss the differences between these kingdoms below, for the purposes of the present discussion we should retain in memory the fact that each is a kingdom

37. "And shall come forth; they who have done good, in the resurrection of the just; and they who have done evil, in the resurrection of the unjust.

38. "Thus saith the Lord concerning all those who know my power, and have been made partakers thereof, and suffered themselves through the power of the devil to be overcome, and to deny the truth and defy my power—They are they who are the sons of perdition, of whom I say that it had been better for them never to have been born; For they are vessels of wrath, doomed to suffer the wrath of God, with the devil and his angels in eternity; Concerning whom I have said there is no forgiveness in this world nor in the world to come—Having denied the Holy Spirit after having received it, and having denied the Only Begotten Son of the Father, having crucified him unto themselves and put him to an open shame. These are they who shall go away into the lake of fire and brimstone, with the devil and his angels—And the only ones on whom the second death shall have any power; Yea, verily, the only ones who shall not be redeemed in the due time of the Lord, after the sufferings of his wrath."

39. "These are they whose bodies are celestial, whose glory is that of the sun, even the glory of God, the highest of all, whose glory the sun of the firmament is written of as being typical."

of glory. Even the very lowest tier of the Telestial Kingdom is described as surpassing all understanding (ibid., verse 89[40]).

The power that God exercises as He reigns over the universe is directly linked with, or flows from, the exercise of His faith. God's faith is perfect. God's power is perfect. He is in perfect harmony with all of the elements, down to the finest particle of matter in the remotest corner of the universe, and they all voluntarily obey His will. His influence and perception penetrate every atom and every sub-particle of matter and spirit (which is refined matter). He knows and understands them, although they are innumerable to the finite mind. Although our bodies are not yet refined to the extent that we can spiritually comprehend and will the elements, we are authorized to tap into the power of the Holy Spirit exercising our faith through that medium, and, by the finger of God, accomplish many of the same things God does as He exercises His vast faith and power. The promise is to all who seek to do His righteous will and follow in the path He has prescribed:

> For what man among you having twelve sons, and is no respecter of them, and they serve him obediently, and he saith unto the one: Be thou clothed in robes and sit thou here; and to the other: Be thou clothed in rags and sit thou there—and looketh upon his sons and saith I am just (D&C 38:26)?

In fact, the Lord God is just. He sustains the efforts of all of His children who righteously seek to accomplish His will, and who exercise sufficient faith in Him.

Justice

To properly comprehend the justice of God, we must first understand the general concept of justice. It is interesting to note how the concept is portrayed in the American and Western legal systems—a woman wearing a blindfold and holding up a scale used for weighing in the balance. Those who search the universe to discover its laws and truths long ago found that it is created against a backdrop of order and

40. "And thus we saw, in the heavenly visions, the glory of the telestial, which surpasses all understanding;"

balance. This balance aspect is inescapable. We express it in universal laws, such as, for every action there is an equal and opposite reaction. We observe it in the toss of a coin and find that, no matter how many times we toss it, half the time it will land on heads and half the time it will land on tails, as long as equal pressure is applied on each throw. There is nothing we can do to circumvent the universal laws that undergird our universe. The best we can do is seek to understand them, to obey them, and to organize the elements in a manner that suits our purposes within the confines of the controlling laws.

This universal balance is illustrative of God's justice. He is impartial (2 Samuel 14:14;[41] D&C 38:16, 26[42]). He applies the law equally to all of His creations, and all receive the natural results that flow from obedience or disobedience to those laws. To seek a desired result, we are instructed to first learn the underlying functionality (law) and then follow the prescribed instructions (commandment) for its operation:

> There is a law, irrevocably decreed in heaven before the foundations of this world, upon which all blessings are predicated—And when we obtain any blessing from God, it is by obedience to that law upon which it is predicated (D& C 130:20–21).

> For all who will have a blessing at my hands shall abide the law which was appointed for that blessing, and the conditions thereof, as were instituted from before the foundation of the world (D& C 132:5).

The implications of this principle are staggering as we begin to comprehend the power involved—God's power to assist us in becoming like Him and doing the things He does. As we learn the laws and how to apply those laws in a manner that achieves certain desired results, we find power in our own lives—the power of Godliness. The

41. "For we must needs die, and are as water spilt on the ground, which cannot be gathered up again; neither doth God respect any person: yet doth he devise means, that his banished be not expelled from him."

42. "And for your salvation I give unto you a commandment, for I have heard your prayers, and the poor have complained before me, and the rich have I made, and all flesh is mine, and I am no respecter of persons. . ."

application of laws and the results that flow therefrom are a two-edged sword, however. The scriptures often speak of the blessings that we receive from obedience to God's laws, but they equally warn of the consequences of violating His laws. We know from our experience of living in God's creation, that violating His laws has natural consequences. A child quickly learns to respect and obey the laws associated with gravitational pull, at the peril of life and limb if they fail to observe them. We obey the law of inertia when we reduce our speed on a winding gravel road, and the law of sanitation when we protect our bodies and food from microbial infestation. We obey subsets of laws as we gingerly navigate the mine fields of interaction with other living creatures, or as we ensure a constant supply of oxygen for our lungs to process. As we violate any such law, we immediately suffer the consequences of disobedience.

The same is true of God's laws, both those which are eternal, and those imposed on us through the prophets who reveal His contemporaneous will to us. The violation of any such law has a requisite "equal and opposite" consequence. There is balance in all things. There is opposition in all things. There is good and evil, sweet and sour, blessing and damnation. We are free to choose these things for ourselves, just as we are free to choose the speed at which we drive on a winding gravel road. As we choose to obey the laws, we receive the benefits associated with those laws. God cannot withhold them from us, nor would He if He could. It is He who declares, "I, the Lord, am bound when ye do what I say;" but He is quick to warn, "but when ye do not what I say, ye have no promise" (D&C 82:10). It is the principle of justice that dictates that when we violate a law, we receive the natural consequence of that violation. God cannot withhold those consequences from us either, nor would He if He could. It is He who likewise declares, "I, the Lord, have suffered the affliction to come upon them, wherewith they have been afflicted, in consequence of their transgressions" (D&C 101:2).

Therefore, we learn that like God's love and blessings, His justice is no respecter of persons—that each one of us, regardless of our pedigree, station, or opportunities, receives the natural result of what we choose to do. It is the law of the harvest—"Fear not to do good, my sons, for whatsoever ye sow, that shall ye also reap; therefore, if ye sow good ye shall also reap good for your reward" (D&C 6:33). Likewise, he warns,

> If my people shall sow filthiness they shall reap the chaff thereof in the whirlwind; and the effect thereof is poison. And again he saith: If my people shall sow filthiness they shall reap the east wind, which bringeth immediate destruction (Mosiah 7:30–31).

History bears this principle out in the cases of many who were called to high and noble stations, but who fell through disobedience, *e.g.*, Lucifer, Cain, Saul, David, Judas, etc.

From our finite, selfish perspective, this principle is a bitter pill to swallow. Because all men transgress God's laws to one degree or another (Romans 3:10, 12[43]), it is inevitable that we will all be cut off from the presence of God seeing that no unclean thing can dwell in His presence (Moses 6:57[44]). Again, it matters nothing who our parents or grandparents were, or what they accomplished in the service of God. It matters nothing what we have sacrificed or accomplished in the name of the Holy One in our own lives. In the end, we are all unprofitable servants (Mosiah 2:21[45]) and fall short of the glory of God (Romans 3:23[46]). In the end, no one can overcome the fall or eternal separation from the presence of God due to the demands of justice—which dictate that no unclean thing can survive the presence of God. God is just and fair because the consequences apply across the board to all people. Through disobedience, we become unclean,

43. "As it is written, There is none righteous, no, not one: . . . They are all gone out of the way, they are together become unprofitable; there is none that doeth good, no, not one."
44. "Wherefore teach it unto your children, that all men, everywhere, must repent, or they can in nowise inherit the kingdom of God, for no unclean thing can dwell there, or dwell in his presence; for, in the language of Adam, Man of Holiness is his name, and the name of his Only Begotten is the Son of Man, even Jesus Christ, a righteous Judge, who shall come in the meridian of time."
45. "I say unto you that if ye should serve him who has created you from the beginning, and is preserving you from day to day, by lending you breath, that ye may live and move and do according to your own will, and even supporting you from one moment to another—I say, if ye should serve him with all your whole souls yet ye would be unprofitable servants."
46. "For all have sinned, and come short of the glory of God;"

and all men and women are disobedient, and therefore, unclean. As a direct result of transgression of eternal law, our separation from God is universal and eternal, and would remain that way forever (Mosiah 13:28[47]) except for the law of mercy, which intercedes and fulfills the demands of justice, providing an equal and opposite effect to sin, providing balance to the justice equation.

Mercy

When an eternal law is broken, its effects are fixed, and its consequences are eternal. There is no escaping the consequences of a broken law. If we go too fast on a winding gravel road, our momentum will carry us forward as the road curves. We will leave the safety of the road. The consequences of the violation will vary, depending on the other laws that come into play, which will be determined in this case by the obstacles that are present. For instance, if no hazards are present, the vehicle will likely skid in the surface materials, and limited damage will result based on the relatively small measure of violence done to the vehicle and its components. If trees or boulders are present, then very serious consequences will result. The greater the violations of law, the greater the probable consequences. If a child climbs a ladder and lets go as they approach the top, the law of gravity will likewise be obeyed. The amount of violence done to the child's wellbeing is dependent on the obstacles that are present in their path. The law will be fulfilled, and unless some opposing force intervenes, there is no escaping the consequences of the fall. In the case of the falling child, a father's loving arms can intervene and slow, then stop the descent of the falling child. The laws governing gravity will be obeyed, and equal and mitigating effort and force must be applied to break the child's fall without harming the child.

In the case of our eternal separation from our Heavenly Father, the intervening force is likewise provided by a loving Father. Only He is capable of applying equal and opposite force sufficient to overcome

47. "And moreover, I say unto you, that salvation doth not come by the law alone; and were it not for the atonement, which God himself shall make for the sins and iniquities of his people, that they must unavoidably perish, notwithstanding the law of Moses."

the natural effects of our fall from grace, or separation from His presence. He can bring balance to the imbalance created by the violation of eternal laws. The prophets speak of this balance, and of the equal and opposite force brought to bear to equalize, mitigate or counterbalance the weight of sin and disobedience. Because the violation of the law is eternal, the equal and opposite force applied must be eternal as well. Because eternal separation from our Heavenly Father spells eternal death for those affected thereby, the only equal and opposite force that can be brought to intercede and neutralize its effects is the force of eternal life. Only a God possesses eternal life. Therefore, the eternal life of a God must be applied to break the fall, to mitigate and neutralize the momentum of its destructive force, and to restore the falling victim to their exalted state.

The prophets have revealed that this is the very nature of the Atonement. Amulek clarified the requirement and nature of the Atonement of the Son of God thus:

> Behold, I say unto you, that I do know that Christ shall come among the children of men, to take upon him the transgressions of his people, and that he shall atone for the sins of the world; for the Lord God hath spoken it.
>
> For it is expedient that an atonement should be made; for according to the great plan of the Eternal God there must be an atonement made, or else all mankind must unavoidably perish; yea, all are hardened; yea, all are fallen and are lost, and must perish except it be through the atonement which it is expedient should be made.
>
> For it is expedient that there should be a great and last sacrifice; yea, not a sacrifice of man, neither of beast, neither of any manner of fowl; for it shall not be a human sacrifice; but it must be an infinite and eternal sacrifice.
>
> Now there is not any man that can sacrifice his own blood which will atone for the sins of another. Now, if a man murdereth, behold will our law, which is just, take the life of his brother? I say unto you, Nay.
>
> But the law requireth the life of him who hath murdered; therefore there can be nothing which is short of an infinite atonement which will suffice for the sins of the world.

> Therefore, it is expedient that there should be a great and last sacrifice, and then shall there be, or it is expedient there should be, a stop to the shedding of blood; then shall the law of Moses be fulfilled; yea, it shall be all fulfilled, every jot and tittle, and none shall have passed away (Alma 34:8–13).

Priesthood leaders have also undertaken the task of explaining Christ's Atonement on several occasions, delineating the opposing roles of justice and mercy. Our Heavenly Father is just, and His justice provides His children with a sense of predictability and fairness. However, He is infinitely merciful, as well, having sacrificed His firstborn son as a ransom for our sins. A favorite modern explanation of the roles of justice and mercy is proffered in a parable by an Apostle of the Lord, Elder Boyd K. Packer, who teaches:

> There once was a man who wanted something very much. It seemed more important than anything else in his life. In order for him to have his desire, he incurred a great debt.
>
> He had been warned about going into that much debt, and particularly about his creditor. But it seemed so important for him to do what he wanted to do and to have what he wanted right now. He was sure he could pay for it later.
>
> So he signed a contract. He would pay it off some time along the way. He didn't worry too much about it, for the due date seemed such a long time away. He had what he wanted now, and that was what seemed important.
>
> The creditor was always somewhere in the back of his mind, and he made token payments now and again, thinking somehow that the day of reckoning really would never come.
>
> But as it always does, the day came, and the contract fell due. The debt had not been fully paid. His creditor appeared and demanded payment in full.
>
> Only then did he realize that his creditor not only had the power to repossess all that he owned, but the power to cast him into prison as well.
>
> "I cannot pay you, for I have not the power to do so," he confessed.
>
> "Then," said the creditor, "we will exercise the contract, take your possessions, and you shall go to prison. You agreed to that.

It was your choice. You signed the contract, and now it must be enforced."

"Can you not extend the time or forgive the debt?" the debtor begged. "Arrange some way for me to keep what I have and not go to prison. Surely you believe in mercy? Will you not show mercy?"

The creditor replied, "Mercy is always so one-sided. It would serve only you. If I show mercy to you, it will leave me unpaid. It is justice I demand. Do you believe in justice?"

"I believed in justice when I signed the contract," the debtor said. "It was on my side then, for I thought it would protect me. I did not need mercy then, nor think I should need it ever. Justice, I thought, would serve both of us equally as well."

"It is justice that demands that you pay the contract or suffer the penalty," the creditor replied. "That is the law. You have agreed to it and that is the way it must be. Mercy cannot rob justice."

There they were: One meting out justice, the other pleading for mercy. Neither could prevail except at the expense of the other.

"If you do not forgive the debt there will be no mercy," the debtor pleaded.

"If I do, there will be no justice," was the reply.

Both laws, it seemed, could not be served. They are two eternal ideals that appear to contradict one another. Is there no way for justice to be fully served, and mercy also?

There is a way! The law of justice can be fully satisfied and mercy can be fully extended—but it takes someone else. And so it happened this time.

The debtor had a friend. He came to help. He knew the debtor well. He knew him to be shortsighted. He thought him foolish to have gotten himself into such a predicament. Nevertheless, he wanted to help because he loved him. He stepped between them, faced the creditor, and made this offer.

"I will pay the debt if you will free the debtor from his contract so that he may keep his possessions and not go to prison."

As the creditor was pondering the offer, the mediator added, "You demanded justice. Though he cannot pay you, I will do so. You will have been justly dealt with and can ask no more. It would not be just."

And so the creditor agreed.

> The mediator turned then to the debtor. "If I pay your debt, will you accept me as your creditor?"
>
> "Oh yes, yes," cried the debtor. "You save me from prison and show mercy to me."
>
> "Then," said the benefactor, "you will pay the debt to me and I will set the terms. It will not be easy, but it will be possible. I will provide a way. You need not go to prison."
>
> And so it was that the creditor was paid in full. He had been justly dealt with. No contract had been broken.
>
> The debtor, in turn, had been extended mercy. Both laws stood fulfilled. Because there was a mediator, justice had claimed its full share, and mercy was fully satisfied (In Conference Report, Apr. 1977, 79–80, or *Ensign*, May 1977, 54–55).

The principles of the debt of sin, justice, and mercy, are beautifully woven together in this explanation of how the Savior has stepped in to pay our debt to justice. In it, we learn that the debt we owe to justice is assumed by the Lord Jesus Christ, and our souls are redeemed by Him. He took upon Himself our debts, and offered in exchange His own life—the life of a God, being the literal son of God. In a way that we cannot fathom, He took upon Himself the suffering for our sins and transgressions of eternal law. He paid the price—a price that we will never fully comprehend. He gives us only allusions to the cost, explaining that the burden was grievous for even Him to bear:

> How sore you know not, how exquisite you know not, yea, how hard to bear you know not. For behold, I, God, have suffered these things for all, that they might not suffer if they would repent; But if they would not repent they must suffer even as I; Which suffering caused myself, even God, the greatest of all, to tremble because of pain, and to bleed at every pore, and to suffer both body and spirit—and would that I might not drink the bitter cup, and shrink—Nevertheless, glory be to the Father, and I partook and finished my preparations unto the children of men (D&C 19:15–19).

Yes, all of this was done for the children of men, to bring to pass the rise from our fall. The fall came in two parts. When Adam and Eve partook of the forbidden fruit, physical death entered the world. Until that time, their bodies were immortal, and they would have lived forever in that state. At the time physical death came upon them, spiritual death came as well, in that they were separated from the presence of God due to their impure state.

> And now, ye see by this that our first parents were cut off both temporally and spiritually from the presence of the Lord; and thus we see they became subjects to follow after their own will (Alma 42:7).

Again, no impurity can dwell in the presence of God (D&C 94:8–9;[48] Moses 6:57;[49] 1 Nephi 10:21[50]). It isn't because our Father lacks love for us that we are unable to dwell in His presence. It is a physical, eternal boundary that keeps us from His presence. We might consider it as we would a more mundane barrier problem. For example, there are certain types of light that create violent reactions in the presence of certain materials. For instance, microwave light is harnessed to heat food and liquids. It accomplishes this by exciting water molecules in the materials placed into a microwave oven. The friction from the molecules rubbing together very quickly creates heat. If water can be thought of as an impurity for the purposes of this example, it illustrates our problem. There are many materials that can be placed into a microwave oven that will not be affected adversely by the light, or this particular wavelength of radiation. The second we place an impure substance into the microwave oven, a material containing water for instance, it will immediately begin to react violently. Water simply cannot dwell in the presence of that type of light. The same is true of

48. "And ye shall not suffer any unclean thing to come in unto it; and my glory shall be there, and my presence shall be there. But if there shall come into it any unclean thing, my glory shall not be there; and my presence shall not come into it."

49. "Wherefore teach it unto your children, that all men, everywhere, must repent, or they can in nowise inherit the kingdom of God, for no unclean thing can dwell there, or dwell in his presence; for, in the language of Adam, Man of Holiness is his name, and the name of his Only Begotten is the Son of Man, even Jesus Christ, a righteous Judge, who shall come in the meridian of time."

50. "Wherefore, if ye have sought to do wickedly in the days of your probation, then ye are found unclean before the judgment-seat of God; and no unclean thing can dwell with God; wherefore, ye must be cast off forever."

God, and all celestial beings. The instant an impure substance is introduced to their presence it is destroyed, unless temporarily shielded or protected by the Holy Spirit or the covenants of the Melchizedek Priesthood (D&C 76:118;[51] 107:19[52]).

From the time of the fall of Adam, mankind has had the problem of the two forms of death to overcome; physical death, and spiritual death. To overcome physical death, Jesus gave up His immortal life, as a ransom for our mortal lives. He entered the world of post-mortal spirits, opened the gates, and immediately men and women began to experience resurrection, the reuniting of their spirits with their reassembled, purified bodies. And it will continue until every last child of the Father is resurrected, concluding at the end of the Millennium.[53] This work of the Savior enables mankind to overcome physical death, and because of it, every person who has ever lived will be resurrected. Thus, all become immortal, and will live forever, thanks to the death and resurrection of Jesus Christ. This is what is generally referred to as salvation, and it comes to all mankind as a free gift from God, through the atoning sacrifice of His beloved Son, the Lamb who was slain from before the foundation of the world (Revelation 13:8;[54] Moses 7:47[55]). All who have ever lived will receive this free gift of salvation from God, and there is nothing that any of us can do to earn or lose the gift.

---

51. "That through the power and manifestation of the Spirit, while in the flesh, they may be able to bear his presence in the world of glory."

52. "To have the privilege of receiving the mysteries of the kingdom of heaven, to have the heavens opened unto them, to commune with the general assembly and church of the Firstborn, and to enjoy the communion and presence of God the Father, and Jesus the mediator of the new covenant."

53. "And the graves were opened; and many bodies of the saints which slept arose, And came out of the graves after his resurrection, and went into the holy city, and appeared unto many" Matthew 27:52–53; See generally, Alma 40.

54. "And all that dwell upon the earth shall worship him, whose names are not written in the book of life of the Lamb slain from the foundation of the world."

55. "And behold, Enoch saw the day of the coming of the Son of Man, even in the flesh; and his soul rejoiced, saying: The Righteous is lifted up, and the Lamb is slain from the foundation of the world; and through faith I am in the bosom of the Father, and behold, Zion is with me."

As we have discussed above, the bestowal of immortality on a fallen race guaranties only a duration of life, not the quality of that life. To overcome spiritual death, the separation of a person, or the entire race from the presence of God, more was necessary. To be readmitted to the presence of God, a price had to be paid to satisfy the demands of justice. The task of making men and women clean again, free of spiritual impurities, in preparation for readmitting them into the presence of God was a great undertaking. As the burden was borne and the Son of God paid the price to cover our debts, He became our debtor—the one to whom we owe our eternal lives. Our debts to justice have transferred to Him, and it is His terms that we must fulfill so that we might enjoy the things He has prepared for us.

To be readmitted to the presence of God is to receive eternal life. There are lesser qualities of immortality than eternal life, but eternal life is the ultimate goal of any intelligent being. It is the highest glory in the eternities, affording the greatest opportunities and possessing the most supreme joys. To receive eternal life is to receive a celestial glory. It is to become like God, in characteristics and pursuits. In the great High Priest's intercessory prayer, Christ said,

> As thou hast given him [Christ] power over all flesh, that he should give eternal life to as many as thou hast given him. And this is life eternal, that they might know thee the only true God, and Jesus Christ, whom thou hast sent (John 17:2–3).

From this we learn that to *know* God and His Son is the very essence of eternal life. Surely, if we knew them well, it would be because we had studied them in depth and pursued their interests. To know anyone well, we must first become completely familiar with every aspect of their life, including their inner life, or their psychological (spiritual) makeup. We must learn to see things from their perspective. The more we immerse ourselves in the person's life and viewpoint, the better we will come to know them. In the case of knowing God and His Son well enough to attain eternal life, we must become entirely familiar with them, by learning all we can about them (2 Nephi 31:20[56]).

---

56. "Wherefore, ye must press forward with a steadfastness in Christ, having a perfect brightness of hope, and a love of God and of all men. Wherefore, if ye

We must pursue the same things they do with the same intensity that they do. The scriptures clarify what it is that they pursue—their entire work and glory is to bring to pass the immortality and eternal life of man. To the extent we desire to have eternal life, we too must engage in the business of bringing to pass the immortality and eternal life of man. We do this by serving others and steering them towards the celestial kingdom by precept, example, and assistance.

Service to others is what Christ has spoken of so often when explaining what it is that He expects of us. "Pure religion and undefiled before God and the Father is this, To visit the fatherless and widows in their affliction, and to keep himself unspotted from the world" (James 1:27). As He explained to His disciples who would receive eternal life, He illustrated the importance of the principle of service to fellow men thus:

> And before him shall be gathered all nations: and he shall separate them one from another, as a shepherd divideth his sheep from the goats: And he shall set the sheep on his right hand, but the goats on the left. Then shall the King say unto them on his right hand, Come, ye blessed of my Father, inherit the kingdom prepared for you from the foundation of the world: For I was an hungred, and ye gave me meat: I was thirsty, and ye gave me drink: I was a stranger, and ye took me in: Naked, and ye clothed me: I was sick, and ye visited me: I was in prison, and ye came unto me. Then shall the righteous answer him, saying, Lord, when saw we thee an hungred, and fed thee? or thirsty, and gave thee drink? When saw we thee a stranger, and took thee in? or naked, and clothed thee? Or when saw we thee sick, or in prison, and came unto thee? And the King shall answer and say unto them, Verily I say unto you, Inasmuch as ye have done it unto one of the least of these my brethren, ye have done it unto me (Matthew 25:32–40; see also Mosiah 2:17[57]).

---

shall press forward, feasting upon the word of Christ, and endure to the end, behold, thus saith the Father: Ye shall have eternal life."

57. "And behold, I tell you these things that ye may learn wisdom; that ye may learn that when ye are in the service of your fellow beings ye are only in the service of your God."

As we can see, God, our Heavenly Father, is a supremely merciful being, sacrificing that which is of greatest value to Him, for us. This He does to afford us the opportunity to overcome the high costs of justice, and to gain that which we had no power to receive on our own—eternal life. Once the sacrifice was made, we became indebted to His Son, Jesus Christ, who redeemed us from the fall with His own blood and suffering. What He expects from us to repay the debt we now owe to Him is that we strive to put off the natural man and become a new, sanctified creature through obedience, sacrifice, and service. In other words, that we do what He and His Father do, bring others to immortality and eternal life. To the extent we devote ourselves to this path, this purpose, and cause, we will receive a measure of forgiveness of the debt we owe Him. To the extent we follow His instructions, *i.e.*, obey His commandments, serve His children, become purified in thought and deed, receive the priesthood ordinances of salvation, and fully repent of all our wrongdoing, we will partially repay the debt in the currency favored by Him, a broken heart and a contrite spirit (2 Nephi 2:7[58]). Then mercy will balance out the equation of justice, and eternal life will be granted to all those who have done what He has asked of them; and those who have performed partially, will receive a portion of eternal glory, appropriately dispensed, based on their degree of adherence to His requirements.

President Nelson has said,

> My plea to you this morning is to find rest from the intensity, uncertainty, and anguish of this world by overcoming the world through your covenants with God. Let Him know through your prayers and your actions that you are serious about overcoming the world. Ask Him to enlighten your mind and send the help you need.[59]

God will help us, as promised by ancient and modern prophets. Through the Atonement of Christ, we are redeemed from our fallen

---

58. "Behold, he offereth himself a sacrifice for sin, to answer the ends of the law, unto all those who have a broken heart and a contrite spirit; and unto none else can the ends of the law be answered."

59. "Overcome the World and Find Rest," October 2022 general conference, Sunday morning session.

state. In this way, we can overcome the world and become like our heavenly parents and Jesus Christ.

Truth

This sixth attribute of our Heavenly Father, truth, is of special importance. The Prophet Joseph Smith cites a number of Old Testament scriptures in *Lectures on Faith* to support this view (*Lectures on Faith*, 4:10). "Mercy and truth shall go before thy face" (Psalms 89:14). "[God is] Long-suffering, and abundant in goodness and truth" (Exodus 34:6). "He is the Rock, his work is perfect: for all his ways are judgment: a God of truth and without iniquity, just and right is he" (Deuteronomy 32:4). "Into thine hand I commit my spirit: thou hast redeemed me, O Lord God of truth" (Psalms 31:5). Isn't it of special significance to us that the Lord Jesus Christ quoted this last scripture as one of His last earthly utterances while fulfilling the final act of ultimate truth and redemption? If ever a "man" loved and lived by every word that proceeds forth from the mouth of God, it was Jesus.

Truth is the ultimate quest, the supreme prize that lies at the end of any journey. God possesses all truth. Many men claim to possess the truth, while many more claim to seek it. What is truth? We recall that just such a question was posed to our Lord as he was interrogated by Pontius Pilate (John 18:37–38). Christ told him, "To this end was I born, and for this cause came I into the world, that I should bear witness unto the truth. Every one that is of the truth heareth my voice." At this point, Pilate asked his question, but had no interest in hearing the answer, and immediately turned to mundane administrative matters before the Lord could speak.[60] How shortsighted he was to have passed up the opportunity to learn the truth from the source of all truth. Pilate was too busy, too important to listen. He was a man of position and strength, a minister in a vast empire. He casually

60. "Pilate therefore said unto him, Art thou a king then? Jesus answered, Thou sayest that I am a king. To this end was I born, and for this cause came I into the world, that I should bear witness unto the truth. Every one that is of the truth heareth my voice. Pilate saith unto him, What is truth? And when he had said this, he went out again unto the Jews, and saith unto them, I find in him no fault at all."

admitted that the nature of truth eluded him, but he didn't have even a moment to listen to what the God who stood before him might have to reveal on the subject. Pilate was a prototype of the men of today—speaking the very word "truth" with disdain, as though the concept were a juvenile inconvenience. Good is called evil in such a society, and evil is called good (Moroni 7:14[61]). Enslavement is called freedom, and selfishness is called love. It is as though anti-Christ is among us already, and anti-truth is his message of counterfeit salvation.

It was nearly two millennia later that the Lord finally found an audience anxious to hear his response to the question Pilate had put to Him. To the Prophet Joseph Smith the Lord revealed: "And truth is knowledge of things as they are, and as they were, and as they are to come" (D&C 93:24); How simple and straightforward is the Lord's description of truth. The concept of time is included—past, present, and future—and we must suppose it is because truth, ultimate truth, like God Himself, is unchangeable. The details of existence might change with the passing of time, like the location of the planets or the progress of particular spirits in the eternities, but the truth doesn't change, as the psalmist declares. "For his merciful kindness is great toward us: and the truth of the Lord endureth for ever" (Psalms 117:2).

Knowledge is often equated with truth, even in the scriptures as we have seen. Certainly, even in the Lord's description of truth, He says that truth is knowledge of all things. There is more to truth than just knowledge, however, as there is more to wisdom than just information or experience. There is an application of knowledge, a certain state of knowledge, that renders it truth. It is further explained as a state of things as they are (or were, or will be), indicating that no amount of interpretation or spin can be present for truth to exist. Only God can know all truth, because only a God can comprehend the actual state of all things, past, present and future. His subservient angels can witness such "details" (D&C 130:7[62]), but only God's eye penetrates and comprehends every atom and every particle of spirit

61. "Wherefore, take heed, my beloved brethren, that ye do not judge that which is evil to be of God, or that which is good and of God to be of the devil."

62. "But they reside in the presence of God, on a globe like a sea of glass and fire, where all things for their glory are manifest, past, present, and future, and are continually before the Lord."

matter in the universe. Only He knows the location of every quark at every moment—past, present, and future. Only He perceives the every thought and impulse of every living creature at any given instant in time. As we seek to become like Him, we will gain more knowledge, and more truth. At the day when we shall become like Him, being quickened by the Spirit and transformed into celestial beings (D&C 88:28[63]), we shall suddenly and fully comprehend all things that are, were, or ever shall be. At that day we will be like Him, and will engage in His work full time, bringing to pass the immortality and eternal life of man (D&C 132:19[64]).

Our Heavenly Father is a God of truth, and all truth is in Him, and He is the source of all truth. We mortals are used to dealing with one another with skeptical reservation, and allow that skepticism to transfer to our relationship with our Eternal Father and His Son, and their appointed oracles. In exercising faith in God and the Savior, it is essential that we learn to put aside our doubt. This is why the prophet taught that it is so important for us to come to understand these essential principles, and to comprehend these attributes of God. Only by accepting the reality that every word spoken by God is absolute truth can we attain the level of faith that endows us with power in our lives, like that exercised by Enoch or the brother of Jared. Our reliance on

63. "They who are of a celestial spirit shall receive the same body which was a natural body; even ye shall receive your bodies, and your glory shall be that glory by which your bodies are quickened."

64. "And again, verily I say unto you, if a man marry a wife by my word, which is my law, and by the new and everlasting covenant, and it is sealed unto them by the Holy Spirit of promise, by him who is anointed, unto whom I have appointed this power and the keys of this priesthood; and it shall be said unto them—Ye shall come forth in the first resurrection; and if it be after the first resurrection, in the next resurrection; and shall inherit thrones, kingdoms, principalities, and powers, dominions, all heights and depths—then shall it be written in the Lamb's Book of Life, that he shall commit no murder whereby to shed innocent blood, and if ye abide in my covenant, and commit no murder whereby to shed innocent blood, it shall be done unto them in all things whatsoever my servant hath put upon them, in time, and through all eternity; and shall be of full force when they are out of the world; and they shall pass by the angels, and the gods, which are set there, to their exaltation and glory in all things, as hath been sealed upon their heads, which glory shall be a fulness and a continuation of the seeds forever and ever."

God must be absolute and our trust in Him unconditional to exercise faith to the degree those prophets did. This is why the prophet taught that it is so important for us to understand that our Heavenly Father is the embodiment of truth, and that He does not waver, vacillate or falter in what He promises or declares. God does not need our excuses or justifications, even though we often find ourselves offering them. It is we who have fallen short of the mark when we have doubted Him. God is worthy of our full devotion and complete trust, because every word He speaks is true, and we must learn to live in accordance with what He says, without hesitation or equivocation.

A "trust" exercise used in counseling is to ask one person to stand in front of the other, and to immediately fall backward and allow the other person to catch him or her. The counselor is immediately able to ascertain the levels of trust, by the amount of hesitation before the person who is to fall backward follows the instruction. The same test can be applied to our relationship with our Heavenly Father. If we hesitate to fall into His arms, the distrust that we feel cannot be the result of His neglect or indifference; it springs from our own lack of reliability, which we project onto Him. In order to exercise the level of faith in our Heavenly Father and His Son that results in blessed lives and frequent heavenly intervention, we must come to understand that we can rely on God's promises because He is a God of truth and cannot lie (Titus 1:2[65]).

We began our discussion of the characteristics and attributes of God, because, as the Prophet Joseph taught, if we understand them, it better enables us to place sufficient faith and confidence in Him to obtain salvation and Eternal Life at His hand. After discussing these six particular attributes in the *Lectures on Faith*—knowledge, faith or power, justice, judgment, mercy and truth—Joseph summarized:

> By a little reflection it will be seen that the idea of the existence of these attributes in the Deity is necessary to enable any rational being to exercise faith in him. For without the idea of the existence of these attributes in the Deity, men could not exercise faith in him for life and salvation; seeing that without the knowledge of all

65. "In hope of eternal life, which God, that cannot lie, promised before the world began;"

> things, God would not be able to save any portion of his creatures; for it is by reason of the knowledge which he has of all things, from the beginning to the end, that enables him to give that understanding to his creatures, by which they are made partakers of eternal life; and if it were not for the idea existing in the minds of men that God had all knowledge, it would be impossible for them to exercise faith in him (*Lectures on Faith*, 4:11).

As we said when we began our discussion about the Supreme Being in whom we exercise our faith, perfect faith becomes a reality in our life if we can grasp three concepts.

1. That God exists
2. God's character
3. Living God's will

We have discussed the existence of God, and the main attributes of His character. Living God's will, the third principle that enables us to develop perfect faith in Him, is more than merely gaining an understanding of God and His character. It is what we must do in our own lives, that empowers us to form a partnership with God, and live our lives as an extension of His own life. It is foundational to engaging with our Father in Heaven in a significant way, and provides the key to invoking the "finger of God" in everything we do. Let us now prayerfully approach this third principle in the next pages.

4

Living According to His Will

An essential aspect of learning to exercise substantial faith in God, is to learn and understand who He is, and that we can trust Him, and His promises. Equally important to our ability to exercise significant faith is our knowledge that the course of life we are pursuing is aligned with the will of God (*Lectures on Faith*, 6:1–3). If God wants me to move to New Mexico, where He can engage me in teaching his children there, but I prefer to go to Florida and buy a fast boat, I am out of alignment with what God wants. He will support me in my choices, as long as they are not unrighteous, but His ability to engage me in His work will be limited. This is the level at which most of us live—we make choices based on what we think is a good course for us, but it really isn't what God prefers we do with our lives.

In this regard, I love the general conference address of October 2007, by Elder Dallin H. Oaks, Of the Quorum of the Twelve Apostles, titled, "Good, Better, Best." Therein, he instructs,

> Most of us have more things expected of us than we can possibly do. As breadwinners, as parents, as Church workers and members, we face many choices on what we will do with our time and other resources. We should begin by recognizing the reality that just because something is good is not a sufficient reason for doing it. The

> number of good things we can do far exceeds the time available to accomplish them. Some things are better than good, and these are the things that should command priority attention in our lives. Jesus taught this principle in the home of Martha. While she was "cumbered about much serving" (Luke 10:40), her sister, Mary, "sat at Jesus' feet, and heard his word" (v. 39). When Martha complained that her sister had left her to serve alone, Jesus commended Martha for what she was doing (v. 41) but taught her that "one thing is needful: and Mary hath chosen that good part, which shall not be taken away from her" (v. 42). It was praiseworthy for Martha to be "careful and troubled about many things" (v. 41), but learning the gospel from the Master Teacher was more "needful." The scriptures contain other teachings that some things are more blessed than others (See Acts 20:35; Alma 32:14–15).

Elder Oaks refers to the Sears, Roebuck catalog, wherein many products were offered in three grades—good, better, and finally, best! The point of the talk, which I highly recommend, is that there are many good things that we can choose—including things that we choose to accomplish with our limited time and resources. Yet, he shares, there are many better things in which we can invest our resources, if we give the matter some thought. And the ultimate, highest and best use of our time, talents and resources is to invest them in those things that are best—which is what our Heavenly Father hopes we will do. Of course, the very best things are those that are dictated by the Holy Spirit, because they tell us what God wants us to do.

The exercise of faith can be manifested in many ways, in diverse circumstances, from daily activities in untroubled waters, to stressful events during which we have great need of the Lord's immediate intervention, at the risk of great loss of that which is very precious to us. It can be manifested in the paths we pursue in life, and whether we choose to share our resources by building a family, and serving others. It can be manifested in how we utilize our time. It can be revealed in our levels of gratitude for the Lord's blessings in our lives, and our willingness to bless the lives of those around us with our own limited time and resources. The Lord has prescribed certain activities and paths for us to follow in our lives, and we learn of these by reading the scriptures, and listening to His prophets. To the extent we follow

His counsel and commandments, we demonstrate our faith in Him, and in His promises.

Beyond doing the things that He asks of all of His Saints, we can seek His will and guidance, and ask what it is He wants us to do specifically. As we do this, and as we become finely attuned to the whisperings of the Holy Spirit, we will find ourselves doing His will more and more. As we discover and perform His will, we demonstrate that He can trust us, and rely on us to do what He asks. Trust and confidence must be mutual in order for us to know that we are living according to His will, and that He trusts us to the extent that He will imbue our actions with power, through the exercise of great faith. Trust and approval come by obedience to all of God's commandments. The Book of Helaman, chapters 10 through 12, remind us how important it is to heed the promptings of the Spirit. Only by doing so can we be sure we are living according to God's will. These chapters also highlight how important it is to want what God wants. The Lord says He knew the prophet Nephi would "not ask that which is contrary to [God's] will" (Helaman 10:5). We likewise must become so reliable to the Lord, so that He knows we will choose righteousness, and His righteous will at all times, in all circumstances. He commands us to ask, yes, that we might receive from Him. Yet, we cannot ask for that which is not right—for that which is contrary to His will.

How can we know what is not "contrary to His will?" That is where living close to the Holy Spirit comes in. The closer we are to God, and to the things He expects, and desires, the more we will find ourselves asking for that which the Spirit approves. As we prove faithful in the small things, the Lord will trust us with the greater things, until we approach perfection in our desires and selections.

Sacrifice

To sacrifice, is not to lose something forever. To make a sacrifice means to give up something of value, for something else of value—often, of greater value. We might think of sacrifice as an exchange, or even an investment. In my personal experience, I have concluded that we are incapable of out-giving the Lord. No matter what we give Him, or sacrifice for Him, the return that He gives us is even greater.

Think a moment upon the plight of Job. After all of his horrible losses, we could say of the sacrifices that were required of him, including his property, livestock and even his beloved children, the holy scripture tells us,

> So the Lord blessed the latter end of Job more than his beginning: for he had fourteen thousand sheep, and six thousand camels, and a thousand yoke of oxen, and a thousand she asses. He had also seven sons and three daughters. . . . And in all the land were no women found so fair as the daughters of Job: and their father gave them inheritance among their brethren. After this lived Job an hundred and forty years, and saw his sons, and his sons' sons, even four generations (Job 42:12–16).

Even the children that were replaced were never really lost to Job, because they will rise with him in the resurrection, and he will have joy and rejoice with them throughout all eternity.

We are sometimes called upon to sacrifice things of value to us, and in fact, as we mature in the gospel, we make covenants with the Lord to sacrifice all that we possess, if called upon to do so. Many of our frequent sacrifices can be small, like stopping when we are in a hurry to greet someone and inquire about their welfare, or baking cupcakes for a neighbor. Many sacrifices, which we recognize as something substantial enough that it costs us something, are in the medium range. The payment of tithes and offerings, serving in callings and on full-time missions, undergoing fertility treatments to have children, and even receiving higher education are examples of the types of substantial sacrifices the Saints often make. Sacrifices can be great as well, as required of many of the former Saints, who withheld nothing from the cause of building the Lord's kingdom, even to the giving up of their lives. In order for us to have the faith necessary to voluntarily make this tremendous level of sacrifice, we must have an unshakeable knowledge that what we are doing, and the path we are pursuing, is exactly what our Heavenly Father desires of us.

The Prophet Joseph Smith explained,

> For a man to lay down his all, his character and reputation, his honor and applause, his good name among men, his houses, his

> lands, his brothers and sisters, his wife and children, and even his own life also, counting all things but filth and dross for the excellency of the knowledge of Jesus Christ, requires more than mere belief or supposition that he is doing the will of God, but actual knowledge; realizing that when these sufferings are ended he will enter into eternal rest, and be a partaker of the glory of God. For unless a person does know that he is walking according to the will of God, it would be offering an insult to the dignity of the Creator were he to say that he would be a partaker of his glory when he should be done with the things of this life. But when he has this knowledge, and most assuredly knows that he is doing the will of God, his confidence can be equally strong that he will be a partaker of the glory of God (*Lectures on Faith*, 6:5–6).

We note the use of the word "confidence" in this final passage, which the Prophet uses somewhat interchangeably with the word "knowledge," although it appears that he didn't mean knowledge in the "ultimate level of certainty" way, but as more of an "understanding." Using the word "confidence" reminiscent of the Lord's admonition to the Saints, which we can view as a formula for being a perfect child of God, or priesthood holder:

> Let thy bowels also be full of charity towards all men, and to the household of faith, and let virtue garnish thy thoughts unceasingly; then shall thy confidence wax strong in the presence of God; and the doctrine of the priesthood shall distil upon thy soul as the dews from heaven (D&C 121:45).

Yes, confidence is key to exercising the type of faith necessary to fill our lives with the power of God. It is akin to the concept of trust, which we develop as we grow in our understanding of the nature and attributes of God. As we develop confidence in our Heavenly Father, it becomes equally necessary that we develop confidence in ourselves—in our ability to live according to His will, and to call upon Him to intervene in our lives, and for Him to respond as we have asked. We can only develop that level of confidence as we add to our knowledge about Him, the knowledge that what we are doing in our life is aligned with His righteous will.

Our willingness and ability to sacrifice our possessions, freedoms, associations and relationships, and even our very lives for the cause of our God, is not the only thing that is important to Him, and most Saints are never called upon to make such extraordinary sacrifices. However, our *willingness* to do so is absolutely fundamental to our ability to call upon Him to bless our lives and to bestow on us eternal life. The Prophet was quite clear when he taught,

> Let us here observe, that a religion that does not require the sacrifice of all things, never has power sufficient to produce the faith necessary unto life and salvation; for from the first existence of man, the faith necessary unto the enjoyment of life and salvation never could be obtained without the sacrifice of all earthly things; it was through this sacrifice, and this only, that God has ordained that men should enjoy eternal life; and it is through the medium of the sacrifice of all earthly things, that men do actually know that they are doing the things that are well pleasing in the sight of God. When a man has offered in sacrifice all that he has for the truth's sake, not even withholding his life, and believing before God that he has been called to make this sacrifice, because he seeks to do his will, he does know most assuredly that God does and will accept his sacrifice and offering, and that he has not nor will not seek his face in vain. Under these circumstances then, he can obtain the faith necessary for him to lay hold on eternal life (*Lectures on Faith*, 6:7).

This concept of sacrifice is key to our relationship with our Heavenly Father, and to developing power in our lives. It began at the time Adam and Eve were expelled from the presence of God, and a redemption was provided to enable mankind's readmittance to His holy presence.

> And Adam and Eve, his wife, called upon the name of the Lord, and they heard the voice of the Lord from the way toward the Garden of Eden, speaking unto them, and they saw him not; for they were shut out from his presence. And he gave unto them commandments, that they should worship the Lord their God, and should offer the firstlings of their flocks, for an offering unto the Lord. And Adam was obedient unto the commandments of the

> Lord. And after many days an angel of the Lord appeared unto Adam, saying: Why dost thou offer sacrifices unto the Lord? And Adam said unto him: I know not, save the Lord commanded me. And then the angel spake, saying: This thing is a similitude of the sacrifice of the Only Begotten of the Father, which is full of grace and truth. Wherefore, thou shalt do all that thou doest in the name of the Son, and thou shalt repent and call upon God in the name of the Son forevermore (Moses 5:4–8).

From that time forward, the children of God were required to sacrifice the first and best of their flocks, to keep their minds focused on God's immeasurable sacrifice of His own Son. Our Heavenly Father made in offering up His Only Begotten Son, the Firstborn and preeminent of all His spiritual offspring, in exchange for our lives—their joint sacrifice, and their joint pursuit of bringing to pass the immortality and eternal life of man.

The principle of mortal sacrifice was finally fulfilled with the culmination of the Lord's Atonement, carried out in the Garden of Gethsemane and on the cross at Golgotha. That which was infinite and eternal, was exchanged as a ransom for our souls, and the price of our debt to justice was paid in full. The ancient prophet Alma explains it very well.

> For it is expedient that there should be a great and last sacrifice; yea, not a sacrifice of man, neither of beast, neither of any manner of fowl; for it shall not be a human sacrifice; but it must be an infinite and eternal sacrifice. Now there is not any man that can sacrifice his own blood which will atone for the sins of another. Now, if a man murdereth, behold will our law, which is just, take the life of his brother? I say unto you, Nay. But the law requireth the life of him who hath murdered; therefore there can be nothing which is short of an infinite atonement which will suffice for the sins of the world. Therefore, it is expedient that there should be a great and last sacrifice, and then shall there be, or it is expedient there should be, a stop to the shedding of blood; then shall the law of Moses be fulfilled; yea, it shall be all fulfilled, every jot and tittle, and none shall have passed away. And behold, this is the whole meaning of the law, every whit pointing to that great and last sacrifice; and that great and last sacrifice will be the Son of God, yea, infinite

> and eternal. And thus he shall bring salvation to all those who shall believe on his name; this being the intent of this last sacrifice, to bring about the bowels of mercy, which overpowereth justice, and bringeth about means unto men that they may have faith unto repentance (Alma 34:10–15).

This is a beautiful explanation of the meaning of God's sacrifice of His Son, for us. Our debt of sin, which separates us from God, is paid in full. The Lord Jesus Christ stepped in and paid our eternal debt, and is now our debtor. As we have learned, the sacrifice that he requires of us is that of a broken heart and a contrite spirit.

> And ye shall offer up unto me no more the shedding of blood; yea, your sacrifices and your burnt offerings shall be done away, for I will accept none of your sacrifices and your burnt offerings. And ye shall offer for a sacrifice unto me a broken heart and a contrite spirit. And whoso cometh unto me with a broken heart and a contrite spirit, him will I baptize with fire and with the Holy Ghost, even as the Lamanites, because of their faith in me at the time of their conversion, were baptized with fire and with the Holy Ghost, and they knew it not (3 Nephi 9:19–20; see also D&C 59:8).

What are a broken heart and a contrite spirit, and why are they considered a sacrifice? As in all things, the Savior's life offers us the perfect example. Though Jesus of Nazareth was utterly without sin, He walked through life with a broken heart and a contrite spirit, as manifested by His submission to the will of the Father. "For I came down from heaven, not to do mine own will, but the will of him that sent me" (John 6:38). To His disciples He said, "Learn of me; for I am meek and lowly in heart" (Matthew 11:29). And when the time came to pay the ultimate sacrifice entailed in the Atonement, Christ shrank not to partake of the bitter cup, but submitted completely to His Father's will. "Then said Jesus unto Peter, Put up thy sword into the sheath: the cup which my Father hath given me, shall I not drink it" (John 18:11)? "And he went a little further, and fell on his face, and prayed, saying, O my Father, if it be possible, let this cup pass from me: nevertheless not as I will, but as thou wilt" (Matthew 26:39). There is no doubt that the Savior was anxious about what he was going through, and had there been any possible way to avoid it, He would have preferred that. Yet, "not as I will," He said to His Father, "but as thou wilt." This is the ultimate demonstration of the character of Christ; that He possessed both a spirit of contrition, and a heart that was deeply saddened because of the things His sinning brothers and sisters put Him through.

Elder Bruce D Porter of the Seventy said,

> The Savior's perfect submission to the Eternal Father is the very essence of a broken heart and a contrite spirit. Christ's example teaches us that a broken heart is an eternal attribute of godliness. When our hearts are broken, we are completely open to the Spirit of God, and recognize our dependence on Him for all that we have and all that we are. The sacrifice so entailed is a sacrifice of pride in all its forms. Like malleable clay in the hands of a skilled potter, the brokenhearted can be molded and shaped in the hands of the Master ("A Broken Heart and a Contrite Spirit," *Liahona*, Nov 2007, 31–32).

Whether we are called upon to sacrifice little or much, our willingness to do all things whatsoever the Lord commands us to do *demonstrates* our faith in Him, and qualifies us to receive all of His promised blessings, including eternal life, the greatest of all blessings. A broken heart and a contrite spirit are also preconditions to another paramount principle of the gospel, which we must ensure is ever present in our lives and consciousness—repentance.

Repentance

The Lord has provided for us a method by which we may become clean, thereby enabling us to enter into His holy presence.[66] As we know, when we left the heavenly realms and took upon us mortal flesh, we entered a fallen world where all things are in a constant state of disintegration. It is Christ's Atonement that rejuvenates and restores life to all dying things. "For as in Adam all die, even so in Christ shall all be made alive" (1 Corinthians 15:22). In order for us to avail ourselves of the full measure of His Atonement, we must maintain a

66. "No unclean thing can inherit the kingdom of heaven" (Alma 11:37).

state of cleanliness, constantly purging ourselves of the sins and transgressions we have committed. Repentance is much more than just acknowledging our wrongdoings. It is a change of mind and heart that provides us a fresh view about God, about ourselves, and about the people and world around us. It includes turning away from sin and turning to God for forgiveness. It is motivated by love for God and the sincere desire to obey His commandments.[67] Repentance is a multi-step process that allows us to cleanse ourselves and become worthy to re-enter our Heavenly Father's presence, in this life and in the world to come.

We have discussed how the foremost sacrifice that the Lord requires of us is that of a broken heart and a contrite spirit, because it opens us up to the nobler feelings and insights that come of the Holy Spirit. It also humbles us to a point of being teachable, by the Spirit and by those who have been called by the Lord to instruct us in important and eternal truths. It strips us of pride and the desire to partake of the things the world would have us indulge in that are inappropriate for the children of God and bearers of His Holy Priesthood. It opens our hearts to view things from a higher perspective, the Lord's perspective, and to consider our true position in the universe. When we have become sufficiently humble to embark on the steps of repentance, we can begin to travel the path that the Lord has prepared to cleanse us of our sins.

What are the steps we are to follow to fully repent of our wrongs? In his book, *The Miracle of Forgiveness*, President Spencer W. Kimball outlines five steps that are necessary in order to rid ourselves of the effects of our mistakes. These are the same steps our missionaries have been teaching to gospel investigators for decades. Perhaps we feel that these steps of repentance are sufficient for those who are new to the gospel, but that those of us who are better established in its precepts and have been given greater light and understanding are beyond the reach of such simple measures. Let us not be like Naaman who hesitated to follow the instructions of the prophet Elisha when directed to

---

67. Repentance Is a Principle of the Gospel, Media Library, Doctrinal Study, Repentance, Overview. Church website: churchofjesuschrist.org/study/manual/gospel-topics/repentance.

wash himself in the river Jordan to cleanse himself of leprosy (2 Kings 5:1–19; Luke 4:27), or like the Israelites who declined salvation from ferocious serpents because the Lord's prescribed method seemed too simple to them (1 Nephi 17:41[68]). The Lord has ordained His method for our repentance from sin, and we must follow His prescription if we are to receive forgiveness and cleanse ourselves of all impurity.

Step One—Sorrow for Sin

Many of us tend to attribute either too little, or too much culpability to ourselves for certain transgressions. Some grind themselves into the depths of humiliation and depression over minor violations of the commandments, while others flippantly wink at sin with frivolous disregard and offer up only the most superficial apologies in hurried prayers. Modern prophets admonish us to study and ponder to determine how serious the Lord defines our particular transgression to be, and to consider it in the appropriate context of how much grief our act has caused to come upon one of Heavenly Father's children, or upon His Son who bore its burden in the Garden of Gethsemane. When we have gained the proper perspective of the gravity of our act and reflected on it sufficiently to internalize its rippling effects, it will produce within us the appropriate level of sorrow and remorse.

We are warned to avoid passing off our culpability with smug and superficial excuses, as is the practice of an insincere world, often observed when public relations gurus instruct erring celebrities to proffer a perfunctory *mea culpa* on a late night broadcast to lay the latest public spectacle to rest. Instead, we must genuinely assimilate a profound and sincere regret for the wrong we have committed, experiencing an appropriate "godly sorrow," as the Apostle Paul put it. (2 Corinthians 7:10[69]) Godly sorrow recognizes the true nature of the wrong, and its

68. "And he did straiten them in the wilderness with his rod; for they hardened their hearts, even as ye have; and the Lord straitened them because of their iniquity. He sent fiery flying serpents among them; and after they were bitten he prepared a way that they might be healed; and the labor which they had to perform was to look; and because of the simpleness of the way, or the easiness of it, there were many who perished."

69. "For godly sorrow worketh repentance to salvation not to be repented of: but the sorrow of the world worketh death."

effects on ourselves, others, the Church, the Savior, and God Himself. This is the type of true sorrow that can lead to a sincere desire for change and a willingness to submit to every requirement for forgiveness. Without this, in appropriate quantities, we cannot move on to the next steps in the process of repentance.

Step Two—Abandonment of Sin

Too often we see among us those who demand forgiveness, without a sincere resolve to wholly abandon an evil or pernicious practice. Even if a resolve to cease committing a particular sin may exist, a permissive attitude of sinfulness in other matters may persist. Not only must we develop an unyielding resolve to avoid repeating a particular transgression to receive forgiveness, but we must adopt such a resolve to avoid all sin. The Lord has declared, "But unto that soul who sinneth shall the former sins return" (D&C 82:7). This appears to be a requirement that escapes many who would seek forgiveness of sins. They seem to operate under the assumption that they can compartmentalize sinfulness, indulging certain weaknesses, while pretending repentance for others. The Lord is not tolerant of such an attitude. He declares, "For I the Lord cannot look upon sin with the least degree of allowance" (ibid., 1:31). He also reveals, "By this ye may know if a man repenteth of his sins—behold, he will confess them and forsake them" (ibid., 58:43). Joseph Smith clarified, "Repentance is a thing that cannot be trifled with every day. Daily transgression and daily repentance is not . . . pleasing in the sight of God" (*Teachings of the Prophet Joseph Smith*, 148).

Men and women are mortal, and as such fall short of the glory of the Perfect One. Therefore, we will all continue to make mistakes throughout our mortal lives. We cannot expect perfection of ourselves, and the Lord doesn't expect it either. The above scriptures are clear that we cannot be lax in our attitudes toward sinful conduct, however. The very principle of repentance takes into consideration our progress from natural man to Godly man. It recognizes that although we seek to be like the Lord, we are not yet like Him. As long as we are determined to become like Him and recognize when we commit sin and immediately repent and resolve to wholly abandon that sin as well as all sin, we can obtain His forgiveness and return to a state of cleanliness. There is an attitude that we must adopt to avail ourselves of the forgiveness that the Lord is willing to extend to us. It was at the conclusion of King Benjamin's address to his people that they experienced a mighty change of heart and had "no more disposition to do evil, but to do good continually" (Mosiah 5:2;[70] see generally Elder Spencer J. Condie, "A Disposition to Do Good Continually," *Ensign*, August 2001). It is this predisposition toward doing good continually that makes true repentance and abandonment of sin possible. The closer we come to this predisposition, the cleaner we become, and remain.

Step Three—Confession of Sin

An indispensable aspect of repentance is confession of our mistakes, sins and transgressions. The Lord has taught us that we are to confess our sins: "I command you again to repent . . . and that you confess your sins" (D&C 19:20). To whom should we confess our wrongs? We must always confess our sins, transgressions, mistakes and weaknesses to the Lord. If they are serious transgressions, such as immorality or other grave acts that may put our Church membership or standing into question, they need to be confessed to our bishop, and possibly our stake president. If we have injured another person we must also confess to that person, and to anyone else who may have been left with a lack of proper understanding about the matter due to our actions (D&C 42:90–91[71]). Partial confession that merely indicates wrongdoing or simply refers to lesser mistakes, is inadequate to confess and resolve a more serious, undisclosed transgression. Essential to forgiveness is our humility, demonstrated by our willingness to fully disclose to the Lord and, where necessary, His priesthood judge, all

70. "And they all cried with one voice, saying: Yea, we believe all the words which thou hast spoken unto us; and also, we know of their surety and truth, because of the Spirit of the Lord Omnipotent, which has wrought a mighty change in us, or in our hearts, that we have no more disposition to do evil, but to do good continually."

71. "And if thy brother or sister offend many, he or she shall be chastened before many. And if any one offend openly, he or she shall be rebuked openly, that he or she may be ashamed. And if he or she confess not, he or she shall be delivered up unto the law of God."

that we have done wrong. Confession of our sins evidences our Godly sorrow for our behavior, and opens our hearts to the predisposition to do no more evil, but to do good continually. There is something in the process of anticipating the confession of sin that enables us to internalize the true nature and severity of our sin—something that we may easily gloss over in the absence of the requirement to confess it. Remember, "He that covereth his sins shall not prosper: but whoso confesseth and forsaketh them shall have mercy" (Proverbs 28:13).

How much corruption have we seen throughout the history of the world by the wicked who have sought to cover their sins? How many crimes have been committed for the sole purpose of hiding other wrongs? How easy it was for our Lord to expose the scribes and Pharisees for their adulterous lives as they presented Him with the woman taken in the act and tempted Him with a question of whether or not she should be stoned. Although they had succeeded in covering their sins from the eyes of the people whom they were appointed to serve, they knew among themselves that their souls were cankered with all manner of adultery, and they were unable to prolong the pretense of having clean hands while looking at one another. Their eyes sank to the ground and from the eldest to the youngest they quietly slunk away until only the Lord and the accused woman remained. Jesus finally looked at her and asked, "Woman, where are those thine accusers? hath no man condemned thee?" She looked around and confirmed that there was no man who condemned her. He then said, "Neither do I condemn thee: go, and sin no more" (John 8:3–11).

Confession of our sins provides a break in the pattern of sin, a "speed bump" to slow the momentum of a sinful disposition. It affords a registration of our acknowledgement of wrongdoing, and puts others on notice that we recognize that the former behavior is unacceptable—even if it is only the Lord that we confess to. It allows us to internalize our remorse, and to face the gravity of our acts. By confessing that we have been inappropriate in our conduct we make a conscious proclamation of wrongdoing, and the next step becomes a natural outlet to appease a troubled conscience and to restore equilibrium to an imbalance caused by our acts.

Step Four—Restitution for Sin

It is such a logical, simple concept that we must restore that which is taken or injured by our acts. It is laid out clearly in our legal system that the goal of the courts is to make victims whole to the extent possible, which means that the court will seek to restore them to their pre-victimized status to the degree it can be done. In cases of financial losses or other injuries the courts seek to put the victim of someone's wrongs into at least as good a position as they were in before the wrong occurred, to the extent financial remuneration or other relief can compensate for the loss or injury. It should not be a matter of wonderment or debate that restoring that which we have diminished is a necessary precursor to receiving forgiveness for an injury we have inflicted on someone. Anyone who assumes otherwise fails to comprehend the principle of balance, of opposition in all things. Surely, where injustice has occurred, an equal and opposite force of justice must be brought to bear to restore balance to the justice equation. This is why we must restore that which we have taken or diminished before we can expect forgiveness, from those we have offended or from the Lord. Jehovah meticulously instructed the Israelites in the requirement of making their victims whole, laying out a number of possible scenarios and remedies in Exodus: "If a man shall steal an ox, or a sheep, and kill it, or sell it; he shall restore five oxen for an ox, and four sheep for a sheep" (22:1; see generally chapter 22). In general, restitution was required for all trespasses or takings, and the payment for such was that the item had to be returned with an additional twenty percent (Leviticus 5:15–16[72]).

We see and hear so little of restoration or restitution these days. It appears to be the forgotten step of repentance. The mindset of entitlement that has overtaken our culture extends even to this realm it

72. "If a soul commit a trespass, and sin through ignorance, in the holy things of the Lord; then he shall bring for his trespass unto the Lord a ram without blemish out of the flocks, with thy estimation by shekels of silver, after the shekel of the sanctuary, for a trespass offering: And he shall make amends for the harm that he hath done in the holy thing, and shall add the fifth part thereto, and give it unto the priest: and the priest shall make an atonement for him with the ram of the trespass offering, and it shall be forgiven him."

appears, leaving offenders to assume that they are no longer required to make their victims whole, due to some type of higher forgiveness that is required of victims, and Christians generally. Again, this is an imbalanced view of matters, and leaves injustice to reign in the stead of justice. Forgiveness is their cry—you must forgive me is their repeated maxim. It is as we discussed with the principle of justice and mercy, justice must be observed, and balance must be restored. To ignore the need to restore a victim of our wrongdoing is to crucify the Savior afresh, failing to do our part to participate in making restoration, and forcing Him to shoulder the entire burden alone (Hebrews 6:6[73]).

Whatever it is that we have done that injures another, we must repay at least that which we have taken. Some injuries are difficult or impossible to restore. Injuring the reputation of another requires a great deal of effort to inform all of those who may have received an incorrect report of the truth of the matter. The loss of reputation and stature may be insurmountable. Certainly, the taking of virtue is a commodity that can never be restored.

Notwithstanding the impossibility of restoring all things that we may have stolen, damaged or defiled, our willingness to restore everything we possibly can is concrete evidence to the Lord that we are committed to do all in our power to make amends, to balance the demands of justice, and to fully repent of our acts. For that part which we cannot restore or replace, despite our attempts and yearnings, the Atonement of Jesus Christ provides the elusive balance. His payment made in recompense for our sins makes up the difference, and those whom we have injured will be made whole as their debts to Him are treated with equal quantities of clemency. As we do all in our power to make restitution for injuries inflicted by our acts, we are prepared to approach the Lord as a cleansed and renewed creature, and demonstrate our willingness to do all things that He has commanded.

---

73. "If they shall fall away, to renew them again unto repentance; seeing they crucify to themselves the Son of God afresh, and put him to an open shame."

Step Five—Obedience to All the Commandments

As we seek strength to overcome our natural inclinations to do things that displease our Heavenly Father and violate His laws, we must focus on full obedience to those laws. The struggle we experience in our transformation from the natural man to the Godly man, will render full adherence to every precept impossible, but a strong desire to live by every word of God will produce necessary strength to keep pushing in the right direction. There are no perfect mortals, and we all fall short of the perfect example of the Savior. There are mortals, however, who have the desire to live righteously and to become like their Father in Heaven, and like His perfect Son. They live each day with a renewed determination to do everything that they can and must do to obey the commandments and bring to pass as much righteousness as they are capable of producing. They approach each of life's situations with a predetermined answer—choose the right. They shun evil at every turn and keep their lives unspotted from inappropriate indulgences that would rob them of the companionship of the Holy Spirit. They are guarded in their responses to others, and in what they allow to enter through their senses. They dwell on worthy and uplifting subjects, and disregard salacious and sensational thoughts that attempt to occupy their minds. They are grateful to God for His constant flow of blessings, and express their gratitude throughout each day and in their prayers. To the extent we struggle every day to become this kind of person, we will find our capacity to put off the natural man increased significantly, and our natures changed. As King Benjamin explained to his people,

> For the natural man is an enemy to God, and has been from the fall of Adam, and will be, forever and ever, unless he yields to the enticings of the Holy Spirit, and putteth off the natural man and becometh a saint through the atonement of Christ the Lord, and becometh as a child, submissive, meek, humble, patient, full of love, willing to submit to all things which the Lord seeth fit to inflict upon him, even as a child doth submit to his father (Mosiah 3:19).

As we learn to incorporate obedience to all of the commandments into our lives we will become Saints, like all of those who dwelled in Enoch's Zion and those who were called to be the chosen oracles and followers of the Lord throughout the earth's history. Each of us can obey the word of the Lord to the fullest extent. As we follow His counsel and instructions, we will find our lives transformed and our attitudes and abilities enlarged and ennobled. As we work through each of the steps of repentance, and come to the point of living in harmony with God's commandments we will find our spirits renewed and our lives sanctified by the ministrations of the Holy Spirit.

> Now this is the commandment: Repent, all ye ends of the earth, and come unto me and be baptized in my name, that ye may be sanctified by the reception of the Holy Ghost, that ye may stand spotless before me at the last day (3 Nephi 27:20).

We will be cleansed from all iniquity, and will stand spotless before God and able to dwell in His holy presence. In short, we will obtain eternal life, the greatest of all the gifts of God (D&C 14:7[74]).

Living as a Saint in the Last Days

We began our current discussion with Joseph Smith's teaching, that essential to our ability to exercise significant faith in our Heavenly Father and His promises is our knowledge that the course of life we are pursuing is in harmony with His will. We have briefly discussed the requirement of obedience to God's commandments that we might qualify for forgiveness of our sins. It is self-evident that living the commandments brings peace of the Spirit, and the blessings of heaven. Also, we have seen that in addition to being blessed for our general obedience to all of the Lord's commandments, obedience to specific commandments qualifies us to receive specific blessings, as outlined by the Lord in D&C 130:20–21.

> There is a law, irrevocably decreed in heaven before the foundations of this world, upon which all blessings are predicated—And when

74. "And, if you keep my commandments and endure to the end you shall have eternal life, which gift is the greatest of all the gifts of God."

we obtain any blessing from God, it is by obedience to that law upon which it is predicated.

We could call the following scripture a companion promise to the above declaration of the Lord: "I, the Lord, am bound when ye do what I say; but when ye do not what I say, ye have no promise" (D&C 82:10). Together these scriptures provide us with a solid understanding of our relationship with the Lord, and how our obedience to His laws automatically qualifies us, or disqualifies us in the case of disobedience, to receive certain blessings from Him.

How are we to know what all of the commandments require of us? There are many commandments. We all know the Ten Commandments, but in ancient Israel the people were burdened with over 600 commandments under the Law of Moses, approximately 365 of which commanded them to abstain from certain acts, and 248 of which commanded them to perform specified positive acts. In addition to these, the leaders of the Jews imposed innumerable permutations and specific steps of implementation on themselves and the Israelites, resulting in the system of strict laws and observances, which Christ specifically denounced during His earthly ministry. His message was that the Jews had substituted ritual and strict procedure for the spirit of love and devotion provided by the Lord in His commandments. Jesus summed up all of God's commandments thus:

> Thou shalt love the Lord thy God with all thy heart, and with all thy soul, and with all thy mind. This is the first and great commandment. And the second is like unto it, Thou shalt love thy neighbour as thyself. On these two commandments hang all the law and the prophets (Matthew 22:36–40).

This is a wonderful summation of the entire law of God. Everything He requires of us is contained in the principle of unfettered devotion to God and fellow men. Can we even imagine a world where all men are focused on their love of God and His children? There would be no need for specific laws detailing various acts to be done, or to be avoided. As long as all men and women were busily about the business of showing their love of God and for each of His children, there would be no crime and no offenses. Of course, while all commandments are founded on this principle of love and devotion, mankind's lack of focus on the underlying principle necessitates our reception of detailed steps to be taken to implement the principle. With each selfish or thoughtless act in the world, there is a reaction to it, purposeful or unconscious, leading to an uncontrolled chain-reaction of negative behavior. Like waves in a small pond, they bounce and reverberate until the entire body of water is driven in confusion. Impelled by a "natural man" sense of self-preservation and self-promotion we observe many who all but forget that they have a Heavenly Father, or that they share a world with fellow beings. So many have adopted an egocentric view of the universe, in stark contrast to that exhibited by the Savior of mankind. Because of these "devilish" tendencies, God gave "commandments," a litany of DOs and DON'Ts intended to guide our every step along an endless path of toil. This was not His wish, however. It is the result of mankind's rejection of higher laws and values that were proffered for our enrichment at times, but reestablished in these latter days for those with an "ear" to hear them.

The higher commandments of the Gospel of Jesus Christ are given to assist us in our transformation from the natural man to the Godly man—until we all eventually arrive at the perfect day when no commandments are required, and we are completely focused on our love of God and our fellow men. The higher gospel law teaches us what manner of men we should be. "Therefore, what manner of men ought ye to be? Verily I say unto you, even as I am" (3 Nephi 27:27). The scriptures reveal that God provides us with testing to see if we will do all things whatsoever the Lord our God shall command us to do. (Abraham 3:25) It gives us opportunities to expand our abilities and elevate our perspective.

> For behold, it is not meet that I should command in all things; for he that is compelled in all things, the same is a slothful and not a wise servant; wherefore he receiveth no reward. Verily I say, men should be anxiously engaged in a good cause, and do many things of their own free will, and bring to pass much righteousness; For the power is in them, wherein they are agents unto themselves. And inasmuch as men do good they shall in nowise lose their reward. But he that doeth not anything until he is commanded, and

> receiveth a commandment with doubtful heart, and keepeth it with slothfulness, the same is damned (D&C 58:26–29).

Generally speaking, the commandments let us know the difference between right and wrong, and point the direction in which we should go—something that many have difficulty determining on their own.

We might ask ourselves, which commandments of the Lord govern which sought after blessings? Many will desire some specific blessing, and will seek out the underlying commandment or principle, which if obeyed will result in the granting of the specified blessing. There is nothing wrong with this thinking, and the above-cited scriptures appear to have been revealed to us to point our minds to the precept. However, as we embark on any path that will lead us to a specific blessing, we must remember that general obedience and devotion to the Lord, and love for His children, are the goal of our Heavenly Father for us. He is not as interested in our ambitions or the acquisition of luxuries as we are, so we must be mindful that expansive compliance is required, as well as particular obedience to specific laws.

Some specific laws are easily identified with corresponding blessings. The Apostle Paul identifies the fifth commandment as the "first commandment with promise" (Ephesians 6:2). The fifth commandment is to honor father and mother, and its corresponding blessing is to enjoy long days on the land (Exodus 20:12[75]), which Paul interprets as, "That it may be well with thee, and thou mayest live long on the earth" (Ephesians 6:3). This is a substantial promise, and certainly a blessing that all should seek for.

Another specific commandment that comes "with promise" is the Word of Wisdom, contained in the 89th Section of the Doctrine and Covenants. The Lord cautions therein, "I have warned you, and forewarn you, by giving unto you this word of wisdom by revelation" (verse 4). Any person would be a fool to ignore whatever might follow such a warning from the Creator of the universe. To the extent we observe and obey the admonitions given in the Word of Wisdom, and

75. "Honour thy father and thy mother: that thy days may be long upon the land which the Lord thy God giveth thee."

generally walk in compliance with the commandments, we are promised the following specific blessings:

> [They] shall receive health in their navel and marrow to their bones; And shall find wisdom and great treasures of knowledge, even hidden treasures; And shall run and not be weary, and shall walk and not faint. And I, the Lord, give unto them a promise, that the destroying angel shall pass by them, as the children of Israel, and not slay them. Amen (verses 18–21).

Each of these promised blessings is marvelous in its scope and implications, and we would do well to fully "obey" the principles enumerated in the Word of Wisdom, so that we can receive the blessings predicated on those principles—health, wisdom, great and hidden treasures of knowledge, vigor and immunity from the destroying angel. Yes, these blessings are well worth following the precepts outlined in Section 89. As we become initiated to the exalting ordinances received in the House of the Lord, we find that these promises have even greater significance than appears on the surface.

Another commandment that we receive with a promised blessing is that of tithing. It is a lesser law of temporal stewardship, but if followed will render tremendous temporal and spiritual blessings, as promised in the scriptures. In the Old Testament the Lord reminded the Israelites of this great commandment with promise, and first informed them that by their disobedience they had missed out on countless blessings. "Will a man rob God? Yet ye have robbed me. But ye say, Wherein have we robbed thee? In tithes and offerings. Ye are cursed with a curse: for ye have robbed me, even this whole nation" (Malachi 3:8–90). After chastising Israel for their lack of obedience to the law of tithing the Lord then reestablished His promised blessings that would flow in abundance from their obedience to the law.

> Bring ye all the tithes into the storehouse, that there may be meat in mine house, and prove me now herewith, saith the Lord of hosts, if I will not open you the windows of heaven, and pour you out a blessing, that there shall not be room enough to receive it. And I

will rebuke the devourer[76] for your sakes, and he shall not destroy the fruits of your ground; neither shall your vine cast her fruit before the time in the field, saith the Lord of hosts.

Again, these are momentous blessings that the Lord promises as a natural result of obeying a particular law. They are a) the windows of heaven will be opened to us, the windows of heaven indicating temporal and spiritual blessings, b) He will pour us out great temporal and spiritual blessings c) in such great abundance that we will have insufficient room to receive and store all that He pours out upon us, and d) He will rebuke the devourer and it will not imperil or rob us of that which the Lord has sent to us. Can we imagine a greater promise of temporal blessings than these? We know that the Lord blessed Israel when they obeyed this law, and the average educational and income levels of the modern camp of Israel certainly reflect that great blessings are poured out on those who obey the law.[77]

The Lord offers us an additional blessing for the payment of tithes. He says, "Behold, now it is called today until the coming of the Son of Man, and verily it is a day of sacrifice, and a day for the tithing of my people; for he that is tithed shall not be burned at his coming" (D&C 64:23; see also meaning of "devourer" in previous footnote). We can add this to our list of promised, appurtenant blessings: we won't be burned when Jesus returns. This principle is affectionately known as "fire insurance" among the more jovial members of the Church, but indicates that the payment of tithes is a key indicator of which of God's children will be adequately prepared for the Savior's Second Coming event.

---

76. "It is contrary to the will and commandment of God that those who receive not their inheritance by consecration, agreeable to his law, which he has given, that he may tithe his people, to prepare them against the day of vengeance and burning, should have their names enrolled with the people of God" D&C 85:3. "But if she observe not to do whatsoever I have commanded her, I will visit her according to all her works, with sore affliction, with pestilence, with plague, with sword, with vengeance, with devouring fire" D&C 97:26.

77. Pew Research Center, "The most and least educated U.S. religious groups," November 4, 2016; Pew Research Center, "Income distribution among members of the Church of Jesus Christ of Latter-day Saints."

Tithing is also a foundational part of the higher law of consecration. Those who live the law of consecration view themselves as stewards of all that they possess, and voluntarily dedicate their time, talents, and material wealth to the establishment and building up of God's kingdom on Earth. It was the law established among the people of the prophet Enoch, and they prospered more than any group on the earth before or since. They "were of one heart and one mind and dwelt in righteousness, and there were no poor among them" (Moses 7:18). Due to the weakness of modern men, the law is not fully invoked by the Lord at this time. All who receive the ordinances of exaltation make such covenants with the Lord, but few consider themselves worthy to be called upon to actively participate. However, all those whose hearts are set upon the principles of Zion, and who view themselves as beggars before the Lord and stewards over the wealth He puts into their hands can be considered to be living the law. The worldwide Church is filled with faithful Saints who dedicate all that they have and all that they are, to building the Lord's kingdom, starting in their homes and congregations. Most couples who have entered into these covenants find themselves living lives centered in the Lord, and raising righteous posterity to build His kingdom. Their time is donated to fulfilling their callings and serving one another, and their generous offerings and sacrifices utilized to ease the burdens of the less fortunate to the end that there are no poor among them. Tremendous outpourings of spiritual, physical and financial blessings are experienced throughout the Lord's kingdom as individual members seek to live this higher law to the extent possible. Whichever level of the law one lives, the results are an increase of temporal and spiritual blessings as promised by the Lord.

Also, the Lord has promised specific blessings to those who obey the commandments to receive the ordinances of salvation. For example, those who obey the commandment of being baptized by one having authority from God, will receive a remission of his sins, and an authorized servant will lay hands on him and bestow the Gift of the Holy Ghost (Acts 2:38[78]). Likewise, those who enter into the New

78. "Then Peter said unto them, Repent, and be baptized every one of you in the name of Jesus Christ for the remission of sins, and ye shall receive the gift of

and Everlasting Covenant of Eternal Marriage will enter into their exaltation, as long as they shed no innocent blood (D&C 132:26[79]). Eternal Life is the greatest gift that God can bestow on us (D&C 14:7[80]). This marvelous, even unspeakable gift will be bestowed on all those who obey the commandment to enter into this new and everlasting covenant. There can be no greater example of the principle we are examining—that the Lord is bound to bless us if we obey the appurtenant commandment.

Similarly, those who obey the commandment to receive the priesthood, with its oath and covenant, and to magnify their callings therein, are likewise promised certain blessings:

> For whoso is faithful unto the obtaining these two priesthoods of which I have spoken, and the magnifying their calling, are sanctified by the Spirit unto the renewing of their bodies. They become the sons of Moses and of Aaron and the seed of Abraham, and the church and kingdom, and the elect of God. And also all they who receive this priesthood receive me, saith the Lord; For he that receiveth my servants receiveth me; And he that receiveth me receiveth my Father; And he that receiveth my Father receiveth my Father's kingdom; *therefore all that my Father hath shall be given unto him* (D&C 84:33–38, emphasis provided).

The Lord concludes,

> And I now give unto you a commandment to beware concerning yourselves, to give diligent heed to the words of eternal life. For you shall live by every word that proceedeth forth from the mouth

---

the Holy Ghost."

79. "Verily, verily, I say unto you, if a man marry a wife according to my word, and they are sealed by the Holy Spirit of promise, according to mine appointment, and he or she shall commit any sin or transgression of the new and everlasting covenant whatever, and all manner of blasphemies, and if they commit no murder wherein they shed innocent blood, yet they shall come forth in the first resurrection, and enter into their exaltation; but they shall be destroyed in the flesh, and shall be delivered unto the buffetings of Satan unto the day of redemption, saith the Lord God."

80. "And, if you keep my commandments and endure to the end you shall have eternal life, which gift is the greatest of all the gifts of God."

> of God. For the word of the Lord is truth, and whatsoever is truth is light, and whatsoever is light is Spirit, even the Spirit of Jesus Christ [The Light of Christ]. And the Spirit giveth light to every man that cometh into the world; and the Spirit enlighteneth every man through the world, that hearkeneth to the voice of the Spirit. And every one that hearkeneth to the voice of the Spirit cometh unto God, even the Father. And the Father teacheth him of the covenant which he has renewed and confirmed upon you, which is confirmed upon you for your sakes, and not for your sakes only, but for the sake of the whole world (verses 43–48).

Yes, the power you wield through the priesthood of God is given to you for your own blessing, and for the blessing of your family, and neighbors, and ultimately—for the entire world. Therefore, those who obey the commandment to obtain the priesthood of God and magnify their calling will 1) be sanctified by the Spirit unto the renewing of their bodies and 2) will be given all that the Father has. What a marvelous blessing that comes from obedience to this specific commandment.

Let us consider a final example of this principle of blessings that are specifically coupled with commandments. It is the principle of preparation. We can see in the natural world around us that if we are unprepared to fill a position or responsibility, our undertaking to do it can have disastrous results. A task that requires training cannot generally be adequately performed by one who lacks the proper training. We cannot ask an inexperienced climber to ascend a rock face to collect honey, and we cannot put a new recruit in charge of the nuclear reactor on a naval war ship, or ask him to pilot a fighter jet. We cannot turn over the reins of government to someone who has no understanding of such matters. Even in volunteer work, wherein one might earnestly seek to serve in a lay capacity and possibly only in a quiet corner of a nearby neighborhood, or sharing the gospel message to neighbors, the Lord warns, "Seek not to declare my word, but first seek to obtain my word, and then shall your tongue be loosed; then, if you desire, you shall have my Spirit and my word, yea, the power of God unto the convincing of men" (D&C 11:21). Similarly, the Lord instructs us: "And see that all these things are done in wisdom and order; for it is not requisite that a man should run faster than he has strength" (Mosiah 4:27; D&C 10:4).

So, what principle do we learn from this? We learn that we must prepare ourselves to meet the challenges that face us. If we are prepared, we will be in a position to enjoy success. Many youths fail to understand the importance of proper education and training, then regret for the remainder of their working lives their decision to cut short their schooling. Even the brethren of the early restored Church were commanded by the Lord to "seek ye diligently and teach one another words of wisdom; yea, seek ye out of the best books words of wisdom; seek learning, even by study and also by faith," so that they would be prepared to face the challenges of interacting with sophisticated men and cultural systems as the gospel was taken to the ends of the earth (D&C 88:118;[81] 109:7, 14[82]). If we obey the commandments pertaining to properly preparing ourselves for the tasks that await us, we will receive the blessings of being up to performing those tasks, and will qualify for the assistance of the Lord and the guidance of the Holy Spirit in fulfilling our duties in life.

Although we have discussed only a few examples of the principle of promised blessings tethered to specific commandments, thoughtful reflection, prayer and study will reveal that nearly every commandment possesses a corresponding blessing, or set of blessings. As we reflect upon each commandment, whether it pertains to personal virtue, honesty, wisdom, or helping others, we can often discover the blessings that flow from observance of each commandment. Surely, we can discern the blessings that flow from moral purity or from dealing fairly with our fellow men. It isn't too difficult to understand the correlation between abstaining from mortal violence and enjoying a

81. "And as all have not faith, seek ye diligently and teach one another words of wisdom; yea, seek ye out of the best books words of wisdom; seek learning, even by study and also by faith."

82. "And as all have not faith, seek ye diligently and teach one another words of wisdom; yea, seek ye out of the best books words of wisdom, seek learning even by study and also by faith; And do thou grant, Holy Father, that all those who shall worship in this house may be taught words of wisdom out of the best books, and that they may seek learning even by study, and also by faith, as thou hast said;"

peaceful existence. Every gospel principle and commandment has a blessing to bestow on anyone willing to adhere to its precepts and fulfill its requirements.

Blessings that naturally flow from living the commandments are not limited to just those who belong to the Church of Jesus Christ. Let me share an example of some men who affirmatively reached out to obtain just such blessings. Jim Power, my High Priest Group Leader, in Queen Creek, Arizona, shared an experience with us involving some migrant workers in our ward. The High Priest Group was called upon to assist a single sister in the ward whose roof was in dire need of repair. After a number of inspections and consultations, it was finally decided by the bishop of the ward that the Church would assist with the cost of a roof replacement, and that the High Priests of the ward could remove the old roofing material to help control the cost of the replacement. When the roofing workers learned that the men of the Church were planning to do the removal themselves, they inquired about why random men in the neighborhood would devote themselves to this type of labor-intensive service. Jim explained to them the principle of service, and the blessings that Church members experience when they freely donate their services to others. The roofers looked at one another, then asked Jim if these blessings were limited to just Church members. Jim smiled, then explained that such blessings were extended to all who live the law of service to others, like the Old Testament scripture that promises that when we cast our bread upon the waters, it will return to us again (Ecclesiastes 11:1[83]). The two roofers then asked if they might avail themselves of the opportunity to receive some blessings at the hand of the Lord by donating the removal service themselves. They said that their work was seasonal, and that they were subject to the ravages of injuries and layoffs, and wondered if the Lord might not better sustain them in some manner if they performed a work of service for this woman. Jim assured them that the Lord was quite aware of their righteous intent and would accept their service and provide blessings in their lives. The men performed the service, and for the first time in their lives knew that their

83. "Cast thy bread upon the waters: for thou shalt find it after many days."

actions on a sunny Saturday morning were being carried out under the watchful eyes of heaven.

As we seek specific blessings of the Lord, we must discover the underlying principles on which each particular blessing operates, then we must obey that law. To the extent we obey the pertinent law we will obtain the sought-after blessing. It should not surprise us at this point in our discussion that for every question, the Lord provides an answer, or for every request, the Lord provides a response. As we have seen it is He who has declared many times, "For every one that asketh receiveth; and he that seeketh findeth; and to him that knocketh it shall be opened" (Matthew 7:7–8; see also Luke 11:10; 3 Nephi 14:8). Our task is to begin thinking seriously about which things to ask or seek, and where to knock, and the eternal laws that govern those particular matters. When we have accurately determined which laws govern which blessings, and faithfully obey those laws in a spirit of love and devotion to the Lord and His children, we will find that our lives are filled with so many blessings that there is insufficient room to receive and store them all.

Say Thank You

How do we develop confidence in the Lord? Elder James E. Faust of the Quorum of the Twelve Apostles shared, "A grateful heart is a beginning of greatness. It is an expression of humility. It helps us develop such virtues as prayer, faith, courage, contentment, happiness, love, and well-being" (April 1990 conference address, "Grateful Heart." See *Ensign*, May 1990, 85). These are certainly enviable characteristics, to which we should all aspire. The Apostle specifically shares that we will develop the virtue of faith through our gratitude. The Lord says, "And he who receiveth all things with thankfulness shall be made glorious; and the things of this earth shall be added unto him, even an hundred fold, yea, more" (D&C 78:19). We read many conference talks over the years that stress how we must learn to be grateful for everything—in all circumstances. We must learn to thank the Lord for every gift, and blessing.

Sometimes we fail to see the value of certain things that come our way. Hardship doesn't really seem like much of a blessing. When we look at a man or woman who has worked hard and developed toned muscles, we tell ourselves that we wish we had such toning. Yet, we look upon "resistence" as something that we must avoid at all costs. In fact, it is in the resistance brought about by life's challenges that we become toned—strong, resilient, wise and insurmountable. We need to learn to see the Lord's hand in all things, and learn to be grateful for everything that He sees fit to share with us—luxury or hardship. "And in nothing doth man offend God, or against none is his wrath kindled, save those who confess not his hand in all things, and obey not his commandments" (D&C 59:21). Whether we merit it or not, the Lord is constantly aware of us and our circumstances, and watches us very closely. He is actively sending people and circumstances into our lives, to provide us with opportunities to learn, grow and prosper. To the extent we recognize this process, and learn to create a partnership with the Lord in the process, we will be able to harness its power, and develop strength and abilities in many aspects of our lives.

I once had a home teacher who asked me and my family, "How many times do you pray each day?" I wasn't sure what the correct answer was, so when he looked at me, I told him, "Fifty or sixty, maybe." I could tell he was surprised. Perhaps startled. Maybe he thought I was embellishing. I smiled, and he knew he was free to challenge my assertion. I then explained that I learned from my stake Patriarch many years ago the secret of developing an intimate relationship with the Father and the Savior. The Patriarch explained to me that his best method of staying close to the Spirit was to be grateful. He made a conscious effort to note every comfort and luxury in his life, and on each occasion when he thought about it, he would thank the Lord for that blessing. I told my home teacher I had adopted the practice as well, each time I sat in my nice car, which zipped me to my destinations much faster than walking would have done, or put on my nice form-fitting comfy shoes, or bit into delicious food—each moment was an occasion to say, "Thank you, Father." Each thank you qualified as a prayer in my mind—so yes, I offered up many short prayers each day.

If we become conscious of every blessing that the Lord provides to us through His generosity, and love for us, we will become grateful.

Gratitude leads to humility, and love. I am grateful—for every little thing and big thing in my life. The chair I sit in is comfortable—much more so than the ground or a stone utilized by millions of others in this very moment. The food I eat is rich and delicious—especially compared to the food eaten by many of my brothers and sisters around the world. My home is warm and clean, and my car is luxurious with its air conditioning and leather seats. I have electricity, and television, and a computer that performs billions of calculations every second, providing me with a very powerful creative tool. My clothes are wonderful—although I usually wear just a cotton t-shirt and cargo shorts. I have books, movies, documentaries, radio and podcast shows I can enjoy at any time of the day or night. I have soft carpet beneath my feet, and live without fear of poverty, violence, or invasion. Every minute of my life is a testimonial to the love that my Heavenly Father has for me, and I have so much abundance that I must rent a storage shed to store the overflow. Yes—I acknowledge God's hand in all things, and it fills my life with abundance and gratitude. Fifty or sixty prayers? I should be offering up two or three every waking moment of my life! Perhaps just one prayer—a never-ending prayer of gratitude throughout the day.

Yes—grow close to the Lord with this simple tool. Have an attitude of gratitude, and no matter where you are in your life, and no matter what trials you face, you will approach it with the wisdom of the eternities, and see your challenges for what they really are—little more than learning and growing opportunities.

My Will, or Thy Will?

Allow me to share an experience with you, where a great, but humble man of God wrestled with the Spirit to know what he should ask for during a serious personal crisis. We are all very much like that man, and I believe we find ourselves at the Lord's feet in dire supplication, struggling to know His will, in desperation that He answer our prayers with His blessings. In our discussions herein, we have discovered that there is a formula we must follow when seeking divine help. The elements of that formula are:

1. Discern if the thing is right—good, and God's will
2. Ask
3. Do not doubt, asking with strong faith
4. Believe that you will receive

Each of these elements is crucial in the process of asking of God, and receiving of Him. Our trust levels in the Lord must be high, and our confidence in His promises to us must be well developed as we seek to know the Lord's will, and accomplish it, through asking and receiving. The Lord revealed to the Prophet Joseph Smith, who himself suffered great anguish and was in the very depths of despair, "Let virtue garnish thy thoughts unceasingly; then shall thy confidence wax strong in the presence of God; and the doctrine of the priesthood shall distil upon thy soul as the dews from heaven" (D&C 121:45). As long as we are in tune with the Spirit, and seek to do the will of our Father in Heaven, we can approach Him with abundant confidence. Those who serve the Lord, through their families, careers and Church callings, seek His blessings in their daily lives, and over their stewardships. Like the prophets of old, we seek to please the Lord in serving His purposes, and not our own. The Lord made this promise to the prophet Nephi, and through extension, to us.

> Blessed art thou, Nephi, for those things which thou hast done; for I have beheld how thou hast with unwearyingness declared the word, which I have given unto thee, unto this people. And thou hast not feared them, and hast not sought thine own life, but hast sought my will, and to keep my commandments. And now, because thou hast done this with such unwearyingness, behold, I will bless thee forever; and I will make thee mighty in word and in deed, in faith and in works; yea, even that all things shall be done unto thee according to thy word, for thou shalt not ask that which is contrary to my will (Helaman 10:4–5).

Many of us in these latter days seek to serve the Lord with all our heart. Most of us are not called to positions of high priesthood authority in the Church, so we assume that we are not called to exercise high levels of priesthood power. This is untrue. Positions of authority in the Church are merely "appendages to this priesthood" (D&C 107:5).

There is a vast difference between exercising priesthood authority, and exercising priesthood power. Priesthood power is bestowed on all who are ordained to the Aaronic and Melchizedek priesthoods, and can only be developed by the personal tutelage of the Father. God Himself teaches us how to develop our priesthood into power sufficient to control the elements, and the course of humanity, and He teaches us only to the extent we seek His divine instruction. We learn through studying scriptures, prayer, and temple worship. The power of Godliness, He informs us, is manifest through the ordinances of exaltation (D&C 84:20).

> The power and authority of the higher, or Melchizedek Priesthood, is to hold the keys of all the spiritual blessings of the church—To have the privilege of receiving the mysteries of the kingdom of heaven, to have the heavens opened unto them, to commune with the general assembly and church of the Firstborn, and to enjoy the communion and presence of God the Father, and Jesus the mediator of the new covenant (D&C 107:18–19).

The Aaronic priesthood has a narrower scope of power than the Melchizedek, but still holds the keys of the ministering of angels (verse 20). All of these powers are extraordinary, and if employed as intended, we can control all aspects of our environment, and influence the world in ways that have never before been experienced, save in the case of Enoch and Melchizedek, and their cities Zion and Salem. In fact, every miracle that we read of in holy writ, from the first man to the present, was performed through faith in Jesus Christ, and with the power of the priesthood—employing the finger of God. From miraculous healings, to raising the dead, to casting out demons, to controlling the weather, and turning away armies, all were and are accomplished through the power of the priesthood. Let's look at the life of the great high priest, Melchizedek,[84] to get a better idea of who he

---

84. The name Melchizedek consists of the two Hebrew words *malkî* ("king") and *sedeq* ("righteousness"), denoting the king of Salem's faith in God—"My king is righteousness." The Apostle Paul interpreted Melchizedek as "King of righteousness" (Heb. 7:2). Salem, the name of Melchizedek's land or city, likely means "peace" or "peaceful." The Bible Dictionary in the LDS edition of the

was, so that we may better emulate him, and perform with the same power that he exercised in behalf of his people.

> Now Melchizedek was a man of faith, who wrought righteousness; and when a child he feared God, and stopped the mouths of lions, and quenched the violence of fire. And thus, having been approved of God, he was ordained an high priest after the order of the covenant which God made with Enoch, It being after the order of the Son of God; which order came, not by man, nor the will of man; neither by father nor mother; neither by beginning of days nor end of years; but of God (JST, Genesis 14:26–28).

In the same way that we will face devastating events in our lives, especially as the last days approach, young Melchizedek, like Enoch, surmounted lethal threats to his life, and other momentous challenges, by exercising his faith in the Lord, even when he was a child. As great as Adam and Enoch were, the prophet Alma informs us that "none were greater" than Melchizedek (Alma 13:19). As the world warred in great violence around them, Melchizedek provided his people of Salem an oasis of peace, as Enoch had done for his people, Zion, through the exercise of priesthood power. In his youth, Melchizedek had delivered himself from ravenous lions, and from raging fires, and had later called his wicked people to repentance, and led them to righteousness—and as a prophet and example to his people, he stood between them and the armies of the kings of the earth. He was ordained to the high priesthood, which is After the Order of the Son of God.

> For God having sworn unto Enoch and unto his seed with an oath by himself; that every one being ordained after this order and calling should have power, by faith, to break mountains, to divide the seas, to dry up waters, to turn them out of their course; To put at defiance the armies of nations, to divide the earth, to break every band, to stand in the presence of God; to do all things according to his will, according to his command, subdue principalities and powers; and this by the will of the Son of God which was from before the foundation of the world (JST, Genesis 14:30–31).

Bible identifies Salem as Jerusalem. (*See Worlds Without Number*, James L. Thompson, Cedar Fort, Inc. (2022), 80–81).

You, who have been ordained to the Melchizedek priesthood, are endowed with this very same power—to exercise the Finger of God, to protect, heal and save, regardless the height of the challenge.

To this end, President Russell M. Nelson, then President of the Quorum of the Twelve Apostles, delivered a conference address titled, "The Price of Priesthood Power," in the October 2015 general conference. He began by saying, "Are we willing to pray, fast, study, seek, worship, and serve as men of God so we can have priesthood power?" He continues his instruction on what it means, and what is required of us, to "bear" the Priesthood of God:

> To bear means to support the weight of that which is held. It is a sacred trust to bear the priesthood, which is the mighty power and authority of God. Think of this: the priesthood conferred upon us is the very same power and authority through which God created this and numberless worlds, governs the heavens and the earth, and exalts His obedient children.
>
> Recently, Wendy and I were in a meeting where the organist was poised and ready to play the opening hymn. His eyes were on the music, and his fingers were on the keys. He began pressing the keys, but there was no sound. I whispered to Wendy, "He has no power." I reasoned that something had stopped the flow of electrical power to that organ.
>
> Well, brethren, in like manner, I fear that there are too many men who have been given the authority of the priesthood but who lack priesthood power because the flow of power has been blocked by sins such as laziness, dishonesty, pride, immorality, or preoccupation with things of the world.
>
> I fear that there are too many priesthood bearers who have done little or nothing to develop their ability to access the powers of heaven. I worry about all who are impure in their thoughts, feelings, or actions or who demean their wives or children, thereby cutting off priesthood power. . . .
>
> In a coming day, only those men who have taken their priesthood seriously, by diligently seeking to be taught by the Lord Himself, will be able to bless, guide, protect, strengthen, and heal others. Only a man who has paid the price for priesthood power will be able to bring miracles to those he loves and keep his marriage and family safe, now and throughout eternity.

As we consider the attributes of God, which make Him the marvelous being He is, and instill confidence, we must begin to realize that we too must develop those very same attributes in our lives—for very similar reasons. President Nelson added,

> How else can we increase our power in the priesthood? We need to pray from our hearts. . . . The Lord loves to do His own teaching in His holy house. Imagine how pleased He would be if you asked Him to teach you about priesthood keys, authority, and power as you experience the ordinances of the Melchizedek Priesthood in the holy temple. Imagine the increase in priesthood power that could be yours.

Power in the priesthood is a very tangible blessing that attends temple worship, and can be developed with frequent exercise of our faith as we present ourselves to the Lord for further light and knowledge, receiving all of the information and keys that have been passed on from the first man to the last in that sacred setting.

President Nelson assures us,

> Priesthood power can calm the seas and heal fractures in the earth. Priesthood power can also calm the minds and heal fractures in the hearts of those we love. Are we willing to pray, fast, study, seek, worship, and serve as men of God so we can have that kind of priesthood power?

That is the price that the Lord requires of us to become men of exceeding faith, who exercise priesthood power in the earth to save and benefit those around us. President Nelson concluded,

> My dear brethren, we have been given a sacred trust—the authority of God to bless others. May each one of us rise up as the man God foreordained us to be—ready to bear the priesthood of God bravely, eager to pay whatever price is required to increase his power in the priesthood. With that power, we can help prepare the world for the Second Coming of our Savior, Jesus Christ.

Exercising Priesthood Power within the Lord's Will

What do I do to employ the finger of God in my life, you ask? What power do I have as a priesthood holder? How do I know that I am exercising my priesthood power within the boundaries of the Lord's righteous will? Marion G. Romney was a faithful priesthood holder, and he served the Lord and His children all the days of his life as a local and general authority in the Church. As a man who was humble in his heart, yet waxed strong in confidence of the Lord, he often struggled, as many of us do, to know what is right in the eyes of God—knowing what is God's will *vs.* what is our own will. Elder Romney was very much aware of the matters we discuss herein. He knew the scriptures quite well, and he understood the Lord's admonitions to us, that we should ask for that which is right, according to His righteous will, doubting nothing, and He will so bless us. He was very aware of the hundreds of miracles reported in the scriptures, and millions more enjoyed by the people of God throughout the history of the world. Yet, when his own sweet wife became very ill, and lay on the doorstep of death, he struggled to know what the Lord would have him do, as a man who was endowed with the Priesthood After the Order of the Son of God.

Brother Romney shared,

> When we pray unto the Father in the name of Jesus for specific personal things, we should feel in the very depths of our souls that we are willing to subject our petitions to the will of our Father in heaven . . . The time will come when we shall know the will of God before we ask. Then everything for which we pray will be "expedient." Everything for which we ask will be "right." That will be when, as a result of righteous living, we shall so enjoy the companionship of the spirit that he will dictate what we ask (In Conference Report, Oct. 1944, 55–56).

Over 20 years after that talk, Elder Romney's wife Ida suffered a serious stroke, and the doctors informed him that there was very little hope for her recovery. They informed him that they could keep her alive on life support for a while, but recommended against it. He and the entire family began to steel themselves for her death. Like so many of us, Elder Romney was heartbroken at the thought of losing his beloved wife, and dreaded the coming years without her love and companionship in his life. He went to his knees in prayer, to learn the Lord's will in the matter. He knew that he had been endowed with the power to raise his quickly fading wife from her deathbed, but that trifling with such power, for such personal, and perhaps even selfish benefit, might temp the Lord in ways that were strictly forbidden. Elder Romney prayed over his wife, and asked the Lord many times that if it was His divine will, that she would recover. Nothing happened, and she did not improve. Elder Romney struggled to know what to do for his wife, and told those nearest him that although he would be lost without her love and companionship, above all he wanted "the Lord's will to be done," and to take what he "needed to take without whimpering." As he prayed for his wife, he even administered to her, anointing her and giving her blessings. Yet, he was circumspect in his pronouncements, because he was "reluctant to counsel the Lord about the matter." Earlier in their life, Elder Romney had often pleaded with the Lord to bless them with children, but the Spirit never confirmed the matter, so he remained shy about asking for personal blessings, no matter how important they were to him. Now, however, his precious Ida was dying, becoming less responsive with each passing day. She would soon be gone. Elder Romney fasted, praying that the Lord would reveal His divine will to him, so he would know what was proper to ask in faith. Elder Romney opened the Book of Mormon to seek inspiration, and read Helaman 10:4–5, which we discussed above. He read,

> And now, because thou hast done this with such unwearyingness, behold, I will bless thee forever; and I will make thee mighty in word and in deed, in faith and in works; yea, even that all things shall be done unto thee according to thy word, for thou shalt not ask that which is contrary to my will.

He says that he was so touched by the power of this passage, that he felt "tangible peace" for the first time since his wife had taken ill. He felt that the Lord was speaking directly to him through this scripture, much as the Prophet Joseph Smith felt when he read a similar passage in James, inviting him to ask of God, to receive knowledge.

Elder Romney prayed, thanking the Lord for this feeling of peace, ending his prayer with the refrain, "Thy will be done."

As he ended his prayer, Elder Romney heard, in his ear or in his heart, a voice that communicated, "It is not contrary to my will that Ida be healed." A feeling of supreme confidence rested on Elder Romney, and although it was two o'clock in the morning, he put on his tie and coat, and went out into the night, driving directly to the hospital. As he walked through her door and approached his nearly lifeless wife, he smiled at her, and went to her, and placed his hands on her head. He was filled with confidence in the promise of the Lord, and he blessed his wife, invoking the power of the holy priesthood, and pronounced that she would recover her health and mental abilities, and would yet perform "a great mission" upon the earth. As he closed the blessing, he opened his eyes to see if she had changed yet. He waited a moment, and watched in amazement as she opened her eyes and looked at him. She hadn't spoken in months, but suddenly said, "For goodness' sake, Marion, what are you doing here?" Ida Romney began her recovery in that moment, and was soon sent home, where she healed quickly and regained her physical and mental abilities. She lived to see her husband. Marion, sustained as a member of the First Presidency of the Church, and she served at his side for many years.[85]

President Romney's struggle is an excellent primer for us all. Distinguishing between our own will, and that of the Lord can be difficult for us—especially when we have so much at stake. We remember Christ's plea from the Garden of Gethsemane, "O my Father, if it be possible, let this cup pass from me: nevertheless not as I will, but as thou wilt." We must come to the point where we know God's will, and we must accept it, and embrace it in our works. Be patient, and be flexible to accommodate the Lord's righteous purposes—even though at times it may seem that all is lost unless our will is fulfilled immediately. Joseph was held in the prison of Egypt for 20 years before he interpreted Pharoah's dream and was released. Moses awaited the Lord's call for 40 years, then wandered with the camp of Israel for another 40 before being translated. If God reveals His own timetable,

85. F. Burton Howard, *Marion G. Romney: His Life and Faith* (Salt Lake City: Bookcraft, 1988), 137–42.

or His own will, and it is not what we had hoped, we must be willing to accept His supremacy. He is all knowing, and understands what can, and what cannot be. Be comforted in the knowledge that no matter the dictates of the Holy Spirit, God's will is ALWAYS the right way. We may not see it in the moment, and we may feel tremendous pain and loss if we don't receive what we will in the moment. But in the end, we are all in a much better position if God's will is victorious.

When we approach the Lord to ask for something, we must allow the Holy Spirit to speak to us, and reveal the will of the Lord in the matter. The more we try to see things from God's exalted perspective, the better we are at being open to His righteous will. Let us all learn to pray always, consulting the Holy Spirit on every matter that passes through our mind throughout the day. As we are prompted to act, do whatsoever the Spirit indicates—and act in the power of the Lord God, because it is He who has ordained you to this very purpose. Learn to say and feel the words, "Thy will be done."

5

What Else Should We Do?

To know that we are living our lives in harmony with the will of God, so that we may be able to exercise strong faith in Him and know that He will bless us as we ask blessings of Him, is paramount to our quest. Certainly, our prayers are often raised with the question, *What should I do*? In fact, many of us would gladly do God's will, because we know that in the end, it is by far the best course for us to take. We are not alone in our question. Upon hearing the good news of the gospel message, we recall that the rich young man asked the same question of the Lord.

> And when he was gone forth into the way, there came one running, and kneeled to him, and asked him, Good Master, what shall I do that I may inherit eternal life? And Jesus said unto him . . . Thou knowest the commandments, Do not commit adultery, Do not kill, Do not steal, Do not bear false witness, Defraud not, Honour thy father and mother. And he answered and said unto him, Master, all these have I observed from my youth. Then Jesus beholding him loved him, and said unto him, One thing thou lackest: go thy way, sell whatsoever thou hast, and give to the poor, and thou shalt have treasure in heaven: and come, take up the cross, and follow me. And he was sad at that saying, and went away grieved: for he had great possessions (Mark 10:17–22).

Similarly, the multitudes at Jerusalem asked the very same question of Peter and the other Apostles, as they heard the gospel message on the day of Pentecost. "Now when they heard this, they were pricked in their heart, and said unto Peter and to the rest of the Apostles, Men and brethren, what shall we do" (Acts 2:37–39)?

> Then Peter said unto them, Repent, and be baptized every one of you in the name of Jesus Christ for the remission of sins, and ye shall receive the gift of the Holy Ghost. For the promise is unto you, and to your children, and to all that are afar off, even as many as the Lord our God shall call (Acts 2:38–39).

Unlike the rich young man who walked away from Jesus grieved, the multitudes at Jerusalem acted on the word of the Lord. "Then they that gladly received his word were baptized: and the same day there were added unto them about three thousand souls" (verse 41).

The answer given to each was essentially the same—follow the commandments. To the young rich man, Jesus first recited the basic commandments that all should live, taken from the Ten Commandments given through Moses—"Do not commit adultery, Do not kill, Do not steal, Do not bear false witness, Defraud not, Honour thy father and mother." But the imprudent youth challenged Him with the assertion that he had kept those commandments since childhood, and wondered what more he could do to ensure himself a place in the eternities in the presence of the Father. Jesus smiled and peered deep into his immature soul with a loving eye, and found something that the youth may not have known was there. His response was, "One thing thou lackest." I wonder what words would follow if the Lord stood before me in this very moment and answered my question, What should I do? The Lord's insightful response to the young rich man was narrowly tailored to his specific need; "sell whatsoever thou hast, and give to the poor." The young man was saddened by this requirement, because he had much wealth, and it appears that giving it all up to follow as one of Jesus's rag-tag troupe of disciples was not something the young man was willing to do. We know nothing of what happened to him afterward, whether he remained close to the Master or drifted into unbelief. We do know that when Jesus responded to his second question, He did so with love, seeking a teaching opportunity for the young man, and for others who could hear. We recall the words of Joseph Smith that "a religion that does not require the sacrifice of all things, never has power sufficient to produce the faith necessary unto life and salvation," and understand that this was exactly what the Savior was teaching—faith, sufficient to save and exalt.

What we learn from this is that there is always room for improvement; always something more that can be done to become more like the Savior. We wonder how this particular scene may have been different if the young man had simply listened to the Master's first response, and smiled his gratitude upon hearing that he was already well on his way to eternal life, and had followed as one of Jesus's disciples, and improved in his ability to serve others as opportunities were afforded him. This is how it's done in the Lord's kingdom in the present day. We learn line upon line, precept upon precept, here a little and there a little, until we eventually arrive at the day of perfection. None of us starts at the top of understanding or commitment. None of us is filled with faith, before we have gone through the process of learning trust through our experiences with the Lord (2 Nephi 28:30;[86] Isaiah 28:10, 13; D&C 98:12 and 128:21). We are imperfect beings, striving to improve with each new day. We control our natural man tendencies by giving service to others and by seeking the Lord's will in our lives. It is in the process of living for others, that we find ourselves. A man or a woman who cares about little more than self-aggrandizement and career advancement may find short term accolades from a worldly culture, but one who becomes a spouse and parent, a friend and listening ear, and a willing servant to all who stand in need will become like the Savior if that path is pursued with love and obedience to the commandments.

In Christ's Church we learn from the common refrain, *Choose The Right.* We are taught in the Primary and Youth programs to implement the concept in all aspects of our life, and all situations in which

86. "For behold, thus saith the Lord God: I will give unto the children of men line upon line, precept upon precept, here a little and there a little; and blessed are those who hearken unto my precepts, and lend an ear unto my counsel, for they shall learn wisdom; for unto him that receiveth I will give more; and from them that shall say, We have enough, from them shall be taken away even that which they have."

we may find ourselves. Surely, if we follow this maxim, we will become like the Holy One, because what is it that sets Him apart from the rest of mankind most but His devotion to the Father, and willingness to do His will in every circumstance (John 14:31[87])? Although we are not yet perfect, our Heavenly Father expects us to follow the Savior's perfect example, and when we fall short He expects us to repent, fully repent as we have discussed, so the Atonement can elevate us again to our unsullied status. If we will learn the general requirements of the Lord for our lives, and strive to live them, we will find that we are becoming righteous—truly righteous—like the prophets and apostles and all who have followed the Lord all the way back to the throne of God. If we are still asking the question, *What shall I do that I may inherit eternal life*?, we should revisit the gospel basics. Christ's answer to the young rich man was simply to obey the commandments, followed by His admonition that the young man begin living his life in the service of others, because when we are in the service of our fellow beings, we are actually in the service of our God (Mosiah 2:17). Peter's response to the men who heard him speak on the day of Pentecost was simply, "Repent, and be baptized every one of you in the name of Jesus Christ for the remission of sins, and ye shall receive the gift of the Holy Ghost" (Acts 2:38). Three thousand converts joined the Church that day, and we have reason to believe that many of them have inherited eternal life as a result of their willingness to ask the question, *What should I do*?, and follow up when they receive the answer.

We can learn all of the commandments and strive to follow them. We can live by the precept "choose the right." We can devote ourselves to service in a marriage and family. We can receive the priesthood and the ordinances of salvation and exaltation and honor the covenants that we make. We can magnify our callings and participate in church meetings and programs. We can fellowship the families assigned to us by our Bishop and strive to fulfill their needs in a spirit of love and stewardship. As we follow the Lord's example and the programs He has established through His modern prophets, He will accept our

87. "But that the world may know that I love the Father; and as the Father gave me commandment, even so I do. Arise, let us go hence."

lives, and reveal to us that we are living them according to His will. Through this knowledge we will be able to approach Him with confidence and in faith, and will be able to exercise our faith in a manner that allows us to draw down the powers of heaven into our lives, and receive the ministering of angels and other miraculous blessings. King Benjamin described the state of those who seek and do the will of the Father.

> And moreover, I would desire that ye should consider on the blessed and happy state of those that keep the commandments of God. For behold, they are blessed in all things, both temporal and spiritual; and if they hold out faithful to the end they are received into heaven, that thereby they may dwell with God in a state of never-ending happiness. O remember, remember that these things are true; for the Lord God hath spoken it (Mosiah 2:41).

What Awaits Us?

Those who do what our Heavenly Father asks in this life will receive His blessings in this world, and in the world to come. Because the blessings we receive in this life are based on obedience to certain commandments and a plan of progress designed for each one of us by our Father, it may be difficult for us to know which blessings to seek, and in what we should exercise our faith. We discuss this topic in greater depth in the next chapter. Something we can predict with great confidence is the future state of all those who obey the commandments of God in the life still to come. Although there are many scriptural resources and commentaries that discuss the world to come and what we can expect when we arrive there, we consider it here to focus our attention on the reason we exercise faith in the first place—to gain salvation and exaltation.

By Grace or by Works?

To begin, we hear much about salvation, the act of being "saved," and the scriptures talk about the concept in some detail. We are surrounded by many millions who tell us that all a person must do to be saved is to confess Jesus Christ, or accept Him as the Lord, or some other simple act of profession. This, they assure us, is the dividing line between those who will burn in the smoldering pits of hell for all eternity, and those who will bask in the heavenly glow of the Lord for all eternity. This simple view of the eternities seems quite attractive to many who subscribe to its bicameral reward system, and in fact it is very flattering to those who feel that any additional effort on their part is unnecessary to gain a full measure of eternal reward. Such beliefs grow out of scriptures that tell us that we are saved not by our own efforts, but rather by the gift of God, through His grace. "For by grace are ye saved through faith; and that not of yourselves: it is the gift of God" (Ephesians 2:8). "Not by works of righteousness which we have done, but according to his mercy he saved us" (Titus 3:5).

Those who center their religious beliefs in this sectarian doctrine, excuse worldly and sinful behavior by declaring that their salvation was granted at the moment they accepted Jesus Christ as their savior. When asked if there is anything else required of them to receive salvation, they are quick to respond there is not. When questioned about what their salvation entails they merely quote isolated biblical passages that indicate that the "saved" will be with Christ in heaven, and they have vague notions about praising Him ceaselessly to pass the eternities. When asked about familial relations or eternal progress, these will always deny that any such things will exist or even be of value to them.

What are we to make of scriptures that indicate that we are saved by the grace of God and not by our own works, seeing there are so many scriptures that tell us we must obey the commandments to receive eternal life? The New Testament is replete with instructions on all we must do to inherit eternal life, as is the Doctrine and Covenants and The Book of Mormon. In fact, we have already discussed Christ's response to the very question put to Him by the young rich man who asked what he must do to have eternal life. If the "Born Again" people are correct in their doctrine, Christ would have said, "Confess that I am the Messiah, and accept me as your savior, and you shall have eternal life." That wasn't His reply to the question, however. In fact, for three years Christ preached His doctrine to hundreds of thousands, and he told them hundreds of things that they must do to merit eternal life. His reply to the young man of what he must do to have eternal life was 1) to remind him of all of the commandments that he must observe, 2) followed with the additional requirement of selling all of his possessions and giving them to the poor, and 3) spending the remainder of his life following Christ in His ministry. Christ seems to be a believer in works, not mere professions of belief or acceptance. Jesus says, "Verily, I say unto thee, Except a man be born of water and of the Spirit, he cannot enter into the kingdom of God," indicating the prerequisite of receiving baptism and the gift of the Holy Ghost, as He had done Himself (John 3:5).

By now we understand from the spoken words of Christ that in order to have eternal life, we must at least 1) obey the commandments, 2) dedicate ourselves to serving others, 3) be willing to sacrifice all that we possess for the Lord's cause, and 4) receive baptism by water and by the Holy Ghost. It is to those who "profess" to accept Him or to represent Him that He said, "Not every one that saith unto me, Lord, Lord, shall enter into the kingdom of heaven; but he that doeth the will of my Father which is in heaven" (Matthew 7:21). Yes, it is clear that Christ Himself is not a believer in the false doctrine that eternal life is automatically granted to all those who merely profess to accept Him as their savior. Upon making His pronouncement, He saw that the people who heard Him were incredulous, so He explained the concept in the clearest terms possible to them:

> Many will say to me in that day, Lord, Lord, have we not prophesied in thy name? and in thy name have cast out devils? and in thy name done many wonderful works?
>
> And then will I profess unto them, I never knew you: depart from me, ye that work iniquity.
>
> Therefore whosoever heareth these sayings of mine, and doeth them, I will liken him unto a wise man, which built his house upon a rock:
>
> And the rain descended, and the floods came, and the winds blew, and beat upon that house; and it fell not: for it was founded upon a rock.
>
> And every one that heareth these sayings of mine, and doeth them not, shall be likened unto a foolish man, which built his house upon the sand:

> And the rain descended, and the floods came, and the winds blew, and beat upon that house; and it fell: and great was the fall of it (Ibid., verses 22–28).

The scripture concludes, "And it came to pass, when Jesus had ended these sayings, the people were astonished at his doctrine:"

Yes—there are many "commandments of men" that will do nothing to improve our eternal standing with God, and there are many commandments of God that men set aside as unimportant. As the Lord clarified, it is those who hear His sayings and do them who will receive His promised blessings. James echoed this precept when he instructed the Saints, "But be ye doers of the word, and not hearers only, deceiving your own selves" (James 1:22). There are many who deceive themselves in their belief that they have no need to obey the Lord's commandments. Entire "Christian" religions are built up on the philosophy that we need do nothing except confess Jesus is Lord, and the followers of those preachers are only too happy to adhere to a religion that requires so little of them—they don't even need to follow the Ten Commandments and they will inherit everything the great Lawgiver Moses will receive, according to their precept. It is a religion of convenience, but it is not the religion of the Lord Jesus Christ, and in it there is no power to bestow eternal life.

The question of whether we are saved by works or by grace can only be answered by first answering the questions, *What is Salvation*? and *What is Eternal Life*?

Salvation

Salvation is something we have already discussed, in our conversation about immortality and eternal life. If we understand that salvation and eternal life are not the same things, then we begin to comprehend what it means to be saved by the grace of God, which gift is bestowed on all humans through the atoning sacrifice of the Son of God. This salvation comes through no effort on our part, and there would be nothing we could do to obtain it on our own, absent the sacrifice of that which was infinite in nature and pure in character. There would be no work we could perform and no amount of repentance for our sins that we could offer up that could redeem us from the fall of all humanity. After all, it is through the transgression of the first man that sin entered the world and polluted the race, and we are all born into a fallen existence (Alma 42:6, 12[88]). It is as we make individual decisions to do things that are contrary to the will of God, that we individually separate ourselves from God's presence, and become personally fallen.

At the time physical death entered the world it became necessary to counteract its effects, to restore the race to its original state of immortality. The process by which we overcome the effects of death is the resurrection, the reuniting of our spirits and our bodies into an immortal state. The prophet Alma explains, "The spirit and the body shall be reunited again in its perfect form; both limb and joint shall be restored to its proper frame, even as we now are at this time" (Alma 11:43; see also 40:21[89]);

Jesus was the very first to experience resurrection, and is called by Paul the firstfruits of them that slept.

> But now is Christ risen from the dead, and become the firstfruits of them that slept. For since by man came death, by man came also the resurrection of the dead. For as in Adam all die, even so in Christ shall all be made alive. But every man in his own order: Christ the firstfruits; afterward they that are Christ's at his coming (1 Corinthians 15:20–23).

Christ's body was separated from His spirit, then reunited again in resurrection. He showed Himself to many of His followers, and allowed the Apostles and His closest disciples to touch His restored physical body. He told them that His resurrected body was made up

88. "But behold, it was appointed unto man to die—therefore, as they were cut off from the tree of life they should be cut off from the face of the earth—and man became lost forever, yea, they became fallen man." "And now, there was no means to reclaim men from this fallen state, which man had brought upon himself because of his own disobedience;"

89. "But whether it be at his resurrection or after, I do not say; but this much I say, that there is a space between death and the resurrection of the body, and a state of the soul in happiness or in misery until the time which is appointed of God that the dead shall come forth, and be reunited, both soul and body, and be brought to stand before God, and be judged according to their works."

of flesh and bone (Luke 24:39[90]). He even had them bring Him some fish and honeycomb to eat, so He could demonstrate that this was a genuine physical body in every apparent respect (Ibid., verses 41–43[91]). When Christ passed out of the spirit realms to be reunited with His now healed and perfected body in resurrection, He opened the gates of the spirit prison that had held the departed spirits of all humanity since the first man had died, and one by one each of the children of God exited that place and experience the resurrection just like Christ did. The scriptures record that immediately following the resurrection of the Savior many of those who had been dead arose from their graves and showed themselves in the cities (Matthew 27:52–53[92]). It is a wonder that so little is mentioned about this marvelous event in holy writ. It must have had a tremendous impact on witnesses, and may be partially responsible for the great numbers of Jews who joined themselves to the Church in the months that followed. Like Christ, and those who rose with Him, at the time of our resurrection, we become physically perfect immortal beings and will never again suffer death.

Resurrection and immortality do not equate with eternal life, however. As we discussed before, immortality is the equivalent of salvation in that it is the process by which we overcome the first death, physical death, and are saved from the grave. "O death, where is thy sting? O grave, where is thy victory" (1 Corinthians 15:55)?

> And if Christ had not risen from the dead, or have broken the bands of death that the grave should have no victory, and that death should have no sting, there could have been no resurrection. But there is a resurrection, therefore the grave hath no victory, and the sting of death is swallowed up in Christ (Mosiah 16:8).
>
> And since man had fallen he could not merit anything of himself; but the sufferings and death of Christ atone for their sins,

---

90. "Behold my hands and my feet, that it is I myself: handle me, and see; for a spirit hath not flesh and bones, as ye see me have."

91. "And while they yet believed not for joy, and wondered, he said unto them, Have ye here any meat? And they gave him a piece of a broiled fish, and of an honeycomb. And he took it, and did eat before them."

92. "And the graves were opened; and many bodies of the saints which slept arose, And came out of the graves after his resurrection, and went into the holy city, and appeared unto many."

> through faith and repentance, and so forth; and that he breaketh the bands of death, that the grave shall have no victory, and that the sting of death should be swallowed up in the hopes of glory (Alma 22:14).

Immortality merely expresses the *duration* of our life in the future world following death and resurrection, not its *quality*. Immortality is not eternal life. The scripture is very clear that after the resurrection we will be brought before the Great Judge, and will be judged for the works which we performed during our mortal lives. "And shall come forth; they that have done good, unto the resurrection of life; and they that have done evil, unto the resurrection of damnation" (John 5:29). As we clearly see from this scripture, and others that agree, salvation from physical death, that free gift of God to all mankind through the grace of the Savior Jesus Christ, merely restores our spirits to our bodies, then brings us to the point of judgment, where our "works" are then weighed in the balance, and rewards are granted based on what we have done (Romans 14:10–12;[93] 2 Corinthians 5:10;[94] Alma 5:15, 12:12, 33:22; 3 Nephi 27:14; Mormon 3:20, 7:6; Ether 12:38). It was the ancient prophet Lehi who explained the entire process so well to his son Jacob:

> And men are instructed sufficiently that they know good from evil. And the law is given unto men. And by the law no flesh is justified; or, by the law men are cut off. Yea, by the temporal law they were cut off; and also, by the spiritual law they perish from that which is good, and become miserable forever.
>
> Wherefore, redemption cometh in and through the Holy Messiah; for he is full of grace and truth.

---

93. "But why dost thou judge thy brother? or why dost thou set at nought thy brother? for we shall all stand before the judgment seat of Christ. For it is written, As I live, saith the Lord, every knee shall bow to me, and every tongue shall confess to God. So then every one of us shall give account of himself to God."

94. "For we must all appear before the judgment seat of Christ; that every one may receive the things done in his body, according to that he hath done, whether it be good or bad."

> Behold, he offereth himself a sacrifice for sin, to answer the ends of the law, unto all those who have a broken heart and a contrite spirit; and unto none else can the ends of the law be answered.
>
> Wherefore, how great the importance to make these things known unto the inhabitants of the earth, that they may know that there is no flesh that can dwell in the presence of God, save it be through the merits, and mercy, and grace of the Holy Messiah, who layeth down his life according to the flesh, and taketh it again by the power of the Spirit, that he may bring to pass the resurrection of the dead, being the first that should rise.
>
> Wherefore, he is the firstfruits unto God, inasmuch as he shall make intercession for all the children of men; and they that believe in him shall be saved.
>
> And because of the intercession for all, all men come unto God; wherefore, they stand in the presence of him, to be judged of him according to the truth and holiness which is in him. Wherefore, the ends of the law which the Holy One hath given, unto the inflicting of the punishment which is affixed, which punishment that is affixed is in opposition to that of the happiness which is affixed, to answer the ends of the atonement (2 Nephi 2:5–10).

The prophet Mormon likewise explains the process to us.

> And because of the redemption of man, which came by Jesus Christ, they are brought back into the presence of the Lord; yea, this is wherein all men are redeemed, because the death of Christ bringeth to pass the resurrection, which bringeth to pass a redemption from an endless sleep, from which sleep all men shall be awakened by the power of God when the trump shall sound; and they shall come forth, both small and great, and all shall stand before his bar, being redeemed and loosed from this eternal band of death, which death is a temporal death. And then cometh the judgment of the Holy One upon them; and then cometh the time that he that is filthy shall be filthy still; and he that is righteous shall be righteous still; he that is happy shall be happy still; and he that is unhappy shall be unhappy still (Mormon 9:13–14).

These scriptures are clear that salvation from the grave, through the resurrection, does not in itself qualify us for any particular quality of life in the eternities. Many will be surprised when they attempt to stake their claim to eternal life and Christ the Great Judge will tell them to depart from Him because He never knew them.

> Many will say to me in that day, Lord, Lord, have we not prophesied in thy name? and in thy name have cast out devils? and in thy name done many wonderful works? And then will I profess unto them, I never knew you: depart from me, ye that work iniquity (Matthew 7:23; Mosiah 26:27; 3 Nephi 14:23).

The Apostle Paul explained, "They profess that they know God; but in works they deny him, being abominable, and disobedient, and unto every good work reprobate" (Titus 1:16).

Jesus Himself asked the people, "And why call ye me, Lord, Lord, and do not the things which I say" (Luke 6:46)? There are many who believe that merely confessing that Jesus is the Christ is sufficient to inherit the mansions on high that He has prepared for His faithful. Yet, His instructions to mankind are very clear and establish the path that we must follow if we desire to arrive where He is—the very path that He walked.

> Enter ye in at the strait gate: for wide is the gate, and broad is the way, that leadeth to destruction, and many there be which go in thereat: Because strait is the gate, and narrow is the way, which leadeth unto life, and few there be that find it (Matthew 7:13–14).

This "life," of which the Master speaks, is Eternal Life. Although many will pass through the gates, few will go on to that place that He calls "life." He expounds on this teaching as recorded in Luke.

> Strive to enter in at the strait gate: for many, I say unto you, will seek to enter in, and shall not be able. When once the master of the house is risen up, and hath shut to the door, and ye begin to stand without, and to knock at the door, saying, Lord, Lord, open unto us; and he shall answer and say unto you, I know you not whence ye are: Then shall ye begin to say, We have eaten and drunk in thy presence, and thou hast taught in our streets. But he shall say, I tell you, I know you not whence ye are; depart from me, all ye workers of iniquity. There shall be weeping and gnashing of teeth, when ye

shall see Abraham, and Isaac, and Jacob, and all the prophets, in the kingdom of God, and you yourselves thrust out (Luke 13:24–28).

This warning message is to all of those who believe that nothing, or little, is required of them, because they followed Christ to some degree. Christ makes it abundantly clear that many good works are required of them if they wish to dwell with Him ad His Father in the eternities.

In summation, the Lord and His apostles and prophets, have abundantly clarified that salvation, which comes to all mankind, is not the equivalent of eternal life. Those who are resurrected gain salvation from death, and it comes to all as a free gift through the grace of a loving Father in Heaven, who willingly sacrificed the life of His Firstborn Son, His Only Begotten in the flesh. The gift of salvation is a marvelous and wondrous endowment. It is not, however, eternal life. It is not exaltation in the eternities. Those who claim to accept Christ as their personal savior but fail to obey Him will not be allowed to dwell with Him eternally. They will be saved by grace. In fact, they will receive a reward more or less like the one they envision—ministering servants who are single, without familial ties or increase of kingdom. But for those who know the Lord and do what He instructs there will be a much better eternity—the one the Lord has prepared for His righteous.

Eternal Life and Exaltation

Salvation raises us from the grave and stands us before the Lord, to be judged for the works we have performed while in the flesh. It is at that point that we will be held accountable for all of our wrongs, or praised and rewarded for our obedience and all of our good works

(Revelation 20:12–15;[95] D&C 128:6–7[96]). In these scriptures we learn that there will be a judgment of those who are resurrected, some being adjudged as good, and others being adjudged evil. Many of those who are resurrected, are saved from the first death, only to be delivered up to a second death! When we speak of faith sufficient to "lay hold on eternal life," as the Prophet Joseph explained it,[97] we speak of faith that keeps us striving to become like the Savior, even when it is difficult to choose the right. It requires great faith on our part to remain honest in all of our dealings with our fellow men when we see them treating us dishonestly. It sometimes appears inevitable that we will be inundated in the sea of corruption that surrounds us, and we feel that

---

95. "And I saw the dead, small and great, stand before God; and the books were opened: and another book was opened, which is the book of life: and the dead were judged out of those things which were written in the books, according to their works. And the sea gave up the dead which were in it; and death and hell delivered up the dead which were in them: and they were judged every man according to their works. And death and hell were cast into the lake of fire. This is the second death. And whosoever was not found written in the book of life was cast into the lake of fire."

96. Joseph Smith instructs: "And further, I want you to remember that John the Revelator was contemplating this very subject in relation to the dead, when he declared, as you will find recorded in Revelation 20:12—And I saw the dead, small and great, stand before God; and the books were opened; and another book was opened, which is the book of life; and the dead were judged out of those things which were written in the books, according to their works. You will discover in this quotation that the books were opened; and another book was opened, which was the book of life; but the dead were judged out of those things which were written in the books, according to their works; consequently, the books spoken of must be the books which contained the record of their works, and refer to the records which are kept on the earth. And the book which was the book of life is the record which is kept in heaven; the principle agreeing precisely with the doctrine which is commanded you in the revelation contained in the letter which I wrote to you previous to my leaving my place—that in all your recordings it may be recorded in heaven."

97. "When a man has offered in sacrifice all that he has for the truth's sake, not even withholding his life, and believing before God that he has been called to make this sacrifice, because he seeks to do his will, he does know most assuredly that God does and will accept his sacrifice and offering, and that he has not nor will not seek his face in vain. Under these circumstances then, he can obtain the faith necessary for him to lay hold on eternal life" *Lectures on Faith*, 6:7.

notwithstanding our struggling against the great tide of immorality and sin, we will be engulfed and lost as it overwhelms our lives. It is understandable that we feel weakened and alone as we frantically fend off the arrows of the wicked, and their chief captain, fired rapidly at us with precision and determination.

Paul teaches, "Above all, taking the shield of faith, wherewith ye shall be able to quench all the fiery darts of the wicked" (Ephesians 6:16). We can feel overwhelmed by the rushing onslaught of filth that bombards our minds and souls with suggestions of how we could be achieving our selfish, vile, prurient, worldly objectives, if only we would engage in certain behaviors that are better attuned to the sensitivities and mores of a modern world. We are incessantly told that we must become more tolerant, more inclusive, and more ecumenical in our views, and that we should be accepting of the differences of others, or be ostracized and branded as bigots by those who are strangers to the Lord Jesus Christ and His path to perfection. This doesn't mean that we shouldn't be kind and inviting to those who choose not to follow the Savior, but it doesn't mean that we should engage in the ceaseless, raucous festivity that occupies the lives of the self-indulgent who are so comfortable in the halls and ballrooms of that great and spacious building observed by the prophets Lehi and Nephi.[98]

The level of faith that we must exercise to rise above such a world is considerable, and Joseph Smith was tireless in teaching the Saints that we seek it at the peril of falling short of the goal of eternal life and exaltation in the eternal worlds. Exercising the level of faith necessary to grasp hold onto eternal life is directly tied to the clearness of our conscience as we approach the Lord in prayer to ask His guidance and protection in our lives. We must know that the things we are doing and the paths we are pursuing are agreeable to His righteous will, and that He smiles upon our lives, and lights our way with His delighted

---

98. "And I also cast my eyes round about, and beheld, on the other side of the river of water, a great and spacious building; and it stood as it were in the air, high above the earth. And it was filled with people, both old and young, both male and female; and their manner of dress was exceedingly fine; and they were in the attitude of mocking and pointing their fingers towards those who had come at and were partaking of the fruit" 1 Nephi 8:26–27.

countenance, before we can enjoy a sufficient level of faith to ensure our exaltation. The Prophet Joseph says:

> This knowledge supplies an important place in revealed religion; for it was by reason of it that the ancients were enabled to endure as seeing him who is invisible.
>
> An actual knowledge to any person that the course of life which he pursues is according to the will of God, is essentially necessary to enable him to have that confidence in God, without which no person can obtain eternal life.
>
> It was this that enabled the ancient Saints to endure all their afflictions and persecutions, and to take joyfully the spoiling of their goods, knowing (not believing merely) that they had a more "enduring substance" (Heb. 10:34).
>
> Having the assurance that they were pursuing a course which was agreeable to the will of God, they were enabled to take, not only the spoiling of their goods and the wasting of their substance joyfully, but also to suffer death in its most horrid forms; knowing (not merely believing) that when this earthly house of their tabernacle was dissolved, they had a building of God, a house "not made with hands, eternal in the heavens" (2 Cor. 5:1).
>
> Such was, and always will be, the situation of the Saints of God, that unless they have an actual knowledge that the course that they are pursuing is according to the will of God, they will grow weary in their minds and faint; for such has been, and always will be, the opposition in the hearts of unbelievers and those that know not God, against the pure and unadulterated religion of heaven (the only thing which ensures eternal life), that they will persecute to the uttermost all that worship God according to his revelations, receive the truth in the love of it, and submit themselves to be guided and directed by his will, and drive them to such extremities that nothing short of an actual knowledge of their being the favorites of heaven, and of their having embraced that order of things which God has established for the redemption of man, will enable them to exercise that confidence in him necessary for them to overcome the world, and obtain that crown of glory which is laid up for them that fear God (*Lectures on Faith*, 6:2–4).

As we obtain salvation and are brought before the judgment bar of God, how will we be judged? What shall we receive as our eternal reward? The Lord explains the details of that great day to us thus:

> And my Father sent me that I might be lifted up upon the cross; and after that I had been lifted up upon the cross, that I might draw all men unto me, that as I have been lifted up by men even so should men be lifted up by the Father, to stand before me, to be judged of their works, whether they be good or whether they be evil—And for this cause have I been lifted up; therefore, according to the power of the Father I will draw all men unto me, that they may be judged according to their works. And it shall come to pass, that whoso repenteth and is baptized in my name shall be filled; and if he endureth to the end, behold, him will I hold guiltless before my Father at that day when I shall stand to judge the world (3 Nephi 27:14–16).

Christ informs us that if we are to be held blameless at the judgment bar, we must repent and be baptized, and endure in obeying Him to the end. He warns,

> And he that endureth not unto the end, the same is he that is also hewn down and cast into the fire, from whence they can no more return, because of the justice of the Father. And this is the word which he hath given unto the children of men. And for this cause he fulfilleth the words which he hath given, and he lieth not, but fulfilleth all his words. And no unclean thing can enter into his kingdom; therefore nothing entereth into his rest save it be those who have washed their garments in my blood, because of their faith, and the repentance of all their sins, and their faithfulness unto the end (verses 17–19).

As we have discussed, no unclean thing can enter the presence of the Lord, and living in the mortal world causes us to become covered in filth, so we must figuratively wash our garments to render ourselves clean. In what can we wash ourselves to become clean from the sins of the world? Christ's Atonement makes this possible, and the Atonement was wrought by His suffering and death. Therefore, He says that we must wash our garments in His holy, spilt blood—which is figurative, and means that we must turn to Him as the one who has paid our debt, and do the things that He instructs us to do, including repent of our sins, and persevere in daily attempts at righteousness until our last breath. Jesus finishes His warning, and invites us,

> Now this is the commandment: Repent, all ye ends of the earth, and come unto me and be baptized in my name, that ye may be sanctified by the reception of the Holy Ghost, that ye may stand spotless before me at the last day. Verily, verily, I say unto you, this is my gospel; and ye know the things that ye must do in my church; for the works which ye have seen me do that shall ye also do; for that which ye have seen me do even that shall ye do; Therefore, if ye do these things blessed are ye, for ye shall be lifted up at the last day (3 Nephi 27:20–22).

Doing the things that we see Christ do so that we might receive eternal life causes us to stop and ask, *What does Christ do that we can do*? His work and His glory—to bring to pass the immortality and eternal life of man. That is what we must be doing also, in our families, wards, neighborhoods and as far as our sphere of influence can reach. We must spend our days blessing the lives of all of those around us, setting a good example, and pointing all to Christ in everything we do.

Justice vs. Mercy in Our Lives

The Savior tells us plainly that we will be judged for our works, whether they were good or evil. He also tells us of the wonderful power of baptism and repentance—that if we receive the authorized priesthood baptism and repent of our sins, both of which are parts of the spiritual cleansing process He has ordained, and if we "endure" in this path of cleanliness, we will receive the Holy Spirit and be sanctified, and He will hold us guiltless before the Father at the day of judgment. This brings us full circle in our discussion about justice and mercy. The Lord steps in and pays the price for our debt to justice, and so doing He becomes our new debtor. He requires something different of us than justice demanded—He requires of us: 1) a humble attitude as evidenced by a broken heart and a contrite spirit, 2) that we repent of our sins that we may become clean, 3) that we help one another, and 4) that we receive the ordinances of salvation and exaltation. If we do these things and endure in this path throughout our lives, He will pronounce us clean before the Father. That which is clean enters the presence of the Father at the last day, and there dwells in eternal glory.

The Lord likewise warns that those who fail to obey His simple and easy requirements will not receive the benefit of His merciful intervention in our behalf, and will be subject to the original demands of justice, and will suffer as He suffered, as though there had been no atonement made, and will be unable to enter the presence of the Father due to their impurity. This is a dire warning. Its implications are ominous. The gospel message is so simple, so lucid, but there are those who have made it their life's work to muddle that which is plain and clear, to lead the souls of men and women eternally away from the presence of our Heavenly Father (1 Nephi 14:3;[99] D&C 10:22[100]). To the degree we repent of our wrongdoing and obey the commandments of the Lord, we will receive blessings in this world, and in the world to come. Not all will receive eternal life. Many will receive only partial glory—something short of the marvelous and glorious life that our Heavenly Father has prepared for us. To the degree we have cleansed ourselves from sin, we will be able to withstand a higher measure of glory. To the extent we were unable to rid ourselves of sin's stain, we will be limited in the amount of glory and light we can endure.

As we discussed earlier, thinking of impurity as a compound that interacts with certain kinds of light, the amount of impurity that rises with us in the resurrection will determine the amount of eternal light we are able to withstand. Some will be able to bear a full measure of the light of eternal glory, most will be able to bear less, many much less, and some will be able to bear none. The Lord outlines the degrees

99. "And that great pit, which hath been digged for them by that great and abominable church, which was founded by the devil and his children, that he might lead away the souls of men down to hell—yea, that great pit which hath been digged for the destruction of men shall be filled by those who digged it, unto their utter destruction, saith the Lamb of God; not the destruction of the soul, save it be the casting of it into that hell which hath no end."

100. "Satan stirreth them up, that he may lead their souls to destruction."

of glory that await His children in the eternities, and even spoke of the multiple planes of eternal inheritance during His earthly ministry, when He told His disciples, "In my Father's house are many mansions . . . I go to prepare a place for you" (John 14:2).

Let us here emphasize that receiving an eternal inheritance is not so much a matter of receiving a reward for a job well done, as it is receiving as much as we are capable of assuming in the eternities. Remember, God's plan for His children is not to put us through an obstacle course, at the end of which He hands out a punishment or a prize—but we are schooled and prepared, to receive a kingdom of glory, and we will receive as much glory as we are equipped to abide. After all, God's sole purpose is to bring to pass the immortality and eternal life of His children. He advances us to the highest level possible, to the extent that He can. God will not, cannot, reward a person with the power to create, if that person is not one hundred percent trustworthy, because inherent in the power to create is the power to destroy. God is God because He is one hundred percent perfect in all attributes, and one hundred percent predictable and trustworthy. To the degree one of us falls short of that level of perfection at the time we are crowned with eternal glory, we must receive a limited amount of power and ability in the eternities.

The Apostle Paul also described the multi-tiered nature of the "mansions" that await us, explaining that our resurrected bodies will be similarly distinguished, and that which is earthly will be raised to a heavenly nature—to one degree of glory or another.

> All flesh is not the same flesh: but there is one kind of flesh of men, another flesh of beasts, another of fishes, and another of birds. There are also celestial bodies, and bodies terrestrial: but the glory of the celestial is one, and the glory of the terrestrial is another. There is one glory of the sun, and another glory of the moon, and another glory of the stars: for one star differeth from another star in glory. So also is the resurrection of the dead. It is sown in corruption; it is raised in incorruption: It is sown in dishonour; it is raised in glory: it is sown in weakness; it is raised in power: It is sown a natural body; it is raised a spiritual body. There is a natural body, and there is a spiritual body (1 Corinthians 15:39–44).

What Paul teaches us in these passages is that as the flesh of bodies differs among the various creations of God, so will it differ among men in the resurrection. He describes three tiers of glory and resurrected bodies, from greatest to least they are compared with the glory of the sun, the moon and the stars. He names the first as the celestial, corresponding to the glory of the sun, and the second terrestrial, corresponding to the glory of the moon. He also explains that in the lowest kingdom of glory, there is a great deal of diversity between the mansions, where some are much brighter than others.

The Lord gave additional information to the Prophet Joseph Smith regarding the degrees of glory that await us in the eternities. He confirmed that there are three major divisions in the heavens, and that they bear the names of the celestial, the terrestrial, and the telestial. He also provided us with information about each of the three divisions or kingdoms of glory. Let us examine the three degrees of glory, beginning with the highest, the Celestial. It is here that each of us desires to reside in the eternities, and whenever the Lord has spoken about what He expects of us or what awaits us in the afterlife, He has always referred to this kingdom.

The Celestial Kingdom

As Joseph Smith administered the ordinances associated with temple attendance in the Kirtland Temple, a vision opened to him, and this is what he recorded regarding what he saw and heard.

> The heavens were opened upon us, and I beheld the celestial kingdom of God, and the glory thereof, whether in the body or out I cannot tell. I saw the transcendent beauty of the gate through which the heirs of that kingdom will enter, which was like unto circling flames of fire; Also the blazing throne of God, whereon was seated the Father and the Son. I saw the beautiful streets of that kingdom, which had the appearance of being paved with gold. I saw Father Adam and Abraham; and my father and my mother; my brother Alvin, that has long since slept; And marveled how it was that he had obtained an inheritance in that kingdom, seeing that he had departed this life before the Lord had set his hand to gather Israel the second time, and had not been baptized for the

> remission of sins. Thus came the voice of the Lord unto me, saying: All who have died without a knowledge of this gospel, who would have received it if they had been permitted to tarry, shall be heirs of the celestial kingdom of God; Also all that shall die henceforth without a knowledge of it, who would have received it with all their hearts, shall be heirs of that kingdom; For I, the Lord, will judge all men according to their works, according to the desire of their hearts. And I also beheld that all children who die before they arrive at the years of accountability are saved in the celestial kingdom of heaven (D&C 137).

This revelation is a treasured jewel to the Saints, and greatly increases our understanding of the nature of God's love and mercy for His children. When the Lord provides glimpses into the heavens, we are not sure of the imagery, but it appears that those things that have been shown in vision are merely representations and images to convey ideas and concepts to us. Although we shouldn't take literally the imagery of the visions, the principles taught are instructive. In this vision the principles are that the Celestial Kingdom is a wonderful place, and that the Father and the Son dwell there with those who inherit that kingdom. We also learn that the Lord judges the hearts of men, not the circumstances in which they lived. Therefore, all will receive that which they truly desired in life, based more on their predispositions toward good or evil, and the righteous desires of their hearts, regardless of the opportunities that came their way during their lives, short or long as they may have been.

On another occasion Joseph Smith was engaged in a translation of the New Testament when a vision of the Celestial Kingdom opened upon him and his associate, Sidney Rigdon, at Hiram, Ohio, on February 16, 1832. In it they beheld the imagery of worship and adoration of the Father and the Son by holy beings who dwell in the Celestial Kingdom.

> And we beheld the glory of the Son, on the right hand of the Father, and received of his fulness; And saw the holy angels, and them who are sanctified before his throne, worshiping God, and the Lamb, who worship him forever and ever. And now, after the many testimonies which have been given of him, this is the testimony, last of

> all, which we give of him: That he lives! For we saw him, even on the right hand of God; and we heard the voice bearing record that he is the Only Begotten of the Father—That by him, and through him, and of him, the worlds are and were created, and the inhabitants thereof are begotten sons and daughters unto God (D&C 76:20–24).

Again, the images provided are not literally what exists in the eternal worlds, but merely a representation of the principle that God and His Son are the Kings of heavenly realms, and that they are the progenitors of all human life throughout the universe. In the same vision Joseph is shown who it is that will inherit the Celestial Kingdom, and what it is that qualifies them for that high level of eternal glory. It's a little lengthy, but reading it in its entirety is very worthwhile, and essentially describes you—the you that you strive to be.

> And again we bear record—for we saw and heard, and this is the testimony of the gospel of Christ concerning them who shall come forth in the resurrection of the just—
>
> They are they who received the testimony of Jesus, and believed on his name and were baptized after the manner of his burial, being buried in the water in his name, and this according to the commandment which he has given—
>
> That by keeping the commandments they might be washed and cleansed from all their sins, and receive the Holy Spirit by the laying on of the hands of him who is ordained and sealed unto this power;
>
> And who overcome by faith, and are sealed by the Holy Spirit of promise, which the Father sheds forth upon all those who are just and true.
>
> They are they who are the church of the Firstborn.
>
> They are they into whose hands the Father has given all things—
>
> They are they who are priests and kings, who have received of his fulness, and of his glory;
>
> And are priests of the Most High, after the order of Melchizedek, which was after the order of Enoch, which was after the order of the Only Begotten Son.

> Wherefore, as it is written, they are gods, even the sons of God—
>
> Wherefore, all things are theirs, whether life or death, or things present, or things to come, all are theirs and they are Christ's, and Christ is God's.
>
> And they shall overcome all things.
>
> Wherefore, let no man glory in man, but rather let him glory in God, who shall subdue all enemies under his feet.
>
> These shall dwell in the presence of God and his Christ forever and ever.
>
> Father, reigns upon his throne forever and ever;
>
> These are they whom he shall bring with him, when he shall come in the clouds of heaven to reign on the earth over his people.
>
> These are they who shall have part in the first resurrection.
>
> These are they who shall come forth in the resurrection of the just.
>
> These are they who are come unto Mount Zion, and unto the city of the living God, the heavenly place, the holiest of all.
>
> These are they who have come to an innumerable company of angels, to the general assembly and church of Enoch, and of the Firstborn.
>
> These are they whose names are written in heaven, where God and Christ are the judge of all.
>
> These are they who are just men made perfect through Jesus the mediator of the new covenant, who wrought out this perfect atonement through the shedding of his own blood.
>
> These are they whose bodies are celestial, whose glory is that of the sun, even the glory of God, the highest of all, whose glory the sun of the firmament is written of as being typical (D&C 76:51–70).

We well understand at this point in our discussion that those who receive a celestial inheritance are those who obey the commandments and received the ordinances of the gospel, including baptism, the Gift of the Holy Ghost, ordination to the priesthood in the case of men, and temple sealing. We note in the scripture that those who inherit this glory are they "who overcome by faith." This is exactly what the Prophet spoke of when he said we must develop faith sufficient to lay hold on eternal life. This particular vision of the Celestial Kingdom closed with the Prophet offering a final description of what he witnessed in the vision.

> And thus we saw the glory of the celestial, which excels in all things—where God, even the Before whose throne all things bow in humble reverence, and give him glory forever and ever. They who dwell in his presence are the church of the Firstborn; and they see as they are seen, and know as they are known, having received of his fulness and of his grace; And he makes them equal in power, and in might, and in dominion. And the glory of the celestial is one, even as the glory of the sun is one (Ibid., 92–96).

We understand from this description of Joseph Smith's vision of the heavenly realms, that those who receive a celestial glory receive a fullness of the grace of God, and that they are equal in power and abilities and dominion, which is different than those who inherit the lowest or Telestial Kingdom. Those of the telestial order vary from person to person in glory. However, there are three subdivisions within the Celestial Kingdom. The Lord revealed through Joseph Smith the following about these divisions.

> In the celestial glory there are three heavens or degrees; And in order to obtain the highest, a man must enter into this order of the priesthood [meaning the new and everlasting covenant of marriage]; And if he does not, he cannot obtain it. He may enter into the other, but that is the end of his kingdom; he cannot have an increase (D&C 131:1–4).

We learn from this scripture that the highest tier of the Celestial Kingdom, essentially the level which enables us to become like God and enjoy eternal increase through the propagation of the human family, is reserved to those who are eternally sealed to a companion, and are thereby able to produce spiritual offspring. It is this ability to propagate the species of God and to create worlds on which to house them that separates those who inherit eternal life (a continuation of the lives or the seeds), from those who cannot, even those who otherwise receive a lesser celestial inheritance.

Although we have already examined this scripture, let us review it in light of the principle now before us.

> And again, verily I say unto you, if a man marry a wife by my word, which is my law, and by the new and everlasting covenant, and it is sealed unto them by the Holy Spirit of promise, by him who is anointed, unto whom I have appointed this power and the keys of this priesthood; and it shall be said unto them—Ye shall come forth in the first resurrection; and if it be after the first resurrection, in the next resurrection; and shall inherit thrones, kingdoms, principalities, and powers, dominions, all heights and depths—then shall it be written in the Lamb's Book of Life, that he shall commit no murder whereby to shed innocent blood, and if ye abide in my covenant, and commit no murder whereby to shed innocent blood, it shall be done unto them in all things whatsoever my servant hath put upon them, in time, and through all eternity; and shall be of full force when they are out of the world; and they shall pass by the angels, and the gods, which are set there, to their exaltation and glory in all things, as hath been sealed upon their heads, which glory shall be a fulness and a continuation of the seeds forever and ever (D&C 132:19).

This scripture is magnificent in its implications and scope. It proclaims that although we are not perfect in this life, and in many cases are somewhat far from that standard, if we attain to marriage in the new and everlasting covenant, meaning if we are sealed to a companion in the holy temple (which entails all of the steps leading to that crowning achievement), we will inherit the highest tier of the Celestial Kingdom and become like our Heavenly Parents, so long as we are not guilty of the unpardonable sin. Notwithstanding all of our weaknesses and all of the admonitions we still need from the Lord, according to this scripture if we go out of this life sealed to our companion without having shed innocent blood (which includes sinning against the Holy Ghost—Matthew 12:31;[101] Alma 39:6[102]),

---

101. "Wherefore I say unto you, All manner of sin and blasphemy shall be forgiven unto men: but the blasphemy against the Holy Ghost shall not be forgiven unto men."

102. "For behold, if ye deny the Holy Ghost when it once has had place in you, and ye know that ye deny it, behold, this is a sin which is unpardonable; yea, and whosoever murdereth against the light and knowledge of God, it is not easy for him to obtain forgiveness; yea, I say unto you, my son, that it is not easy for him to obtain a forgiveness."

we will eventually receive eternal life as enjoyed in the highest level of the Celestial Kingdom. This is not to say that we have arrived. There is yet, learning and work that remains to be done to properly avail ourselves of the Savior's Atonement. However, after the price has been paid, either by the Redeemer or by the unrepentant party, we are assured that the stripes will eventually be healed and the qualifying candidate will be received into celestial glory, there to enjoy all of the blessings pronounced upon them as they knelt at the altar with their companion and were sealed up to come forth in the morning of the first resurrection and inherit thrones, kingdoms, principalities, powers, dominions, glories, and a continuation of the seeds forever. This level of mercy is nearly impossible for mortals to fathom. It is made possible only through the merciful Atonement of the Savior and Redeemer, Jesus Christ.

The revelation then tells us something more about the destiny of those who inherit this glory, and why many fail to obtain it.

> Then shall they be gods, because they have no end; therefore shall they be from everlasting to everlasting, because they continue; then shall they be above all, because all things are subject unto them. Then shall they be gods, because they have all power, and the angels are subject unto them. Verily, verily, I say unto you, except ye abide my law ye cannot attain to this glory. For strait is the gate, and narrow the way that leadeth unto the exaltation and continuation of the lives, and few there be that find it, because ye receive me not in the world neither do ye know me. But if ye receive me in the world, then shall ye know me, and shall receive your exaltation; that where I am ye shall be also. This is eternal lives—to know the only wise and true God, and Jesus Christ, whom he hath sent. I am he. Receive ye, therefore, my law (D&C 132:20–24).

After describing the marvelous destiny of those who fulfill the plan of exaltation, the Lord here emphasizes His earlier declarations that unless we know Him intimately and do the simple things He asks us to do, we cannot attain to this glory. We hear His admonition to relinquish the institutions of men, and their flattering and false teachings and philosophies. We perceive that there are many doctrines floating throughout the world that are designed to keep us from fulfilling our eternal destiny if it were possible. It is the result of the problem described by Lehi as he witnessed the vision of the iron rod and the great and spacious building, wherein the path to eternal life was obscured by enticements and inducements to wander off course into paths that led away from eternal life and into destruction. (1 Nephi 8:9–34) There are counterfeits of those things that God has established, things that take us in the right direction, and improve us and make us more godly, but fail to get us all the way to eternal life. For instance, marriage itself is a God given institution, and in all circumstances of marriage, "the sacred powers of procreation are to be employed only between man and woman, lawfully wedded as husband and wife," even if not sealed in the New and Everlasting Covenant.[103] By entering into civil marriage a man or woman fulfills the plan of the Father to people the earth with His spirit children, and provide them with experience and opportunity for growth, even exaltation. Each partner in the marriage learns valuable lessons in service and sacrifice, and progresses toward godliness in attitude and character. If the marriage is not sealed by the Holy Spirit of Promise, however, it will have an end when one of the partners passes to the next realm. The Lord has thus revealed the fate of those who fail to seal their marriages in the temple.

> Therefore, if a man marry him a wife in the world, and he marry her not by me nor by my word, and he covenant with her so long as he is in the world and she with him, their covenant and marriage are not of force when they are dead, and when they are out of the world; therefore, they are not bound by any law when they are out of the world. Therefore, when they are out of the world they neither marry nor are given in marriage; but are appointed angels in heaven, which angels are ministering servants, to minister for those who are worthy of a far more, and an exceeding, and an eternal weight of glory. For these angels did not abide my law; therefore, they cannot be enlarged, but remain separately and singly, without exaltation, in their saved condition, to all eternity;

103. "The Family: A Proclamation to the World," *Ensign* or *Liahona*, Nov. 2010, 129.

> and from henceforth are not gods, but are angels of God forever and ever (D&C 132:15–17).

These righteous and upright people will eventually populate the kingdoms that are lower in glory than those that receive the heirs of exaltation and eternal life. Many may even inherit the second and third tiers of the Celestial Kingdom, and continue as angels, but they will not enjoy the blessings of eternal increase and becoming heavenly parents to countless children working their way through the phases of eternity. They have an end to their kingdom and a limitation to their glory in the eternities—something less than that hoped for them by the Father and the Savior.

Other counterfeits of those things that God has established are religions, churches, institutions, teachings and philosophies, all of which bring people closer to the truth and eternal life, but fail to provide a path leading all the way to the final destination. Many of these speak of God and the Savior, or supply substitutes to be adored or worshipped, and have an appearance of godliness, but as the Lord warned Joseph Smith, their hearts are far from God and eternal truth. (Joseph Smith—History 1:19[104]) These can lead men in the right direction, and eventually to the Church of Jesus Christ, but on their own they have no ability to lead us to exaltation. Many of these institutions and philosophies are encouraged, or even founded by the evil one, whose goal it is to prevent men from fulfilling their eternal destiny.

The Terrestrial Kingdom

Having discussed at length what it means to inherit Eternal Life, let us consider what awaits those who in some measure finish short of the glory that God provides His obedient children. In the same vision beheld by Joseph Smith and Sidney Rigdon, wherein they saw and heard things pertaining to the Celestial Kingdom, they also beheld

---

104. "I was answered that I must join none of them, for they were all wrong; and the Personage who addressed me said that all their creeds were an abomination in his sight; that those professors were all corrupt; that: 'they draw near to me with their lips, but their hearts are far from me, they teach for doctrines the commandments of men, having a form of godliness, but they deny the power thereof.'"

details pertaining to the lesser kingdoms and those who inherit them. The kingdom just below the celestial is the terrestrial, and it differs in glory from the celestial as the moon differs in glory from the sun.

> And again, we saw the terrestrial world, and behold and lo, these are they who are of the terrestrial, whose glory differs from that of the church of the Firstborn who have received the fulness of the Father, even as that of the moon differs from the sun in the firmament (D&C 76:71).

The Lord reveals to the Prophet in this revelation, what it is about these children of God that distinguishes them from those who were worthy of a far greater glory and inheritance.

> Behold, these are they who died without law; For he who is not able to abide the law of a celestial kingdom cannot abide a celestial glory. And also they who are the spirits of men kept in prison, whom the Son visited, and preached the gospel unto them, that they might be judged according to men in the flesh; Who received not the testimony of Jesus in the flesh, but afterwards received it. These are they who are honorable men of the earth, who were blinded by the craftiness of men. These are they who receive of his glory, but not of his fulness. These are they who receive of the presence of the Son, but not of the fulness of the Father. Wherefore, they are bodies terrestrial, and not bodies celestial, and differ in glory as the moon differs from the sun. These are they who are not valiant in the testimony of Jesus; wherefore, they obtain not the crown over the kingdom of our God (D&C 76:72–79).

We might well think of many good Christian, and otherwise religious or genuinely kindhearted people, who fit into this category—those who perform acts of kindness and may even profess belief in Christ, and do many things that seem religious, yet fail to do all that the Lord asks them to do. They obey many of the commandments, but not all, and they fail to embrace the gospel in its fulness, or receive the priesthood and the ordinances of salvation and exaltation. They approach the things of God with their lips, yet their hearts are far from Him. They reject the testimony of God's authorized servants, and in their zeal may even hand out pamphlets "exposing" the doctrines of the restored gospel.

The revelation further informs us that those in the Terrestrial Kingdom receive the occasional presence of the Son, although not of the Father, and that they are ministered to by those ministering angels of the Celestial Kingdom (D&C 76:77). The scripture gives us the reason that good people are consigned to a lesser glory than the celestial.

> And they who are not sanctified through the law which I have given unto you, even the law of Christ, must inherit another kingdom, even that of a terrestrial kingdom, or that of a telestial kingdom. And he who cannot abide the law of a terrestrial kingdom cannot abide a terrestrial glory (D&C 88:21).

We can see the Lord's justice and consistency as He requires us to obey the simple instructions He's given to us. Those who just can't quite manage obedience are not rewarded with the high blessings of eternal increase, or eternal life in the presence of the Father. This lack of blessing is not due to God's lack of love or compassion for His children, but is governed by eternal principles that dictate that we are assigned to the highest possible kingdom whose law we are able to abide. We might refer to our microwave oven example to understand the limiting factors that govern this eternal assignment principle. Those who inherit the Terrestrial Kingdom, however, are rewarded with an eternal existence that far exceeds the dreams of mankind. The Prophet explained that human language is simply unable to convey the wondrous beauty and extreme joy that exist in heavenly realms, even those of a terrestrial or telestial glory. He closes his description of the Terrestrial Kingdom thus: "And thus we saw the glory of the terrestrial which excels in all things the glory of the telestial, even in glory, and in power, and in might, and in dominion" (D&C 76:91).

The Telestial Kingdom

We do not aspire to receive a telestial inheritance. The gospel of Jesus Christ was proclaimed so that all mankind might be instructed in how to rise above telestial glory. However, salvation comes to all of

Heavenly Father's children, and they all receive an inheritance of glory in the eternal worlds, regardless of their level of obedience or good works. After Joseph and Sidney had seen the glorious realms of the celestial and terrestrial worlds, they then beheld what happens to all of those who lacked the goodness, kindness and integrity to earn such a wonderful reward. Joseph records:

> For all the rest shall be brought forth by the resurrection of the dead, through the triumph and the glory of the Lamb, who was slain, who was in the bosom of the Father before the worlds were made. And this is the gospel, the glad tidings, which the voice out of the heavens bore record unto us—That he came into the world, even Jesus, to be crucified for the world, and to bear the sins of the world, and to sanctify the world, and to cleanse it from all unrighteousness; That through him all might be saved whom the Father had put into his power and made by him; Who glorifies the Father, and saves all the works of his hands (D&C 76:39–43).

The works of His hands who are saved only through His grace, and not because of anything they did or accomplished during their lives, are those who will inherit the Telestial Kingdom. Of all those who do not receive a celestial or terrestrial inheritance, everyone else will receive a telestial inheritance. The only ones who live on earth at any point in its history who will not receive an inheritance in one of these three kingdoms of glory are the few who are designated Sons of Perdition, who denied the testimony of the Holy Ghost and shed innocent blood. Therefore, many will populate the Telestial Kingdom in the eternities.

> And again, we saw the glory of the telestial, which glory is that of the lesser, even as the glory of the stars differs from that of the glory of the moon in the firmament. These are they who received not the gospel of Christ, neither the testimony of Jesus. These are they who deny not the Holy Spirit. These are they who are thrust down to hell. These are they who shall not be redeemed from the devil until the last resurrection, until the Lord, even Christ the Lamb, shall have finished his work. These are they who receive not of his fulness in the eternal world, but of the Holy Spirit through the ministration of the terrestrial; And the terrestrial through the ministration

> of the celestial. And also the telestial receive it of the administering of angels who are appointed to minister for them, or who are appointed to be ministering spirits for them; for they shall be heirs of salvation. And thus we saw, in the heavenly vision, the glory of the telestial, which surpasses all understanding (D&C 76:81–89).

All of those whose unrepentant souls are stained with the sins of worldly living, will dwell in the telestial world. These are the liars, the thieves, the cheats, the abusers, the murderers, the thugs, the immoral, and those who fight against good and against the Kingdom of God. They persecute the Saints of God and glory in their foul deeds. They are enemies of mankind, and children of evil. They will not receive the ministrations of the Father or the Son, whom they rejected in mortality, but of angels whose lot it is to minister to those of lower kingdoms. Yet, these will live in a kingdom of great glory, which surpasses all understanding. Their sins will be purged in the exquisite burnings of what we refer to as hell, which is a figurative reference to a state or process of purification. We know nothing about it except that it is extremely unpleasant, as testified of by the Savior Himself (D&C 19:15–18[105]) and by Alma the younger (Alma 36:16[106]). When the punishment and purging or cleansing process is complete, each of these formerly unrepentant children of God will be resurrected and judged by the Savior, and will finally bow the knee to the Son of God and confess that Jesus is the Christ, their Savior and Redeemer, and the Son of the Living God, then they will be consigned to the Telestial Kingdom.

---

105. "Therefore I command you to repent—repent, lest I smite you by the rod of my mouth, and by my wrath, and by my anger, and your sufferings be sore—how sore you know not, how exquisite you know not, yea, how hard to bear you know not. For behold, I, God, have suffered these things for all, that they might not suffer if they would repent; But if they would not repent they must suffer even as I; Which suffering caused myself, even God, the greatest of all, to tremble because of pain, and to bleed at every pore, and to suffer both body and spirit—and would that I might not drink the bitter cup, and shrink."
106. "And now, for three days and for three nights was I racked, even with the pains of a damned soul."

> Yea, every knee shall bow, and every tongue confess before him. Yea, even at the last day, when all men shall stand to be judged of him, then shall they confess that he is God; then shall they confess, who live without God in the world, that the judgment of an everlasting punishment is just upon them; and they shall quake, and tremble, and shrink beneath the glance of his all-searching eye (Mosiah 27:31; see also Philippians 2:10; D&C 76:110; 88:104).

Joseph Smith speaks of the number of those who populate the Telestial Kingdom, "We saw the glory and the inhabitants of the telestial world, that they were as innumerable as the stars in the firmament of heaven, or as the sand upon the seashore" (D&C 76:109). We can well understand that most of humanity finds itself in the comfortable and familiar surroundings of the telestial world following the resurrection and judgment of humanity. They learned to live no better in mortality, because it was not intrinsic to their spirits to rise above the natural man. Nevertheless, they will live for eternity in what most of them actually dreamed would be heaven—and they will not be disappointed.

Exercising Faith Brings Salvation and Exaltation

For the Saints of the Most High, our only eternal goal is obtaining the highest level of the Celestial Kingdom. That is what all of the scriptures and revelations speak of when describing heaven. That is the only place the Lord has ever pointed us toward. We learn what the Lord has instructed us to do, and we do all things necessary to obtain the blessings reserved for those who obey His voice. We adopt an attitude of obedience and service, and learn to choose the right in every circumstance and situation. We receive the Priesthood After the Order of the Son of God, and we receive the ordinances of salvation and exaltation. We love our fellow men and sacrifice for the welfare of those around us. We fulfill the measure of our creation by marrying, and bringing children into our families, and we teach our children about the Lord and His plan of exaltation. We don't just speak of religious principles, and we don't merely sit in pews on Sunday and listen while a hired preacher fires up our souls with speeches about religion—we *act* on our faith by living by every word that proceeds forth from the mouth of God (Matthew 4:4; Moroni 7:25; D&C 84:44, 98:11).

We learn our "religion" from the Apostle James, who instructs: "Pure religion and undefiled before God and the Father is this, To visit the fatherless and widows in their affliction, and to keep himself unspotted from the world" (James 1:27). His admonition reminds us of the covenant that we make upon entering the waters of baptism.

> Yea, and are willing to mourn with those that mourn; yea, and comfort those that stand in need of comfort, and to stand as witnesses of God at all times and in all things, and in all places that ye may be in, even until death, that ye may be redeemed of God, and be numbered with those of the first resurrection, that ye may have eternal life (Mosiah 18:9).

And finally, the Lord Himself describes what our *religion* consists of, as we discussed above.

> Then shall the King say unto them on his right hand, Come, ye blessed of my Father, inherit the kingdom prepared for you from the foundation of the world: For I was an hungred, and ye gave me meat: I was thirsty, and ye gave me drink: I was a stranger, and ye took me in: Naked, and ye clothed me: I was sick, and ye visited me: I was in prison, and ye came unto me . . . And the King shall answer and say unto them, Verily I say unto you, Inasmuch as ye have done it unto one of the least of these my brethren, ye have done it unto me (Matthew 25:32–40; see also Mosiah 2:17).

There are many who stand in need of comfort and the necessities of life. There are many who find themselves in circumstances that try their souls—some because of their own decisions, and some because of the decisions of others. They are all precious children of the Father, and He loves them and seeks their comfort and joy in life. He allows us to grow spiritually by providing service to others, by supplying them with the comfort they seek and the joy they desire. He does not wish to compel us in every act of kindness (D&C 58:26–29[107])

---

107. "For behold, it is not meet that I should command in all things; for he that is compelled in all things, the same is a slothful and not a wise servant;

because we must desire to do good and voluntarily sacrifice something of our personal comforts and resources in order to qualify for the soul-ennobling blessings that flow from giving service to others. The Lord instructs: "Verily I say, men should be anxiously engaged in a good cause, and do many things of their own free will, and bring to pass much righteousness" (D&C 58:27).

Faith is action—the things that we do naturally in response to what we are certain is true. It is when we are lifting others toward the Celestial Kingdom, that we lift ourselves. As we lift together and share one another's burdens we begin to enjoy the synergy of Zion—that blessed state when we have added to our own efforts those of angels. We must have the spirit of the Lord with us in our collective work, and we must be united in our cause and look upon our brothers as ourselves. "I say unto you, be one; and if ye are not one ye are not mine" (D&C 38:27). "And the Lord called his people Zion, because they were of one heart and one mind, and dwelt in righteousness; and there was no poor among them" (Moses 7:18).

President Nelson has shared his own formula for overcoming the pull of the world and soaring in the heights with the Church of the Firstborn. He says,

> Overcoming the world is not an event that happens in a day or two. It happens over a lifetime as we repeatedly embrace the doctrine of Christ. We cultivate faith in Jesus Christ by repenting daily and keeping covenants that endow us with power. We stay on the covenant path and are blessed with spiritual strength, personal revelation, increasing faith, and the ministering of angels. Living the doctrine of Christ can produce the most powerful virtuous cycle, creating spiritual momentum in our lives. As we strive to live the higher laws of Jesus Christ, our hearts and our very natures begin to change. The Savior *lifts* us above the pull of this fallen world by

---

wherefore he receiveth no reward. Verily I say, men should be anxiously engaged in a good cause, and do many things of their own free will, and bring to pass much righteousness; For the power is in them, wherein they are agents unto themselves. And inasmuch as men do good they shall in nowise lose their reward. But he that doeth not anything until he is commanded, and receiveth a commandment with doubtful heart, and keepeth it with slothfulness, the same is damned."

blessing us with greater charity, humility, generosity, kindness, self-discipline, peace, and *rest.*[108]

Conversely, as the spirit of anti-Christ spreads its dark tentacles upon the land and fills the halls of government and other institutions in these last days preceding the Second Coming of the Lord, Jesus Christ, may we so live to ensure that the Savior is our exemplar and our leader. May we learn to bring to pass the immortality and eternal life of man and make that activity our central desire and pursuit. May we establish Zion among us and ensure that there are no poor in our midst, especially any poor of heart or spirit. Let there be no child's cry that goes unanswered, or tear of loneliness or worry that goes unwiped by a comforting and caring hand. Let us be like the Holy One and visit the sick, the outcast, the lonely, the imprisoned and the afflicted daily, in His holy name. Our faith that the Lord is at the head of His kingdom and that we are following in the path He has created with His own footsteps is what will bring us close to Him in this world, and into His holy presence in the world to come. We gain that faith by doing the things He asks us to do, which are the very things He has done Himself. We come to know Him by doing the things He does. The better we know Him, the closer we come to gaining eternal life until we finally arrive at the perfect day, when we will see as we are seen, and know as we are known (D&C 76:94–95[109]).

---

108. "Overcome the World and Find Rest," October 2022 general conference, Sunday morning session.

109. "They who dwell in his presence are the church of the Firstborn; and they see as they are seen, and know as they are known, having received of his fulness and of his grace; And he makes them equal in power, and in might, and in dominion."

6

The Power of Faith

Among the many blessings of the Restored Gospel is the coming forth of the Book of Mormon, received by Joseph Smith, and translated by the power of God—through the exertion of faith. Within the pages of the book is the history of the Jaredites, so named after their leader, Jared. Jared and his brother were warned by the Lord during the construction of the Tower of Babel that they must take their families and flee "at the time the Lord confounded the language of the people" (Ether 1:33). The brother of Jared was the one who cried to the Lord for relief from the impending calamities, and the Lord gave him instructions that their families, and the families of their friends should hide themselves in a remote wilderness, awaiting the time when the Lord would lead them to a "land of promise, which was choice above all other lands, which the Lord God had preserved for a righteous people" (Ether 2:7). The brother of Jared waited for four years, not thinking to ask the Lord for further instructions. The Lord finally appeared to him, and chastised him "for the space of three hours" (verse 14). The Lord then instructed the brother of Jared how they should build special ships for the journey, and they went to work to fulfil the Lord's will in the matter. When the eight "barges" were completed, and the Lord had explained how to make them watertight while providing a supply of air for the people and creatures inside, the brother of Jared asked the Lord how they would be able to see during their long journey, because the ships had no portals. In anticipation, he "did molten out of a rock sixteen small stones; and they were white and clear, even as transparent glass; and he did carry them in his hands upon the top of the mount, and cried again unto the Lord," (Ether 3:1) asking,

> And I know, O Lord, that thou hast all power, and can do whatsoever thou wilt for the benefit of man; therefore touch these stones, O Lord, with thy finger, and prepare them that they may shine forth in darkness; and they shall shine forth unto us in the vessels which we have prepared, that we may have light while we shall cross the sea (verse 4).

In response to what the brother of Jared asked of Him,

> The Lord stretched forth his hand and touched the stones one by one with his finger. And the veil was taken from off the eyes of the brother of Jared, and he saw the finger of the Lord; and it was as the finger of a man, like unto flesh and blood; and the brother of Jared fell down before the Lord, for he was struck with fear (Ether 3:6).

From this we know that the brother of Jared had faith sufficient to ask the Lord, doubting nothing, to touch the stones he had prepared (action), to give them light. We don't know everything about the background of this man, but we know that he acted as spokesman for the tribe, and that he received direct revelations from the Lord in response to his inquiries. The Lord, in fact, touched the stones with his finger, and they lit up—just as the brother of Jared had asked. The ensuing discussion between him and the Lord is instructive to us all.

> And the Lord saw that the brother of Jared had fallen to the earth; and the Lord said unto him: Arise, why hast thou fallen? And he saith unto the Lord: I saw the finger of the Lord, and I feared lest he should smite me; for I knew not that the Lord had flesh and blood. And the Lord said unto him: Because of thy faith thou hast seen that I shall take upon me flesh and blood; and never has man come before me with such exceeding faith as thou hast; for were it not so ye could not have seen my finger. Sawest thou more than this (verses 7–9)?

It is more than interesting that Adam and Enoch both walked with God, and knew Him quite well—as did the patriarchs between them. Adam launched the entire human family, acting as the Patriarch and Prophet, and under his direction young Enoch led the people of God, traveled between Earth and heaven, and performed countless miracles for the sake of his people. Yet, the Lord here declares that "never has man come before me with such exceeding faith as thou hast." Moroni completes the account, and explains to his readers that the brother of Jared went from exceeding faith to knowledge in his level of certainty,

> And because of the knowledge of this man he could not be kept from beholding within the veil; and he saw the finger of Jesus, which, when he saw, he fell with fear; for he knew that it was the finger of the Lord; and he had faith no longer, for he knew, nothing doubting. Wherefore, having this perfect knowledge of God, he could not be kept from within the veil; therefore he saw Jesus; and he did minister unto him (verses 19–20).

As the prophet Moroni later recounts the wonders and marvels accomplished by faith, he first shares the relationship of belief, hope and faith, expounding some of the very principles that we have discussed.

> Wherefore, whoso believeth in God might with surety hope for a better world, yea, even a place at the right hand of God, which hope cometh of faith, maketh an anchor to the souls of men, which would make them sure and steadfast, always abounding in good works, being led to glorify God. And it came to pass that Ether did prophesy great and marvelous things unto the people, which they did not believe, because they saw them not. And now, I, Moroni, would speak somewhat concerning these things; I would show unto the world that *faith is things which are hoped for and not seen; wherefore, dispute not because ye see not, for ye receive no witness until after the trial of your faith* (Ether 12:4–6, emphasis added).

Following his explanation of the nature of faith, Moroni shares with his readers many examples where people acted on their faith, resulting in blessings and miracles by the finger of God. He first instructs us that those who saw Christ, did so through their faith.

> For it was by faith that Christ showed himself unto our fathers, after he had risen from the dead; and he showed not himself unto them until after they had faith in him; wherefore, it must needs be that some had faith in him, for he showed himself not unto the world. But because of the faith of men he has shown himself unto the world, and glorified the name of the Father, and prepared a way that thereby others might be partakers of the heavenly gift, that they might hope for those things which they have not seen. Wherefore, ye may also have hope, and be partakers of the gift, if ye will but have faith (verses 7–9).

We note that the prophet here builds a formula for his readers, first showing how others exercised faith and eventually beheld Christ, and hinting that the same will happen to them if they too exercise faith. He continues,

> Behold it was by faith that they of old were called after the holy order of God. Wherefore, by faith was the law of Moses given. But in the gift of his Son hath God prepared a more excellent way; and it is by faith that it hath been fulfilled. For if there be no faith among the children of men God can do no miracle among them; wherefore, he showed not himself until after their faith. Behold, it was the faith of Alma and Amulek that caused the prison to tumble to the earth. Behold, it was the faith of Nephi and Lehi that wrought the change upon the Lamanites, that they were baptized with fire and with the Holy Ghost. Behold, it was the faith of Ammon and his brethren which wrought so great a miracle among the Lamanites. Yea, and even all they who wrought miracles wrought them by faith, even those who were before Christ and also those who were after. And it was by faith that the three disciples obtained a promise that they should not taste of death; and they obtained not the promise until after their faith. And neither at any time hath any wrought miracles until after their faith; wherefore they first believed in the Son of God. And there were many whose faith was so exceedingly strong, even before Christ came, who could not be kept from within the veil, but truly saw with their eyes the things which they had beheld with an eye of faith, and they were glad. And behold, we have seen in this record that one of these was the brother of Jared; for so great was his faith in God, that when God put forth his finger he could

> not hide it from the sight of the brother of Jared, because of his word which he had spoken unto him, which word he had obtained by faith. And after the brother of Jared had beheld the finger of the Lord, because of the promise which the brother of Jared had obtained by faith, the Lord could not withhold anything from his sight; wherefore he showed him all things, for he could no longer be kept without the veil. And it is by faith that my fathers have obtained the promise that these things should come unto their brethren through the Gentiles; therefore the Lord hath commanded me, yea, even Jesus Christ (verses 10–22).

We have discovered a number of promises extended to us by the Lord, assuring us that He will bless us and sustain us as we exercise our faith in Him. He has multiplied His appeals to us that if we will ask anything that is expedient of Him in faith, He will give it to us. He has declared, "Prove me now, herewith" (Malachi 3:10[110]), that if we will obey certain commandments, He will respond with certain correlated blessings, and He promises to pour out such great blessings that we do not possess adequate space to receive and store them all. Concerning His promised blessings, He proclaims, "I, the Lord, am bound when ye do what I say" (D&C 82:10), clearly promising that if we will but perform our part, He will perform His. We recall His impassioned plea for His chosen yet faithless people to do the simple things He asks of them so He can bless them. ". . . how often would I have gathered thy children together, even as a hen gathereth her chickens under her wings, and ye would not" (Matthew 23:37)! Yes, the Lord stands ready, desirous, and eager to bless us and to grant us the blessings that we seek at His caring hand. Let us not be faithless in seeking the promised blessings of the Lord.

The prophet Moroni shared with us a few of the teachings of his father, Mormon, in which he expounded the principles of good and evil, and demonstrated how faith helps us to overcome the world, and secure eternal life.

---

110. "Bring ye all the tithes into the storehouse, that there may be meat in mine house, and prove me now herewith, saith the Lord of hosts, if I will not open you the windows of heaven, and pour you out a blessing, that there shall not be room enough to receive it."

> And now I come to that faith, of which I said I would speak; and I will tell you the way whereby ye may lay hold on every good thing. For behold, God knowing all things, being from everlasting to everlasting, behold, he sent angels to minister unto the children of men, to make manifest concerning the coming of Christ; and in Christ there should come every good thing (Moroni 7:21–22).

Mormon tells us that angels were sent forth to proclaim the message from God to men on the earth, resulting in the establishment of the truth among them. They predicted the advent of Christ, and men began to exercise faith in God, and enjoyed His marvelous blessings as a result. The Prophet Mormon continues,

"Wherefore, by the ministering of angels," the prophet Mormon begins,

> By every word which proceeded forth out of the mouth of God, men began to exercise faith in Christ; and thus by faith, they did lay hold upon every good thing; and thus it was until the coming of Christ. And after that he came men also were saved by faith in his name; and by faith, they become the sons of God. And as surely as Christ liveth he spake these words unto our fathers, saying: Whatsoever thing ye shall ask the Father in my name, which is good, in faith believing that ye shall receive, behold, it shall be done unto you (ibid., 25–26).

This specific promise was extended to the people, by Jesus Christ at the time of His appearance to them in the Americas, and repeated by His prophets thereafter, that whatever they asked God in faith, which was good, would be granted by the Lord. Blessings flowed among them for generations as a result of their asking the Lord in faith. Mormon asked them why they supposed miracles had ceased among them in their day.

> Wherefore, my beloved brethren, have miracles ceased because Christ hath ascended into heaven, and hath sat down on the right hand of God, to claim of the Father his rights of mercy which he hath upon the children of men? For he hath answered the ends of the law, and he claimeth all those who have faith in him; and they who have faith in him will cleave unto every good thing; wherefore

> he advocateth the cause of the children of men; and he dwelleth eternally in the heavens. And because he hath done this, my beloved brethren, have miracles ceased? Behold I say unto you, Nay; neither have angels ceased to minister unto the children of men (Moroni 27–29; see also Mormon 9:15–19).

Mormon's declaration to his people was that miracles had not ceased, and angels had not failed to minister among them. Mormon reminds the Church in his own writings that God is a God of miracles, and that because He is an unchangeable God, He must continue to perform miracles among the children of men. He then tells them the reason they see so few miracles among them—and we are wise to listen to his wisdom and logic, and apply them equally in our day.

> And now, O all ye that have imagined up unto yourselves a god who can do no miracles, I would ask of you, have all these things passed, of which I have spoken? Has the end come yet? Behold I say unto you, Nay; and God has not ceased to be a God of miracles.
>
> And who shall say that Jesus Christ did not do many mighty miracles? And there were many mighty miracles wrought by the hands of the apostles.
>
> And if there were miracles wrought then, why has God ceased to be a God of miracles and yet be an unchangeable Being? And behold, I say unto you he changeth not; if so he would cease to be God; and he ceaseth not to be God, and is a God of miracles.
>
> And the reason why he ceaseth to do miracles among the children of men is because that they dwindle in unbelief, and depart from the right way, and know not the God in whom they should trust.
>
> Behold, I say unto you that whoso believeth in Christ, doubting nothing, whatsoever he shall ask the Father in the name of Christ it shall be granted him; and this promise is unto all, even unto the ends of the earth (Mormon 9:15, 18–21).

The answer was simple and clear—the only reason we don't see more miracles among us is our own disbelief, or lack of faith. We might initially recoil at the thought that we lack faith, but on further reflection, perhaps we are more like the father of the young man possessed by an evil spirit who tearfully exclaimed, "Lord, I believe," then realizing his faith was lacking in practical application, cried out to the Master, "help thou mine unbelief" (Mark 9:21–24).

In Matthew 14, we read about a trial of faith of a close follower of the Master. Peter, an Apostle of the Lord, was on a boat in the middle of the sea with the other Apostles,

> And in the fourth watch of the night Jesus went unto them, walking on the sea. And when the disciples saw him walking on the sea, they were troubled, saying, It is a spirit; and they cried out for fear. But straightway Jesus spake unto them, saying, Be of good cheer; it is I; be not afraid (verses 25–27).

Peter, seeing that the Lord was able to walk on top of the water, suddenly realized that as an Apostle of Christ, he too could do the same thing—something Jesus had told them often. "Lord, if it be thou, bid me come unto thee on the water" (verse 28). Jesus was pleased, and told him, "Come. And when Peter was come down out of the ship, he walked on the water, to go to Jesus" (verse 29). The scripture then informs us, "But when he saw the wind boisterous, he was afraid; and beginning to sink, he cried, saying, Lord, save me" (verse 30). This is a very interesting point of how faith works—and how it fails to work. It is clear that Peter was walking on the water, just as Christ was doing. The promise was valid—Ask, and ye shall receive. Peter asked, and Christ granted his request, and Peter miraculously walked on the water. Yet, even though he was in the middle of doing the same miraculous act he was witnessing the Lord do in that very moment, the howling winds distracted him and reminded him of the dangers around him. His own mind began to create doubt within him, and his faith waned to the point of failing him. In that moment he began to sink, and exclaimed, "Lord, save me." It has always struck me as so odd, yet so predictably human, that Peter faltered even as he was succeeding. We note that his faith did not suddenly disappear, and he did not simply drop into the sea, sinking beneath the surface of the water as we would expect if we were to suddenly step off of a boat into the water. No, he began to sink, as he walked toward the Lord; still succeeding partially, even as his faith fled from him. The scripture tells us, "And immediately Jesus stretched forth his hand,

and caught him, and said unto him, O thou of little faith, wherefore didst thou doubt?"

Jesus's response to Peter's failing is extremely simple, and instructive. Jesus seems almost baffled that someone in Peter's position could snatch failure from the jaws of victory with such certain precision. In my own life, I acknowledge Peter's bold request of the Lord, and his initial success.

I have never walked on water, and can barely contemplate the state of mind required to accomplish the act. However, I would like to think that if the Lord were walking on the water, and called to me to do the same, I would do it. As I contemplate the scene, however, the familiar term "make the attempt" comes to mind, acknowledging the probability of failure in the "attempt." No—we do, or do not . . . there is no try, to quote that fuzzy little Jedi. In fact, the fictional high priest of Star Wars fame states the law of exercising faith perfectly—we do it. President Spencer Kimball was famous for his decree, "Do it." There is no try. There is no maybe. Faith is yes. Faith is do. Faith is accomplish. We simply do what the Lord tells us to do. "I can do all things through Christ which strengtheneth me." Philippians 4:13. No barrier prevents us from doing it. We push through, overcoming all obstacles, even the laws of physics if necessary. Christ is the Creator of all matter, and through His power and authority, we, His servants, are granted an extension of His power and authority to perform all acts, without deference to the normal workings of those laws. The atoms obey His will, as we speak it with His holy authority. "I can do all things through Christ," no matter how difficult, or out of the ordinary they might be, because Christ strengthens me that I might accomplish it. In the same way that the wind and water obey Him, they obey me, through His authority. That must be the mindset of the disciple of Christ, who exercises faith in power.

Moroni provided further wisdom from his father as he affirmed the Savior's promise that if we exercise faith in Him He will give us power above that of the world—power that comes from God. The prequalifying condition to receiving this power is to repent, be baptized, and have faith, and Mormon reminds us of the promise of the Savior.

> And Christ hath said: If ye will have faith in me ye shall have power to do whatsoever thing is expedient in me. And he hath said: Repent all ye ends of the earth, and come unto me, and be baptized in my name, and have faith in me, that ye may be saved. And now, my beloved brethren, if this be the case that these things are true which I have spoken unto you, and God will show unto you, with power and great glory at the last day, that they are true, and if they are true has the day of miracles ceased? Or have angels ceased to appear unto the children of men? Or has he withheld the power of the Holy Ghost from them? Or will he, so long as time shall last, or the earth shall stand, or there shall be one man upon the face thereof to be saved (Moroni 7:33–36)?

Mormon promises that God will show us in the last day that all these things are true, repeating the rhetorical questions, have miracles ceased, have angels ceased appearing to mankind, or has God withheld the power of the Holy Ghost from Church members? He replies:

> Behold I say unto you, Nay; for it is by faith that miracles are wrought; and it is by faith that angels appear and minister unto men; wherefore, if these things have ceased wo be unto the children of men, for it is because of unbelief, and all is vain. For no man can be saved, according to the words of Christ, save they shall have faith in his name; wherefore, if these things have ceased, then has faith ceased also; and awful is the state of man, for they are as though there had been no redemption made. But behold, my beloved brethren, I judge better things of you, for I judge that ye have faith in Christ because of your meekness; for if ye have not faith in him then ye are not fit to be numbered among the people of his church (Moroni 7:37–39).

Mormon speaks directly to us in the present day, as much as to the members of the Church in his day. He assures us that miracles have not ceased and that angels have not stopped intervening in the lives of Church members, or appearing to them—that it is by our faith that these miracles and wonders exist in our lives. He assures us that if we are fit to be numbered as members of Christ's Church, then we have faith sufficient to call upon Him and to receive from Him miracles, and the intervention and visitation of angels in our lives.

We can exercise priesthood power, and the power of the Holy Spirit, exactly as it has been done among us since the first man called upon God for blessing and assistance. We can learn to exercise "the finger of God," as did Christ in His life (Luke 11:20;[111] Hebrews 5:8). Mormon reminds his people what the Lord has said they can expect to accomplish through the intervention of heaven if they will let go of their faithlessness, and seek to serve the Lord in sincerity and humility.

> And these signs shall follow them that believe—in my name shall they cast out devils; they shall speak with new tongues; they shall take up serpents; and if they drink any deadly thing it shall not hurt them; they shall lay hands on the sick and they shall recover; And whosoever shall believe in my name, doubting nothing, unto him will I confirm all my words, even unto the ends of the earth. And now . . . hearken unto the words of the Lord, and ask the Father in the name of Jesus for what things soever ye shall stand in need. Doubt not, but be believing . . . strip yourselves of all uncleanness; ask not, that ye may consume it on your lusts, but ask with a firmness unshaken, that ye will yield to no temptation, but that ye will serve the true and living God (Mormon 9:24–28).

Mormon speaks these words directly to us, as though we were seated before him. It was the Lord Himself who performed all of these works in the sight of hundreds of thousands of witnesses. He healed every sort of illness and deformity, even raising the dead from their beds. He cast out wicked spirits, turned water to wine, walked on water, withered the unproductive tree and calmed the turbulent gale. His apostles, seventies, and disciples likewise performed these miracles in their own ministries, in both hemispheres. Jesus promised that all of His followers would be able to perform these same miracles and more, when He said, "Verily, verily, I say unto you, He that believeth on me, the works that I do shall he do also; and greater works than these shall he do; because I go unto my Father" (John 14:12).

---

111. "But if I with the finger of God cast out devils, no doubt the kingdom of God is come upon you."

What Can We Accomplish through Faith?

We come to a critical juncture in our discussion. We know what Christ has promised, and that He is not a liar. We know that He has restored the high priesthood which is After the Order of the Son of God, among us, and has endowed us with power from on high. He tells us that we can do all of the miracles that He performed, and greater, including gaining salvation and exaltation, if we believe on Him. We do believe on Him. We have reviewed herein the numerous occasions that Christ has invited us to ask God, in His holy name, for all things that are expedient, and as long as we ask in faith, He promises that He will so bless us. He says, "Ask, and it shall be given you; seek, and ye shall find; knock, and it shall be opened unto you" (Luke 11:9; 3 Nephi 14:7). He does not equivocate in His instruction. He merely tells us to ask in faith, and we *will* receive that which we ask.

The question that looms brightly, blindingly before us, is *Do we believe the promises of the Lord*? The Apostle Peter said of us, "But ye are a chosen generation, a royal priesthood, an holy nation, a peculiar people; that ye should shew forth the praises of him who hath called you out of darkness into his marvelous light" (1 Peter 2:9). This is an important declaration from he who looked upon the lame man who had never walked a step in his life and said, "Silver and gold have I none; but such as I have give I thee: In the name of Jesus Christ of Nazareth rise up and walk," and the man arose and walked. Peter was initially doubtful of His ability to serve the Lord, and wavered when Jesus beckoned to him to walk on the surface of the sea, and was put to the test of loyalty to the Master when it seemed from his perspective that all was crashing down around him. His periodic unbelief remained with him until Christ's death, and resurrection. Then when he was finally "converted," as Christ put it, Peter exercised faith, and was able to accomplish all the things he had seen the Master do.

We must vanquish our unbelief. It is unbelief that holds men and women back from doing what the Lord has asked them to do, including asking, that they might receive. It is unbelief that prevents the Lord from sending His miracles among us. We recall that He was unable to perform miracles among the unbelieving people of His own land, due to their lack of faith in Him (Mark 6:5–6[112]). Mormon clarified that it was the same with his own people, that miracles could not be poured out among them in their state of disbelief.

> For it is by faith that miracles are wrought; and it is by faith that angels appear and minister unto men; wherefore, if these things have ceased wo be unto the children of men, for it is because of unbelief, and all is vain (Moroni 7:37).

It is only as we accept the truth of the Lord's promises to us, and exercise our faith in Him that He will answer our prayers and send His miracles and angels among us. When we learn to exercise that level of faith, our lives will be filled with these rich blessings from heaven.

The Savior blessed the lives of many of those among whom He walked during His earthly ministry, and there is a specific case in which we see how He exercised His own faith in their behalf, and to provide the world a witness of His divine calling.

> Now a certain man was sick, named Lazarus, of Bethany, the town of Mary and her sister Martha. (It was that Mary which anointed the Lord with ointment, and wiped his feet with her hair, whose brother Lazarus was sick.) Therefore his sisters sent unto him, saying, Lord, behold, he whom thou lovest is sick. When Jesus heard that, he said, This sickness is not unto death, but for the glory of God, that the Son of God might be glorified thereby (John 11:1–4).

It is interesting that the Lord said that the sickness was not unto death, but was sent of God to provide an opportunity to glorify God. In fact, the scripture relates that Jesus delayed going to visit and administer to his dear friend, and Lazarus died. "Then when Jesus came, he found that he had lain in the grave four days already" (verse 17). Under Jewish law, there was no disputing that a person was dead after three days had passed. This was important, because Jesus needed there to be no disputations from the Jewish leaders that Lazarus was dead. By Moses's own decree, Lazarus was dead.

---

112. "And he could there do no mighty work, save that he laid his hands upon a few sick folk, and healed them. And he marvelled because of their unbelief. And he went round about the villages, teaching."

Jesus arrived in Bethany, and the sisters of Lazarus heard He was there, and Martha went to Him. "Then said Martha unto Jesus, Lord, if thou hadst been here, my brother had not died. But I know, that even now, whatsoever thou wilt ask of God, God will give it thee" (verses 21–22). This was a wonderful declaration of Martha's faith in God, and in His willingness to grant whatever Jesus would ask of Him.

"Jesus saith unto her, Thy brother shall rise again" (verse 23). Martha responded in a way that relieved Jesus of the burden of acting against the will of God. "I know that he shall rise again in the resurrection at the last day." Yes, Lazarus would rise one day, in the resurrection of the just. But, as Martha hoped, Jesus would not cause Lazarus and his loved ones to wait for that glorious day.

> Jesus said unto her, I am the resurrection, and the life: he that believeth in me, though he were dead, yet shall he live: And whosoever liveth and believeth in me shall never die. Believest thou this (verses 25–26)?

This was exactly what Martha had prayed He would say to her. She happily replied, "Yea, Lord: I believe that thou art the Christ, the Son of God, which should come into the world" (verse 27). Martha had now declared her faith in Jesus as the One sent by the Father to save the world. She knew that He was empowered to give life, now, and in the resurrection. She knew that Jesus would raise her brother from death, even after he had been dead these four days. Jesus called for the people with Martha to go fetch her sister, Mary, and they did. And as Mary and her relatives and friends came, they were weeping, and Jesus likewise wept with them. He instructed them to take the stone away from the mouth of the cave where Lazarus's body was entombed, and He groaned,

> And Jesus lifted up his eyes, and said, Father, I thank thee that thou hast heard me. And I knew that thou hearest me always: but because of the people which stand by I said it, that they may believe that thou hast sent me. And when he thus had spoken, he cried with a loud voice, Lazarus, come forth (verses 41–43).

Lazarus came forth from his tomb, still wrapped in the burial cloths, and the glory of God was manifested among the people, who spread word of the mighty miracle to all in the area, including the Pharisees, who were perplexed by His extraordinary ability.

The scriptures are filled with occurrences of God's intervention in the affairs of His children on Earth. Their pages reveal His love for His children, and the many times He has come to their aid, protected them, sent angels to minister to their needs, provided for them, and sent His prophets among them to guide them toward a better life, today and tomorrow. If we learn anything from our study of God's historical dealings with mankind, it is that the more we follow His instructions, or commandments given to us, the better our lives are. We find protection from evil, enemies, poverty, disease and burdensome governments as we collectively exercise our faith in Him and in His promises to us. We find increase in our productivity and the preservation of our assets and freedoms as we obey His instructions and do all of the things He asks us to do.

Our Heavenly Father has historically endowed faithful servants with tremendous power to bless their lives and the lives of their loved ones. The only requirement is that they obey Him, which includes observing His commandments and exercising their faith, by asking for His blessings. We read of great examples of this in all of the scriptures, beginning with Adam and His children. The prophet Enoch exercised vast power, including the ability to move mountains and rivers with a word, all because he obtained the Holy Spirit, and asked according to the Spirit (Moses 6:34). Moses performed mighty miracles in the sight of Pharaoh and all of Israel. The Brother of Jared performed many mighty miracles as did the followers of Christ on both continents. Many will read these numerous accounts and offer the excuse that these men were called of God and ordained to serve Him, resulting in their extraordinary abilities. What these fail to understand is that all who have made a covenant with God in the waters of baptism have been called of Him. All who have received the priesthood of God have been specifically called of Him. All who have received the ordinances of exaltation in the holy temples, have been ordained to receive all that He has. There is nothing that makes any one of us different from those who enjoyed great outpourings of His Spirit, and blessings at any time in the earth's history. The only thing we need is a little faith.

Spiritual Gifts

Jesus explained to His followers that faith is graded by purity, not quantity. Although we are all able to exercise faith sufficient to lay hold on salvation and exaltation in the world to come, which is the ultimate application of faith, we wonder if we are able to call upon the powers of heaven to bless our lives, and those of others, in this world. We have discussed the occasion when Christ was approached by His Apostles, who in His absence had been unable to cast a wicked spirit from a young man. They asked Him about their inability, and He merely replied,

> Because of your unbelief: for verily I say unto you, If ye have faith as a grain of mustard seed, ye shall say unto this mountain, Remove hence to yonder place; and it shall remove; and nothing shall be impossible unto you (Matthew 17:20).

He used the grain of mustard seed comparison on another occasion when He taught them, "If ye had faith as a grain of mustard seed, ye might say unto this sycamine tree, Be thou plucked up by the root, and be thou planted in the sea; and it should obey you" (Luke 17:6). We hear many sophisticated explanations by learned scholars for the grain of mustard seed teaching of the Lord, and they are all compelling. For our purposes nothing more is necessary to understand the principle than the truth that the Lord conveyed to His followers, that by exercising the smallest quantity of faith, as long as it contains no doubt, we can perform any miracle, and accomplish anything we wish, so long as our lives are in conformity with the will of God, and we ask His help. Whenever any disciple of the Lord asked why there was difficulty in performing a miracle, the response was always the same—lack of faith. It is the only time that miracles fail, and the Lord says it many times in the scriptures.

Faith is a gift from God. It is one of many spiritual gifts that our Father provides to His children on earth—which means that some have it more naturally, and more abundantly, than others. Nevertheless, even those who do not enjoy it as a natural gift may develop it through effort and exertion. Furthermore, we should understand that those members of God's Kingdom who are not endowed with special power from on high, in the form of the holy priesthood, or other specific covenants and endowments, may nevertheless develop power to exercise the Finger of God, through the power of the Holy Ghost, the Light of Christ, or the priesthood authority to which they are sealed. Even single sisters in the Church, with no specific link to one who is ordained to the priesthood, may exercise faith and power through the priesthood authority to which they are appurtenant, through their bishop and other priesthood leaders.

Women have authority to perform their callings, under the direction of one who holds priesthood keys, just as men do. President M. Russell Ballard, Acting President of the Quorum of the Twelve Apostles, stated, "Those who have priesthood keys . . . literally make it possible for all who serve faithfully under their direction to exercise priesthood authority and have access to priesthood power."[113]

President Oaks explained,

> We are not accustomed to speaking of women having the authority of the priesthood in their Church callings, but what other authority can it be? When a woman—young or old—is set apart to preach the gospel as a full-time missionary, she is given priesthood authority to perform a priesthood function. The same is true when a woman is set apart to function as an officer or teacher in a Church organization under the direction of one who holds the keys of the priesthood.[114]

113. M. Russell Ballard, "Men and Women in the Work of the Lord," New Era, Apr. 2014, 4; see also Daughters in My Kingdom: The History and Work of Relief Society (2011), 138–39.

114. Dallin H. Oaks, "The Keys and Authority of the Priesthood," 51.

President Ballard taught,

> All who have made sacred covenants with the Lord and who honor those covenants are eligible to receive personal revelation, to be blessed by the ministering of angels, to commune with God, to receive the fulness of the gospel, and, ultimately, to become heirs alongside Jesus Christ of all our Father has.[115]

President Joseph Fielding Smith likewise instructed,

> The blessings of the priesthood are not confined to men alone. These blessings are also poured out upon . . . all the faithful women of the Church. . . The Lord offers to his daughters every spiritual gift and blessing that can be obtained by his sons.[116]

The Lord promised Joseph Smith that the Saints, both men and women, would be endowed with "power from on high" (D&C 95:8). We are specifically granted power over the spirits in the world (D&C 50:30–33). We are endowed with many gifts, powers and abilities. President Ballard explained temple blessings thus: "The endowment is literally a gift of power. All who enter the house of the Lord officiate in the ordinances of the priesthood. This applies to men and women alike."[117] All worthy members who have received their endowment and keep the covenants they have made in the temple have priesthood power. Thus, women, married or single, can have priesthood power in their homes regardless of a visit from a priesthood holder.[118] Remembering the difference between authority and power, children and sisters have every right to call upon the power of the Finger of God, through the power of the priesthood of their father, husband or

---

115. M. Russell Ballard, "Men and Women in the Work of the Lord," 4–5.
116. Teachings of Presidents of the Church: Joseph Fielding Smith (2013), 163. For a more in-depth discussion on the blessings of the priesthood, see Bruce R. McConkie, "The Ten Blessings of the Priesthood," *Ensign*, Nov. 1977, 33–35.
117. M. Russell Ballard, "Let Us Think Straight" (Brigham Young University devotional, Aug. 20, 2013), 7, speeches.byu.edu.
118. See generally, Barbara Morgan Gardner, "Connecting Daughters of God with His Priesthood Power." March 2019.

Bishop, or through the angels that are available to intervene. Demons of every stripe may certainly be rebuked, invoking the name of the very highest priesthood authority, the great High Priest, Jesus Christ, the Savior of all humanity. All of these things are accomplished through power, circuiting from God, through Jesus Christ, Adam-Michael, angels, prophets, apostles, and bishops, to the smallest and meekest of the children of God in His earthly Kingdom, through the medium of the Holy Spirit and the Light of Christ. The power of God is limitless, as is our ability to tap into it and exercise and direct it as the Spirit directs.

Lamenting those who lose their way, President Nelson has said,

> Dear brothers and sisters, I grieve for those who leave the Church because they feel membership requires too much of them. They have not yet discovered that making and keeping covenants actually makes life easier! Each person who makes covenants in baptismal fonts and in temples—and keeps them—has increased access to the power of Jesus Christ. Please ponder that stunning truth! The reward for keeping covenants with God is heavenly power—power that strengthens us to withstand our trials, temptations, and heartaches better. This power eases our way. Those who live the higher laws of Jesus Christ have access to His higher power. Thus, covenant keepers are entitled to a special kind of rest that comes to them through their covenantal relationship with God.[119]

As the ancient prophet Moroni contemplated the end of his mission, he shared with us his last testimony, and implored us to learn for ourselves that God truly lives, and that He is a loving Father who seeks our welfare in all things. He says,

> And ye may know that he is, by the power of the Holy Ghost; wherefore I would exhort you that ye deny not the power of God; for he worketh by power, according to the faith of the children of men, the same today and tomorrow, and forever (Moroni 7:7).

119. "Overcome the World and Find Rest," October 2022 general conference, Sunday morning session.

This passage is key to our understanding that God, the Creator of the universe, always works by power, "according to the faith of the children of men." Yes, it is my faith, and your faith, that makes possible the miracles and blessings of God. The prophet exhorts us to open ourselves to the blessings of our loving and gracious Heavenly Father, and the many gifts of the Spirit that He sends among us to bless our temporal lives while we feel so alone, and often abandoned, here on the earth.

> And again, I exhort you, my brethren, that ye deny not the gifts of God, for they are many; and they come from the same God. And there are different ways that these gifts are administered; but it is the same God who worketh all in all; and they are given by the manifestations of the Spirit of God unto men, to profit them.
>
> For behold, to one is given by the Spirit of God, that he may teach the word of wisdom;
>
> And to another, that he may teach the word of knowledge by the same Spirit;
>
> And to another, exceedingly great faith; and to another, the gifts of healing by the same Spirit;[120]
>
> And again, to another, that he may work mighty miracles; And again, to another, that he may prophesy concerning all things; And again, to another, the beholding of angels and ministering spirits;
>
> And again, to another, all kinds of tongues;
>
> And again, to another, the interpretation of languages and of divers kinds of tongues.
>
> And all these gifts come by the Spirit of Christ; and they come unto every man severally, according as he will.

---

120. "Respecting the female laying on hands," the Nauvoo Relief Society minutes record, Joseph said that "it is no sin for any body to do it that has faith," and admonished, "if the sisters should have faith to heal the sick, let all hold their tongues, and let every thing roll on." Nauvoo Relief Society Minutes, Apr. 28, 1842. Joseph Smith taught that the gift of healing was a sign that would follow "all that believe whether male or female." Eliza R. Snow explained in 1883, "Women can administer in the name of JESUS, but not by virtue of the Priesthood" (Morgan Utah Stake Relief Society Minutes and Records, 1878–1973, Church History Library, Salt Lake City, vol. 1, Apr. 28, 1883, 88).

> And I would exhort you, my beloved brethren, that ye remember that every good gift cometh of Christ.
>
> And I would exhort you, my beloved brethren, that ye remember that he is the same yesterday, today, and forever, and that all these gifts of which I have spoken, which are spiritual, never will be done away, even as long as the world shall stand, only according to the unbelief of the children of men (Moroni 10:7–19).

In fact, not every one of us possesses the same spiritual gifts, in the same quantities. As the Lord explains through His prophet, it is as we combine our gifts that all gifts are manifest among us. Diverse gifts are enjoyed by various people, to profit mankind. By uniting our gifts and our prayers to the Lord, all blessings and manifestations of the Spirit come to us. By raising our requests in unison we combine our faith and petition the Lord for His blessings with power, as if the voice of the lone widow who petitions the judge is multiplied in its effect. Think of the effect of millions of Latter-day Saints raising their petitions in unison to the Lord, or of hundreds in a ward or stake doing the same. Think of the effect of those in the stakes of Zion developing their spiritual gifts and sharing them among one another.

Many gifts of the Spirit tend to dwell in us in a latent state most of the time, because we fail to exercise them. Often, we ignore them, forgetting to utilize them to bless our lives and the lives of those around us. Sometimes we just fail to recognize that we enjoy an ongoing outpouring of the Spirit.

If you will indulge your author a personal experience, I served my mission in northern Italy, and we were introduced to family members of a member of the branch. The Church in Italy was quite young at the time and we struggled to find those who were willing to listen to our message. The opportunity to teach relatives of active members was rare. We were introduced to the couple and their small children and learned that they had spoken with missionaries before, but had only a little curiosity at that time. Now, however, they had been studying with evangelicals and had developed some questions, and their relatives were quick to suggest a talk with the missionaries. We enjoyed the first four or five discussions with the young family and challenged them to be baptized by those having priesthood authority. They were in favor of the move, but harbored a small reservation based on something their evangelical friends had told them. They asked if we would be willing to meet with them and their evangelical missionary friends together, and we agreed.

At the appointed time my missionary companion and I arrived at the home of the family, and found the evangelicals there already. We greeted their guests warmly and asked if we could be of any assistance. The evangelicals took that as a challenge and began to pepper us with doctrinal questions, interjecting as often as possible their assertion that one is not saved until they have spoken in tongues; something that they had done by their own report. We politely answered their questions, understanding that the important aspect of the evening was to help the young couple feel the Holy Spirit, not to win a debate. As the evangelicals escalated their tone, we remained calm, and finally one of them loudly proclaimed that we certainly did not possess the gift of the Holy Ghost, as evidenced by our lack of ability to speak in tongues. At that moment the Spirit testified to me that I was in the right place at the right time doing that which the Lord had asked me to do, and told me exactly what to do. I looked at the young couple, then at the evangelicals and I began to speak in a tongue that was foreign to all of them—English. I said in my native tongue,

> How can you tell me that I do not enjoy the gift of tongues, when I have been speaking all evening in a foreign language, preaching the gospel of my Master? If you enjoyed the gift of tongues, you would understand what I am saying to you at this very moment, but I can see from the dull shock on your faces that you fail to understand a single word of what I'm saying.

Everyone was frozen in place, unsure what to do. Then their eyes began to dart around at one another, and my companion looked at me smiling, as did the young couple. The evangelicals were speechless, in any tongue, and the husband of the family we were teaching turned to me and immediately asked about setting up a baptismal date.

Faith is a principle of *action* and *power* in all intelligent beings, and to implement it we must "act." Until one does something, they have not yet exercised faith. Can you imagine a Missionary Training Center where young missionaries sit around for months praying for the gift of tongues, without doing anything to learn the languages? The Lord will not bless such faithlessness. The Lord rebuked Oliver Cowdery saying, "Behold, you have not understood; you have supposed that I would give it unto you, when you took no thought save it was to ask me" (D&C 9:7). Yes, Oliver asked, as we have discussed, but he failed to ask in faith—a necessary prerequisite to receiving the blessings of the Lord. We must do something to initiate the process, to complete the task, and the Lord will make up the difference between what we can do, and what must be done. We see the principle in action in the case of the Brother of Jared, who knew better than to merely ask for light in the barges, but decided he would design and manufacture stones that the Lord could touch and give light to. Certainly, as long as we're doing our best to serve the Lord as He has asked, He will bless us, and in those moments when there was nothing we could have done to better prepare, He will make up the difference, and bestow the miraculous gift.

James, the Apostle of the Lord, explained this very principle to the ancient Saints.

> What doth it profit, my brethren, though a man say he hath faith, and have not works? can faith save him? If a brother or sister be naked, and destitute of daily food, And one of you say unto them, Depart in peace, be ye warmed and filled; notwithstanding ye give them not those things which are needful to the body; what doth it profit? Even so faith, if it hath not works, is dead, being alone. Yea, a man may say, Thou hast faith, and I have works: shew me thy faith without thy works, and I will shew thee my faith by my works. Thou believest that there is one God; thou doest well: the devils also believe, and tremble. But wilt thou know, O vain man, that faith without works is dead? Was not Abraham our father justified by works, when he had offered Isaac his son upon the altar? Seest thou how faith wrought with his works, and by works was faith made perfect? And the scripture was fulfilled which saith, Abraham believed God, and it was imputed unto him for righteousness: and he was called the Friend of God. Ye see then how that by works a man is justified, and not by faith only. Likewise also was not Rahab the harlot justified by works, when she had received the messengers,

> and had sent them out another way? For as the body without the spirit is dead, so faith without works is dead also (James 2:14–26).

Without acting on filling a need or desire, there is no faith. We can hope or believe the Lord will do something, and to that extent, many believe that they exercise faith. It is not so. Belief in a thing, even a correct thing, will not produce anything without being combined with an act or an exertion. We can think of several examples of this principle. For example, we can believe that Christ will exalt us at the last day, but if we fail to do what He has instructed us to do, there will be no exaltation. Many will be surprised when they stand before Him and He says, "I know you not whence ye are; depart from me, all ye workers of iniquity" (Luke 13:27). We can believe that the Lord will bless us with productive crops, but unless we do our part to sow the seed and care for it while it grows, we have no promise of success.

The prophet Joseph Smith taught the School of the Prophets that when we exercise faith in performing extraordinary tasks by the finger of God, it is by mental or spiritual exertion. The key word is exertion. It is work. He explains:

> Let us here offer some explanation in relation to faith that our meaning may be clearly comprehended. We ask then, what are we to understand by a man's working by faith?
>
> We answer, We understand that when a man works by faith he works by mental exertion instead of physical force.
>
> It is by words instead of exerting his physical powers, with which every being works when he works by faith.
>
> God said, "Let there be light: and there was light" (Gen. 1:3). Joshua spake, and the great lights which God had created stood still. Elijah commanded, and the heavens were stayed for the space of three years and six months, so that it did not rain. He again commanded, and the heavens gave forth rain.
>
> All this was done by faith, and the Savior says, "If ye have faith as a grain of mustard seed, ye shall say unto this mountain, Remove hence to yonder place; and it shall remove" (Matthew 17:20); or "ye might say unto this sycamine tree, Be thou plucked up by the root, and be thou planted in the sea; and it should obey you." (Luke 17:6)
>
> Faith then works by words, and with these its mightiest works have been, and will be, performed (*Lectures on Faith*, 7:3).

Joseph further explained that this is the very method employed by angels to move about, and to carry out their varied assignments, as well as God's method of organizing the planets and maintaining them in their orbits.

> Angels move from place to place by virtue of this power—it is by reason of it that they are enabled to descend from heaven to earth; and were it not for the power of faith, they never could be ministering spirits to them who should be heirs of salvation, neither could they act as heavenly messengers; for they would be destitute of the power necessary to enable them to do the will of God. It is only necessary for us to say that the whole visible creation, as it now exists, is the effect of faith. It was faith by which it was framed, and it is by the power of faith that it continues in its organized form, and by which the planets move round their orbits and sparkle forth their glory. So then faith is truly the first principle in the science of Theology, and when understood, leads the mind back to the beginning and carries it forward to the end; or in other words, from eternity to eternity (*Lectures on Faith*, 7:4–5).

Faith is the ultimate principle, the first and the last principle, upon which all things rest for a foundation. There can be no joy in this life or in the world to come without the exercise of our faith. This is why there is so much depression and misery in the world, especially among those who have no faith in the Lord; they fail to obtain the blessings of a loving Father, by asking Him in faith.

> As faith then is the principle by which the heavenly hosts perform their works, and by which they enjoy all their felicity, we might expect to find it set forth in a revelation from God as the principle upon which his creatures here below must act, in order to obtain the felicities enjoyed by the Saints in the eternal world; and that when God would undertake to raise up men for the enjoyment of himself, he would teach them the necessity of living by faith; and the impossibility there was of their enjoying the blessedness of eternity without it, seeing that all the blessings of eternity are the effects of faith. Therefore it is said, and appropriately too, that "without faith it is impossible to please him [God]" (Hebrews 11:6) (*Lectures on Faith*, 7:6–7).

The Prophet sums up his teachings about faith by reminding us that the history of the universe is a history of the exercise of faith. Everyone obtains that which they have the faith to receive. All blessings and privileges from God are entirely dependent on our individual faith to obtain them, and men and women, exactly like us, have called down the powers of heaven and received extraordinary gifts and Godly acts of intervention by asking God in faith.

> And through the whole history of the scheme of life and salvation, it is a matter of faith: every man received according to his faith. According as his faith was, so were his blessings and privileges; and nothing was withheld from him when his faith was sufficient to receive it. He could stop the mouths of lions, quench the violence of fire, escape the edge of the sword, wax valiant in fight, and put to flight the armies of the aliens; women could by their faith receive their dead children to life again. In a word, there was nothing impossible with them who had faith. All things were in subjection to the Former Day Saints, according as their faith was. By their faith they could obtain heavenly visions, the ministering of angels, have knowledge of the spirits of just men made perfect, of the general assembly and church of the Firstborn whose names are written in heaven, of God the Judge of all, of Jesus the Mediator of the new covenant, and become familiar with the third heavens, see and hear things which were not only unutterable, but were unlawful to utter (*Lectures on Faith*, 7:17).

The Prophet's objective in teaching us this principle was to assure us that we are in no worse a position to receive these many blessings from the hand of the Lord than were the former Saints. We are every bit as qualified to receive miracles and visitations as they were. Visions, the ministering of angels, the restoration of dead children—the Prophet specifically mentions these as things that the Lord stands ready to give us if we will ask in faith. If we haven't been receiving them, we by now understand the reason—lack of faith. There is no need to doubt, however, because the Savior has been clear and unequivocal in His promise that these blessings are waiting to be bestowed on us as we begin to exercise our faith in Him. He stands ready to bless us, and not only asks us to knock at the door so that it may be opened to us, but He knocks and asks to be admitted into our lives. "Behold, I stand at the door, and knock: if any man hear my voice, and open the door, I will come in to him, and will sup with him, and he with me" (Revelation 3:20).

Joseph seals his testimony of the principle of faith with a recitation of what we can expect in our lives as we begin to exercise our faith.

> For when faith comes, it brings its train of attendants with it—apostles, prophets, evangelists, pastors, teachers, gifts, wisdom, knowledge, miracles, healings, tongues, interpretation of tongues, etc. All these appear when faith appears on the earth, and disappear when it disappears from the earth. For these are the effects of faith and always have, and always will attend it. For where faith is, there will the knowledge of God be also, with all things which pertain thereto—revelations, visions, and dreams, as well as every other necessary thing in order that the possessors of faith may be perfected and obtain salvation . . . And he who possesses it will through it obtain all necessary knowledge and wisdom, until he shall know God and the Lord Jesus Christ whom he has sent, whom to know is eternal life. Amen (*Lectures on Faith*, 7:20; see generally, gifts of the spirit, D&C 46:7–30).

It is through faith that we gain salvation, and eventually, exaltation and Eternal Life, as the Prophet clarifies. It is through faith that we obtain divine help, guidance, and intervention in this life as well. It is through faith that we accomplish all things relative to joy and rejoicing in this world, and in the next. It is through faith that we accomplish all things, and that we come to know God—because it is through faith that we do the things He does. Faith is everything. Exercising faith in our Heavenly Father sets a life filled with miracles apart from all of the mundane existences we see around us. Going to the temple, as did Peter and the Apostles, and keeping our eyes open for needs around us, and discerning God's will, and asking God to bless our efforts by reaching forth His mighty finger—these are the "acts" of faith that result in a lame man taking up his bed and walking. When we exercise our faith by doing good things that are in agreement with God's divine will and plan, doubting nothing as we ask for God's help, the Lord blesses our efforts and rains down miracles.

Trial of Our Faith

Adversity comes into every life. Human history is a desolate parade of hardship, danger, persecution and destruction—usually inflicted by those who are enemies of good. Jesus clearly taught His disciples:

> Ye have heard that it hath been said, Thou shalt love thy neighbour, and hate thine enemy. But I say unto you, Love your enemies, bless them that curse you, do good to them that hate you, and pray for them which despitefully use you, and persecute you; That ye may be the children of your Father which is in heaven: for he maketh his sun to rise on the evil and on the good, and sendeth rain on the just and on the unjust (Matthew 5:43–45).

We learn from this that even the followers of the Lord: a) would have enemies, b) some would curse them, c) some would hate them, d) some would despitefully use them, e) some would persecute them, f) the rains would fall on them the same as they fall on the unjust, and g) they would watch as the sun rose on the evil as well. A moment earlier, He had warned the people, "Blessed are ye, when men shall revile you, and persecute you, and shall say all manner of evil against you falsely, for my sake" (verse 11).

The message is clear that being a faithful member of the Church of Jesus Christ will not exempt us from the evils and heartbreaks of our mortal existence. We learn that quite the opposite is true. The prophet Moroni specifically instructed us that the very nature of faith is its unseen quality, and that exercising it, like exercising a muscle in the body, necessarily requires opposing force, which often comes in the form of a trial of our faith.

> And now, I, Moroni, would speak somewhat concerning these things; I would show unto the world that faith is things which are hoped for and not seen; wherefore, dispute not because ye see not, for ye receive no witness until after the trial of your faith (Ether 12:6).

Let's look at the "unseen" aspect of faith for a moment. We began our discussion looking at two definitions of faith provided in the Book of Mormon.

> And now as I said concerning faith—faith is not to have a perfect knowledge of things; therefore if ye have faith ye hope for things which are *not seen*, which are true (Alma 32:21).

> And now, I, Moroni, would speak somewhat concerning these things; I would show unto the world that faith is things which are hoped for and *not seen*; wherefore, dispute not because ye see not, for ye receive no witness until after the trial of your faith (Ether 12:6).

Most definitions of faith contain this "not seen" aspect. As a result, many attribute a mystical quality to faith—which tends to put it out of our reach. That is entirely untrue, however. The unseen nature of faith is that unlike God, we can't see the end from the beginning. When the farmer plants seeds, they do not yet see the harvested crops in his storehouse. When a student walks through the university doors for the first time, they do not yet hold the diploma in their hands. When a glassblower melts the glass, they do not yet see the goblet sitting on the shelf. When the writer sits down at the keyboard, they do not yet see the bound book on the shelf. The "unseen" nature of faith is that we set the creation of the thing into motion, and follow the steps to ensure its fruition, without yet seeing the results. We can envision the result, yes. We can create it spiritually in our mind, as does God, and we can work toward the finished product with our efforts. But the unseen nature of faith is merely that we "trust" or have "confidence" that the exertion will produce a completed effort. At the point that we see the result of our effort, if ceases to be faith, and is transformed into knowledge.

If we expect to receive the unrestricted flow of miracles from heaven without having our faith proved by the Lord, we ignore the clear teachings of the prophets. If we expect Him to merely give us things without exercising our faith—that is, doing something, doubting nothing—we are equally mistaken. He will test us, and He will allow us the opportunity to question His veracity. It is as we push beyond those doubts and into the light of His truth and love that we enter the realms of the prophets and angels. Despite heartbreak, loss, tearful nights, and gut-wrenching trials, we must remain faithful and always seek to see things from the Lord's eternal perspective. As we look at things from His higher viewpoint, we often see that the immediacy of our panicked desires is insignificant in the eternal perspective. Some minor loss or change of course may not be the curse that we fear it is from our shortsighted and obstructed point of view.

We also must be careful to limit our exposure to adversity to those things that the Lord sees fit to inflict upon us. All too often we heap misery on ourselves through our own foolish choices. The trials we suffer from our own mistakes are often not those that the Lord would have selected for us, so the suffering and trial is wasteful in that it fails to produce any desirable improvements in our character. As we submit ourselves to Him, and subdue our own will in favor of His righteous will, we will see that His way is best, and that we should exercise our faith to bring about His will. This is why the Lord instructs us that if we ask in faith, which includes asking in righteousness and in alignment with His will, and as long as the thing which we ask is "right," which again indicates it is in alignment with His will, or that the thing is "expedient," which means it is necessary and in alignment with His will, He will give it to us. In other words, if we ask something of our Heavenly Father that is good for us and is not contrary to His will, and we exercise our faith with respect to the matter, the Lord is bound to bless us. If we ask something that is amiss, or something that is contrary to His will, it indicates that we have failed to ask in faith, because we have failed to obtain the confirmation of the Holy Spirit that we are permitted to ask for the item. "Ye ask, and receive not, because ye bask amiss, that ye may consume it upon your lusts" (James 4:3; 2 Nephi 4:35[121]).

Let us remember the Lord's statement about why He swore He would fulfill any word spoken by the prophet Enoch:

---

121. "Yea, I know that God will give liberally to him that asketh. Yea, my God will give me, if I bask not amiss; therefore I will lift up my voice unto thee; yea, I will cry unto thee, my God, the rock of my righteousness. Behold, my voice shall forever ascend up unto thee, my rock and mine everlasting God. Amen."

> Behold my Spirit is upon you, wherefore all thy words will I justify; and the mountains shall flee before you, and the rivers shall turn from their course; and thou shalt abide in me, and I in you; therefore walk with me (Moses 6:34).

The Holy Spirit was upon Enoch, and he spoke the words the Lord wanted him to speak, and remained close to Him in his daily life, therefore, the Lord justified anything that Enoch spoke. Enoch spoke the words of power, invoking the finger of God and the intervention of heavenly hosts. He turned away great and fierce armies as they approached to destroy the people of Zion, by the speaking of a word. Joseph Smith instructed us that it is by the speaking of the word that faith is exercised in performing miracles by the finger of God. It is by mental exertion as opposed to physical exertion, that these things are accomplished. Again, the word exertion connotes an act, and in this case, more of a repeated act—like exercise. It is instructive that the word exercise is appropriate when speaking about strengthening our faith through use—we exercise our faith, and strengthen it through repetitious use. We can think of it as muscle tissue that grows and becomes stronger through repeated use and by pushing to new limits. There is discomfort involved, and even some pain. We understand the process and accept it in the realm of physical exercise. The moment many of us begin to feel a little discomfort when exercising faith, we immediately end the workout, becoming encircled by fear and doubt. It is fear and doubt that destroy faith. Let us not be faithless in the exercise of this splendid gift from God. Let us trust Him who has earned our trust, and believe His words.

The Ministering of Angels

As we consider the methods that the Lord utilizes to bless us in answer to our requests, often through the ministering of those around us and sometimes in extraordinary ways, we must be mindful of the wonderful resource of angelic intervention. We hear from our earliest training that the Aaronic Priesthood holds the keys of the ministering of angels (D&C 13:1;[122] 84:26; 107:20; Joseph Smith—History 1:69). In relation to this principle, we often hear the infrequent story of how someone was assisted by an angel in a desperate circumstance and wonder under what circumstances the Lord decides to send angelic ministers to assist us. So that we may know what we ask when requesting the assistance of angels, let us consider what we know about the subject.

Angels are messengers from God. They are frequently sent to minister to mankind in many capacities. Angels are children of God like us, at various stages on their own path of eternal progress. Angels can be:

1. Spirits that have not yet come to earth and received a body;
2. Spirits that have come to earth and received a body but have been temporarily separated from their body in death and currently await the resurrection;
3. People who have lived, died, and been resurrected;
4. People who have been translated as were Enoch and the inhabitants of Zion, John the Beloved, and the Three Nephite Disciples;[123]
5. In some circumstances, mortal men and women can be sent as angels to fulfill a specific mission from God, as *possibly* in the case of those who were sent to rescue Lot from the fate of Sodom.

---

122. "Upon you my fellow servants, in the name of Messiah I confer the Priesthood of Aaron, which holds the keys of the ministering of angels, and of the gospel of repentance, and of baptism by immersion for the remission of sins; and this shall never be taken again from the earth, until the sons of Levi do offer again an offering unto the Lord in righteousness."

123. There is a class of beings called Watchers, who are barely mentioned in the canonized scriptures, but are expounded in great detail in many apocryphal works. They appear to be something akin to translated humans, sent by God to assist each new world as its "Adam and Eve" exit the Garden. See generally, *Worlds Without Number*, James L. Thompson, Cedar Fort International (Springville, Utah, 2022), 86.

An in-depth discussion of the rich and fascinating nature of, and doctrines surrounding these heavenly messengers, is beyond the scope of this work.[124] It is sufficient for the purposes of our discussion that we understand that angels are beings empowered by God to intercede in our lives to bring about the blessings we seek from the Lord. They are sent to inspire us, to protect us, to administer priesthood blessings to us, to teach us, or to intervene in a circumstance to avert its natural result. We can read of many visitations and interventions by angels in the scriptures. First, let us re-examine a scripture describing angels coming to earth to teach men the gospel, and instill in them great faith.

> And now I come to that faith, of which I said I would speak; and I will tell you the way whereby ye may lay hold on every good thing. For behold, God knowing all things, being from everlasting to everlasting, behold, he sent angels to minister unto the children of men, to make manifest concerning the coming of Christ; and in Christ there should come every good thing . . . Wherefore, by the ministering of angels, and by every word which proceeded forth out of the mouth of God, men began to exercise faith in Christ; and thus by faith, they did lay hold upon every good thing; and thus it was until the coming of Christ (Moroni 7:21–22, 25).

Moroni then declares that miracles continue to exist among men and that angels continue to minister to the children of men (verse 29[125]), and that their mission is "to minister according to the word of (Christ's) command, showing themselves unto them of strong faith and a firm mind in every form of godliness" (verse 30). In modern times, the very restoration of the Church and priesthood was accomplished through the visitation and administration of several heavenly messengers. There are billions of such beings at our disposal, and the Lord stands ready to send any number of them to bless our lives, or

124. For an excellent treatment on the subject of angels, see generally, *Angels*, Oscar W. McConkie, Jr., Deseret Book Company, (Salt Lake City, Utah, 1978)

125. "And because he hath done this, my beloved brethren, have miracles ceased? Behold I say unto you, Nay; neither have angels ceased to minister unto the children of men."

intervene in perilous circumstances whenever one "of strong faith and a firm mind" calls upon Him for a blessing.

An example of how God intervenes with His angels is found in the Old Testament, where the prophet Elisha is going about the business of the Lord, and an enemy encompasses the city he is in.

> Therefore sent he thither horses, and chariots, and a great host: and they came by night, and compassed the city about. And when the servant of the man of God was risen early, and gone forth, behold, an host compassed the city both with horses and chariots. And his servant said unto him, Alas, my master! how shall we do? And he answered, Fear not: for they that be with us are more than they that be with them. And Elisha prayed, and said, Lord, I pray thee, open his eyes, that he may see. And the Lord opened the eyes of the young man; and he saw: and, behold, the mountain was full of horses and chariots of fire round about Elisha (2 Kings 6:14–17).

How simple and clear the prophet's response to his young assistant: "Fear not: for they that be with us are more than they that be with them." This is always the case when we obey the commandments of our Heavenly Father, and ask His help in faith.

At other times it was the prophet Elisha who was sent to minister as an angel of God. In 2 Kings, chapter 4, we read of a few of the times that he administered relief to the people through the finger of God. We first read of a widow whose two sons were to be taken into bondage as payment of her dead husband's debt. Elisha asked what she had left in the house, and she reported there was nothing, save a small pot of oil. He instructed her to collect all of the empty jars and other vessels she could find, and to pour the small pot of oil into them. She obeyed, and was surprised that the small pot of oil kept pouring and pouring, eventually filling all of the vessels they could locate. She was able to sell all of the oil, and pay the debt. Also, while Elisha traveled to Shunem, there was a wealthy middle-aged woman who kindly made sure that Elisha and his servant had food for their journey, and she even constrained her elderly husband to build Elisha a special room on their roof, which he used each time he traveled that direction. He blessed her and told her that although she had been barren, she would produce a son within the year. She was incredulous, and said, "Nay, my lord, thou man of God, do not lie unto thine handmaid." The baby boy was born that following season, and the woman rejoiced. When the boy was a little grown, he fell ill one day, and died. The woman had him carried up to Elisha's cot, and rushed to Mount Carmel to ask for the prophet. Elisha instructed his servant to go to the boy, and to lay his staff on him, and he should live—but the attempt was unsuccessful. Elisha himself went to the woman's house and administered to the child, and he lived again. Also, during a great famine, a man from Baal-shalisha came to Elisha to pay an offering of food. Elisha instructed him to prepare the food and give it to all of the men of the area, but the man said, "What, should I set this before an hundred men?" Elisha repeated what he had said, "Give the people, that they may eat: for thus saith the Lord, They shall eat, and shall leave thereof." The man did as he was told, and "set it before them, and they did eat," and when they had all eaten, there was food left over.

Perhaps we will say to ourselves that we are not Elisha, or any other person of historical importance, or Godly preference. Perhaps we feel that we are not special enough to merit the attention of our Heavenly Father. We have reviewed several scriptures that testify otherwise. Something to think about is just how rare each of us is in the eyes of heaven. Those who have entered into the waters of baptism and made a covenant with Heavenly Father can be numbered in the mere millions, accounting for the entire history of the earth. That is a small fraction of the approximately 100 billion children that have been on the earth thus far—less than a small fraction of just one percent. That already makes each of us extremely noteworthy to our Father in Heaven, and His angels, who all watch us with great interest and concern. Jesus taught this principle to his audience, that they were of great interest to their Father in heaven.

> Are not five sparrows sold for two farthings, and not one of them is forgotten before God? But even the very hairs of your head are all numbered. Fear not therefore: ye are of more value than many sparrows (Luke 12:6–7).

A son or daughter of God is much more valuable to him than a mere bird, or grasshopper—yet He is constantly aware of the condition of each and every one of His creatures, and He admires them as they grow and develop within their sphere of creation. As one of His children, you are of enormous concern to Him, and His loving and caring eye is unceasingly upon you. As a member of His Church, and one who has entered into covenants with Him, you are of even more interest to Him. Additionally, think now upon the small fraction of the children of God who have received the holy priesthood. If you are ordained to the holy priesthood, are sealed to someone who possesses the priesthood, or even if it is present in your household, you are a rare jewel in the crown of the Father. The Lord says to those who have received ordination to the priesthood,

> And wo unto all those who come not unto this priesthood which ye have received, which I now confirm upon you who are present this day, by mine own voice out of the heavens; and even I have given the heavenly hosts and mine angels charge concerning you (D&C 84:42).

To receive the priesthood is to be assigned to the angels who are given stewardship over us. What is it that we can suppose they are charged to do for us? Because it is mentioned in direct connection with the bestowal of the priesthood, we can assume that it is at least connected to protecting us, and to fulfilling the words that we speak in the name of God. When I was a full-time missionary serving in northern Italy, I was on the train during a transfer, and it suddenly occurred to me as I looked out of the window at the passing farmlands, that I was probably the only priesthood holder within many miles. My thought was that if the Lord needed a priesthood holder in this part of the world, in this moment, I was the only one. I felt the weight of that moment very keenly, and understood somewhat that God knew where I was, and we were acting in a very real partnership—I was literally serving Him, as He brings about the immortality and eternal life of His children.

If we would like to consider further just how unique we are in the eyes of heavenly beings, consider how few children of earth have been sealed together in the temples of God. How many have knelt at the alters of God and received the pronouncement,

> Ye shall come forth in the first resurrection . . . and shall inherit thrones, kingdoms, principalities, and powers, dominions, all heights and depths . . . and they shall pass by the angels, and the gods, which are set there, to their exaltation and glory in all things, as hath been sealed upon their heads, which glory shall be a fulness and a continuation of the seeds forever and ever (D&C 132:19).

What fraction of God's children have received this pronouncement by one ordained to that power? Do you really think that angels do not follow your every move and hang on your every word? Do you think that they do not stand in awe of the life you are living, despite your weaknesses and human frailties?

There can be no doubt that God, our Heavenly Father, and His holy angels are very much aware of each of us, and that they are cheering us on toward the finish line of our lives. They are anxious to help us in all circumstances and stand ready to assist any of us who do what the Lord has instructed us to do—ask in faith, doubting nothing, that we might receive. The exercise of our faith is essential to our eternal progress. It is essential to obtaining the blessings the Lord has in store for us here and now, and in the life that awaits us. Don't doubt that you can fill your life with miracles from heaven. Like the servant of Elisha, if your eyes were suddenly opened, you would see that we are surrounded by angels at all times. If you were permitted to look into the background matrix of the universe, you would see that God is creating miracles constantly, and your life is a series of billions and billions of miracles, all stacked in your favor to bring to pass your immortality and eternal life. Those who study the nature of the universe and our reality have come to understand that our very existence is the result of complex planning, and execution of those plans. Even those who have no faith in a creator are beginning to understand that the odds of the universe existing in its present form, and creating and sustaining life in environments that are hospitable to life, are incredibly low. Exponentially low, in fact. They are beginning to realize that if not for billions upon billions of "happy accidents" and serendipitous circumstances, there would be no life at all, even in our small corner of the universe.

Your life is an incessant series of miracles, and God radiates His majestic governance of the universe from His throne in a manner that provides you with life and light. It is the Light of Christ that emanates from God and fills the universe, and governs every particle, including all matter and spirit in your environment.

> Which light proceedeth forth from the presence of God to fill the immensity of space—The light which is in all things, which giveth life to all things, which is the law by which all things are governed, even the power of God who sitteth upon his throne, who is in the bosom of eternity, who is in the midst of all things (D&C 88:12–13).[126]

If you will allow His glorious light to fill you and enlighten your soul and understanding, you will see who you truly are, and what you are capable of doing. You are a son or daughter of Heavenly Parents, and like Jesus Christ, you lived for eons before coming to this earth, and you practiced faith to travel millions of light years in an instant, and to help create this very planet on which we reside. You have always lived by faith, and performed countless miracles through the finger of God. We should not allow the temporary veil of forgetfulness to rob us of the will to live by faith in God any longer. "Awake, awake; put on thy strength, O Zion; put on thy beautiful garments" (Isaiah 52:1).

The Last Days

The Lord has warned us that we live in the last days, just preceding His Second Coming. The Prophet Joseph Smith was allowed to see our days as he read the Bible using the Urim and Thummim, and he updated portions of the Book of Matthew with a more accurate translation as a result of his expanded knowledge. The last days will begin with the events enumerated in The Revelation of the Apostle John, starting with a devastating worldwide earthquake, causing the sun to be darkened and the moon to appear red, through the heavy

126. See generally, *Worlds Without Number*, Thompson, 20–29.

debris in the atmosphere.[127] This is the beginning, and the Apostle tells us that the ensuing calamity is so destructive, that "the kings of the earth, and the great men, and the rich men, and the chief captains, and the mighty men, and every bondman, and every free man, hid themselves in the dens and in the rocks of the mountains," to survive the aftermath.

Reading on into chapter 7 of the Revelation and elsewhere, we learn more about the physical calamities that will plague the earth. Christ warns us that spiritual trials will likewise torment us,

> For in those days there shall also arise false Christs, and false prophets, and shall show great signs and wonders, insomuch, that, if possible, they shall deceive the very elect, who are the elect according to the covenant (Joseph Smith—Matthew 1:22).

Jesus warns,

> Behold, I speak these things unto you for the elect's sake; and you also shall hear of wars, and rumors of wars; see that ye be not troubled, for all I have told you must come to pass; but the end is not yet. Behold, I have told you before (verses 23–24).

Jesus continues with His description of those days.

> And they shall hear of wars, and rumors of wars. Behold I speak for mine elect's sake; for nation shall rise against nation, and kingdom against kingdom; there shall be famines, and pestilences, and earthquakes, in divers places (verses 28–29).

We note that the Lord tells us specifically that He shares this information with us, for the sake of the elect. You are the elect. He wants you to be prepared, and to know what to do as those difficulties come upon us.[128]

---

127. Revelation 6:12.

128. A thorough treatment of last days events preceding the Second Coming of the Lord is beyond the scope of this discussion, although it is during those tumultuous difficulties that the power of faith will be of extreme value to the Saints of God.

During these calamities that keep the earth and its inhabitants in extreme turmoil, the Man of Sin and Antichrist will rise to world dominion, working great miracles and deceiving most of the people to worship false gods, under the penalty of death. Survival during this reign will be very difficult—especially for those who refuse to receive the Mark of the Beast, that they may buy and sell. (Revelation 13:16–17) President Russell M. Nelson says of our times, and those that are about to break upon us:

> Our Savior and Redeemer, Jesus Christ, will perform some of His mightiest works between now and when He comes again. We will see miraculous indications that God the Father and His Son, Jesus Christ, preside over this Church in majesty and glory. But in coming days, it will not be possible to survive spiritually without the guiding, directing, comforting, and constant influence of the Holy Ghost. My beloved brothers and sisters, I plead with you to increase your spiritual capacity to receive revelation.[129]

But Christ tells us,

> And whoso treasureth up my word, shall not be deceived, for the Son of Man shall come, and he shall send his angels before him with the great sound of a trumpet, and they shall gather together the remainder of his elect from the four winds, from one end of heaven to the other (Joseph Smith—Matthew 1:37) .

We are the elect, and the Lord has done everything to prepare us for those difficult times. He has warned us of what to expect, and He has told us what to do to be prepared for those times. Most importantly, He has endowed us with great power from on high, and put His own mark upon us, and imbued us with His power in the Holy Priesthood, which is after the Order of the Son of God, and extended His own finger to us that we might exercise His power in the protection and blessing of His children. This is all done through faith, and each day we look around ourselves and see the grip of totalitarian fascism tightening ever more threateningly, we must provide resistance

---

129. "Revelation for the Church, Revelation for Our Lives," in Conference Report, April 2018.

to this evil that will overtake the world in the last days, by warning its inhabitants of the perils at its doorstep, and of the evil that is gathering like an ominous storm cloud.

The Challenge

We have read the words of the Lord, wherein He promises certain blessings if we will do a few, simple things that He requests of us. Most of us exercise a certain level of faith in our daily lives, but grow immediately uncomfortable when asked to rely on the Lord's promises, and trust Him completely. Our challenge is to believe Him. In all things He declares, "Prove me now herewith," meaning He stands ready to prove to us that which He has promised, if we will only put Him to the test. The Saints have been somewhat comfortable in the world for the past few decades, and have drifted in their contentment. As the veil of darkness begins to encroach and the spirit of Antichrist further permeates the earth, we will find ourselves in a position that we must rely on the Lord and His protective power more than we have in a long while. We will find that we will receive His promised blessings when we do the things He has requested us to do, and that we will feel that we are abandoned and left to ourselves when we fail to follow His instructions.

Our prophet recently bestowed on the Saints his Apostolic Blessing in this very regard.

> With the power of the holy apostleship vested in me, I bless you in your quest to overcome this world. I bless you to increase your faith in Jesus Christ and learn better how to draw upon His power. I bless you to be able to discern truth from error. I bless you to care more about the things of God than the things of this world. I bless you to see the needs of those around you and strengthen those you love. Because Jesus Christ overcame this world, you can too. I so testify in the sacred name of Jesus Christ, amen.

Let us be true to the Lord in exercising our faith. Let us ask for that which we desire, asking according to the Spirit, and knowing that the Lord has promised that He will so bless us. Let us learn the will of the Lord for our lives and allow it to become the path that we choose to follow, that He might abide with us as He did with Enoch and the people of Zion. As we do what He has asked us to do, we will receive of His rich blessings.

Seek unto my Father, and it shall be done in that very moment what ye shall ask, if ye ask in faith, believing that ye shall receive.

—JST, Mark 9:45

Author's Note

For those who wouldn't mind, your author would appreciate receiving your reports of how you came to believe the promises of the Father and His Beloved Son and how you were able to implement and apply their promises in your life to obtain the blessings you sought through faith. Please share your experiences with the author at the following email address and leave a brief note if you wouldn't mind sharing your experience with others in a future publication.

MiracleOfFaith1@gmail.com

About the Author

James Thompson, JD, is an award-winning writer and well-known professional ghostwriter. He has ghostwritten dozens of books for the nation's top business, motivational, and political leaders and is also known for his work in religious historical fiction.

James holds a Juris Doctor degree from Brigham Young University's J. Reuben Clark Law School, where he served as articles editor of the *BYU Law Review.*

Scan the QR code to visit
James' writing den
and see his latest projects.

Look for James's book *Worlds without Number* on Amazon, cedarfort.com, and at other fine retailers. An excellent addition to any library, *Worlds without Number* is a gospel discussion about the creation and nature of the universe, the life that fills it, and recent government admissions that unknown objects in our skies may not be from here.

Scan to visit

cedarfort.com/products/worlds-without-number